Without Forgetting
the Imam

Without Forgetting the Imam

Lebanese Shi'ism
in an American Community

LINDA S. WALBRIDGE

WAYNE STATE UNIVERSITY PRESS   DETROIT

00 99 98 97   5 4 3 2 1

Library of Congress Cataloging-in-Publication Data

Walbridge, Linda S.
    Without forgetting the Imam : Lebanese Shi'ism in an American
community / Linda S. Walbridge.
        p.   cm.
    Includes bibliographical references (p.   ) and index.
    ISBN 0-8143-2675-7 (alk. paper)
    1. Shi'ah—United States—Michigan.   2. Lebanese—Michigan—
Dearborn.   3. Dearborn (Mich.)—Religious life and customs.
I. Title
BP192.7.D4W35   1997
297'.82'0956920977433—dc20   96-32617

Designer: Betty Pilon
Cover art: Sayed Moustafa al-Qazwini giving a sermon during Ramadan, 1995, at the Imam Ali ibn Talib Mosque in San Diego, California. (Photo provided by the author.)

For the

PEOPLE OF LEBANON

and

MY DEAR HUSBAND, JOHN

Contents

Preface

EVERYONE WHO STUDIES a group of people should be grateful to them for their time and consideration. Perhaps, though, I feel a deeper sense of gratitude than usual because of the constant flow of hospitality and friendship shown to me. The Lebanese in Dearborn owed me nothing yet have given me so much. Aside from the Lebanese, there is also an Iraqi family who assisted me tremendously with their knowledge and insights. Unfortunately, they must remain anonymous.

In my writing, I use pseudonyms when referring to individuals, simply to protect their privacy. However, I make an exception when talking about clerical leaders. I consider these men to be more or less public figures, and I believe that nothing I have written about them could be in any way detrimental to them. I am deeply indebted to several of them for their hospitality and patience and for the openness with which they answered my questions.

I want to express special thanks to Dr. Barbara Aswad, my mentor and my friend, and also to Drs. Juan Cole, Aleya Rouchdy, Guerin Montilus, and Frances Trix, all of whom offered thoughtful comments.

There are some "Americans" in Dearborn whose hospitality and friendship were also of great importance to me: Roxanne and Al Firman, who actually helped move us to Dearborn, and Sherry Miller, who not only provided room and board during return trips to Dearborn but also arranged for me to interview her Polish-American Catholic father and mother, Emil and Evangeline Wozniak. Their stories of parochial school and church in the 1920s and '30s in Detroit added a sense of verisimilitude to my readings.

Above all, I must express my deepest gratitude to my husband, Dr. John Walbridge. My greatest critic, he also was my greatest supporter. His deep knowledge of Shi'ism and of Arabic and Persian was indispensable to this work.

Then there are our sons, John IV and Nathaniel. They adjusted adequately to my field research, taking any solace they needed from the delights produced in our neighbors' kitchens. They found it helpful at times to be known as the sons of a mother who "likes Arabs." They also grew to take some interest in my research, making their own astute observations from time to time, some of which are included in this book.

Finally, I would like to express my gratitude to all of those who worked so hard to produce this book at Wayne State University Press, particularly Alice Nigoghosian.

Introduction:
On Entering Dearborn

WHEN MY HUSBAND and I and our two elementary-aged sons planned to move to Dearborn so that I could conduct my research among the Arabic population there, I was warned by "Americans" (white non-Arabs) not to move to the east side or south end of Dearborn. They alluded to "the poorer quality of the schools" and "problems" in those parts of town. They urged us to move to the more affluent western section of Dearborn. It became apparent that these people, though perhaps well-meaning, were simply intimidated by what they perceived as an alien culture, one often associated in the media with violence and turmoil.

At first, we did move to the western part of the town because, with little time for house hunting, we were unable to find a suitable rental house in the eastern portion of Dearborn. Fortunately, we soon found ourselves in a position to purchase a house. We selected one that was a block away from a mosque and in a neighborhood in which Lebanese Shi'a predominated. But while we still lived on the west side, I met a woman who provided my first significant entrée into the Lebanese community.

Shortly after beginning school, my sons came home with two boys whose parents had migrated from Lebanon. We spoke Arabic with them, which obviously pleased them. As their friendships developed, our sons invited the boys to spend the night with us in our home. The boys told us that we would have to ask their mother. We sent them home with a note to her written in Arabic. She sent

11

her sons back to say that she would be arriving at our home in a few moments to meet us.

Their mother, who is referred to as "Wafa" in this book, was positively dazzling in her Italian wool two-piece dress, dangerously high heels, and a glorious display of gold jewelry. I recall vividly that I wore a pair of rather shabby jeans. My husband was no better attired. In her conversation, Wafa mentioned that Americans were jealous of the Lebanese because "they see us dressed in our nice clothes in the shopping malls, and they are wearing blue jeans and sneakers." The initial stiffness broke down, though, as she surveyed our walls full of books and artifacts from her part of the world. She flipped through the Arabic textbook from which I had been studying before her arrival. The Arabic coffee was not done to her taste, but she still was pleased that it was Arabic and not American. The boys were allowed to stay overnight, and two years later she recounted our first meeting to one of her friends while in my presence. "Wallah (by God)," she said, "I liked these people the first time I met them." Wafa developed an interest in my study and believed that she had an obligation to assist me. A gifted person with keen insight into the community and broad contacts because of her family's business, she was an invaluable informant. It was she who made the initial telephone contact with two of the sheikhs for me and arranged for appointments.

Good fortune continued to befall me as I came to know more and more people and felt free to spend time informally socializing in homes and on porches. Being a mother was a great asset. Furthermore, I was a mother who allowed other children into our home, a home cluttered with electric trains, Legos and GI Joes. Mothers began to refer to me jokingly as *kheltu*, a child's maternal aunt. In this patrilineal society, then, I was being viewed as a "close outsider." I also developed a reputation in the neighborhood for being good with babies, and I was consulted for advice and in times of emergencies. When my seventeen-year-old neighbor returned from the hospital with her newborn, I was the one to show her how to bathe the infant girl.

My children's attendance at a school in which at least two-thirds of the children are Arabic (and mostly Lebanese) was also a significant advantage to this study. Attending school functions, speaking with teachers, receiving school mailings, and simply listening to my sons describe their classroom situations all assisted me in developing a fuller picture of this community.

Being only a block and a half from Warren Avenue, the major street that runs through East Dearborn, with its mosque (there are now two mosques on this street) and predominantly Lebanese shops allowed me to observe and meet people. The fact that we frequented these places and relied on them for many of our daily needs also served to develop a certain trust. Aside from the bakeries, fruit markets, and grocery stores, there were bookshops, one of which I mention throughout this book. I spent countless hours there discussing theology and the dynamics of the Dearborn religious establishment with the store's very knowledgeable owners. I still count them among my dearest friends.

Having lived in Chiah, Lebanon, a Beirut suburb with a large Shi'i population, assisted me in both general and concrete ways. Shortly after arriving in Dearborn in 1987, I heard that a certain Lebanese family had recently moved to town. Although I had never known this particular branch of the family, I had known some of their relatives in Lebanon. I was accepted with great warmth into the lives of these people, who always spoke quite frankly with me about their own travails and about the Shi'i community in Dearborn as they saw it.

When I told people that my husband and I had lived in Chiah, this news was always greeted with a look of astonishment (accompanied by a spontaneous "No!" or "Wallah?") But they were also pleased. Westerners simply did not live in a place like that. Indeed, we had been the only Westerners there at the time. Americans and Europeans lived in the upscale places such as Ras Beirut. I had seen Lebanon's more humble side but still could have affection for it. Furthermore, I had seen it before the war, so I "knew" that the Lebanese were basically good people and that the civil war with its seemingly never-ending aftermath was an aberration, not the natural state of things. When I was introduced to one Lebanese by another, the person doing the introduction obviously felt compelled to explain my presence. Why was an outsider drinking coffee in an Arab's kitchen or TV room? The first piece of information uttered about me was, invariably, that I had lived in Chiah.

My position was enhanced even further because of my husband's background. As Anglo-Saxon as myself, he holds a Ph.D. in Islamic Studies from Harvard. His Arabic library, shelved conspicuously in our living room, impressed even one of the sheikhs who visited our home. His knowledge conferred upon him great prestige in a community in which religious knowledge is equated with an elite position. As the wife of a learned man who easily communicated with sheikhs, I also gained respect.

And thus I spent four very happy years among research subjects who, in actuality, became my friends and dear acquaintances. I formally interviewed sheikhs, but I also just spoke with some of them informally. I went, quite inconspicuously, to the mosques, where I was called "sister." Since I could not attend all mosque functions, I relied also on the cable TV ethnic access channel. By spring of 1990, services from the three mosques then open in Dearborn were being recorded and played on this station. I also had access to published information from the mosques, such as announcements of special events, calls for elections, and information about fasting. Also of great importance were texts that have been written and published locally, usually books or booklets written by the local 'ulama.

Toward the end of my research, I used interview schedules to question certain beliefs and attitudes of a wide spectrum of people. This was done after I had established certain "categories" of people along lines of political affiliation, religious orientation, education and social class, mosque affiliation, region of origin, and so on. But, mostly, I simply spent vast amounts of time with people in various situations. And we talked until I felt I had something worthwhile to write about them. I hope they agree.

East Dearborn (a.k.a. Little Beirut)

It is not like the south end of Dearborn at all. The south end, "depressing" and "foreboding" because of its proximity to the polluting Ford factory, does capture one's imagination.[1] The Yemeni Zaydi Mosque on Dix Avenue looks like a Middle Eastern mosque. The coffeehouses and the colorful peasant dress bear no mark of "American" life. These are transplants from the towns and villages of the Arab world. Even the architecture of the recently renovated shops is reminiscent of Middle Eastern styles.

East Dearborn (i.e., the northeast corner of the city) is less colorful. And it is not a ghetto such as the south end has become. For one thing, there are still large numbers of non-Arabs, many of whom are immigrants from Italy and eastern European countries. While the Lebanese are making their mark on this side of town, they are not "recreating" their villages here. Perhaps it is because the Lebanese, a mercantile people, are accustomed to transplanting themselves. While they love their land with its mountains and sea coast, they seem to accept the fact that their lives may not be spent there. They may have to join their countless predecessors who have found their livelihoods in alien lands.

On the main business street in northeast Dearborn, Warren Avenue, stands one of the Shi'i mosques. It is simply a refurbished bank building with a sign in the front in English: "Islamic Institute."

A similar sign appears in Arabic on the building's east side, away from Warren Avenue. Several blocks away is another mosque, one that is even easier to mistake for a business rather than a religious center.

Dress is not that of the village. It is modern dress, either Western or Islamic. The people in this neighborhood do not want to appear to be peasants. Most aspire to look like either wealthy Beirutis or the ideal good Muslim. Therefore, while head coverings and various cover-ups abound, these are often the type worn by the "new breed" of Muslim and are not usually reminiscent of village life. True, signs are in Arabic as well as English, and they advertise imports from Lebanon, but, compared to the south end, the Middle Eastern ambience is lacking.

Lebanese restaurants in East Dearborn are plentiful, and the food is prepared by men who are often fresh from the villages of the south and the Bekaa. But these places strongly cater to Americans. One entrepreneur who opened a restaurant on Warren Avenue was sure that he would have a mostly American clientele and wanted it that way. He consulted me on how to make it most attractive to Americans.

There are no "male domain" coffeehouses on Warren Avenue as there are on Dix. They would not fit with the lifestyle of the Lebanese of this district. The men frequently work two jobs. After all, houses in East Dearborn run between $45,000 and $90,000 and even more on the fancier streets. When the man is not at work, he is expected to be with his wife and children, either receiving guests in his home or visiting friends and relatives with them. The man who leaves his wife to sit alone while he is out enjoying himself subjects himself to criticism. Suad Joseph has made the same observation about life in the Beirut suburb of Borj Hamoud, saying that "most men came directly home after work, relatively few being accustomed to coffee houses or bars. But since their work kept them until late in the evening, many men came home exhausted, only wanting to eat, rest and sleep."[2]

On the south end's Dix Avenue, largely, though not exclusively, inhabited by people from Yemen, women and girls are rarely seen.[3] Not so on Warren Avenue. Unaccompanied women, exuding self-confidence, go in and out of the shops and the mosque continually, although they don't loiter in, say, the meat market as the occasional male might do. Again, Joseph describes a similar situation in Borj Hamoud.

The services provided on Warren Avenue can now meet most needs, though the Lebanese certainly do utilize shopping centers in other parts of the city. Over the past ten years or so, Lebanese-owned businesses and other services have multiplied and prospered. Arabic bakeries, patisseries, produce markets, specialty grocers, restaurants, bookstores, beauty salons, gas stations—all of these can be found on Warren Avenue. Medical and dental problems can be dealt with by Lebanese physicians on Warren as well.

Furthermore, an ethnic access cable TV station broadcasts programs mostly in Arabic addressing a multitude of issues, interests, and tastes. Common are features on Lebanon and broadcasts from the three Lebanese Shi'i mosques.

What has made all this development possible? Part of the answer is simply that there has been such a great influx recently of Lebanese immigrants eager to escape the violence that has continued in Lebanon since 1975. They follow their kinsmen here, some of whom immigrated before the war, seeking a way out of their grinding poverty and an oppressive political system. This pattern of settling around one's fellow countrymen and relatives is common among immigrants and, though it seems to contradict America's ideals of individualism, has been a successful strategy for both economic development and maintaining social and psychological stability.[4]

Frequently, these new immigrants, and the ones who came earlier, do not start off in East Dearborn. They may begin life in America in the south end, where housing is much cheaper. Then, when able, they move northward.

The other half of Dearborn, the northwest and southwest sides, are largely untouched by this migration activity, except insofar as some political decisions might affect them. The west side is almost entirely white and, particularly the northwest side, increasingly trendy. The entire east side of Dearborn appears much more urban, with its many multifamily homes and more crowded conditions. Dearborn, with its population of 90,000 to 100,000 people, shares a long border with Detroit, which the Dearborn police patrol heavily. Extensive Ford Motor Company properties divide the two parts of Dearborn, which originally were not one entity but two. The west side was the original Dearborn, the east side a town named Fordson. The two old towns merged in 1929, becoming the city of Dearborn.

Dearborn's Arabic History

Detroit may be the oldest Muslim community in America. The Muslims followed their Christian countrymen, who preceded them by twenty to sixty years.[5] In those early days, between 1900 and 1915, the days of the Ottoman Empire, anyone coming from the Levant region was known as a Syrian, but most of these early immigrants came from villages of the Bekaa Valley and South Lebanon, the regions from whence the Shiʿa in Dearborn originated.[6] They were largely from the lower strata of society, peddlers, laborers, and small business owners who were drawn to Detroit because of the presence of the Ford Motor Company in Highland Park, a city within the borders of Detroit. These "pioneers" were usually men who, even if married, came alone. Most had the idea of returning to their homelands with money in their pockets but eventually came to realize that they would never return. While for some the freedom and opportunities of America, so unlike anything in the Middle East, made this country appear like paradise on earth, for others the disappointments and obstacles they faced—including prejudice— were staggering.

Between 1918 and 1922, immigrants from the Arab countries poured into the Detroit area, as did people from all over the world. World War I had been devastating to the Middle East, and it was followed by years of drought, various epidemics, and plagues of locusts. The Ottoman Empire was dismantled, and in its place came occupation by the great Western powers: France and England. New countries were created, one of them being Lebanon.

By then, a new Ford plant had been constructed on the Rouge River in southeast Dearborn. Many Muslims settled in this corner of town. The Lebanese Christian Orthodox, on the other hand, moved to the northern suburbs, having attained white-collar and professional employment. Slightly later, Palestinians, particularly single men or men who had left their families back home, also began arriving as a result of the Arab revolt in Palestine in the 1930s. Yemenis, too, began to appear on the scene. But in the 1920s and '30s, immigration decreased. Several immigration laws were passed in the 1920s reducing the number of people the United States would accept. The act of 1929, for example, restricted immigration from Lebanon and Syria jointly to 123 individuals.[7] Still, people from the Arab world managed to find their way to America. These were usually relatives of those who had already established themselves here. Commonly, families sent their grown children back to the homeland to marry; they would then return with their spouses. But with immigration policy liberalizing after World War II, we see another large influx of immigrants to the United States in general and to the Detroit area in particular.[8] The greatest numbers were still from Lebanon, but Palestinians also came in waves following each of the

Arab-Israeli wars, with the Yemenis coming in the 1960s and 1970s. The typical immigrant from any of these areas was among the least educated and skilled of his countrymen. Probably the most extreme example is that of the Yemenis, as described by Nabeel Abraham: "Most immigrants are in their twenties and thirties, although boys as young as twelve years old and many men over forty can also be found among the immigrants. With notable exceptions, the population is generally illiterate or semiliterate, unskilled peasants, who have little or no knowledge of English."[9]

The early Muslims living in the Dearborn area found themselves sharing their neighborhoods—and, to some degree, their mosques—with people with whom they never would have previously associated. The area, aside from containing a large number of Southern Christian whites, grew to consist of Lebanese and Palestinian Sunnis, Yemeni Shafeis (a Sunni sect), Lebanese Shi'a, and Yemeni Zaydis (a Shi'i sect). Mosques came into being at that time to attempt to meet the spiritual and social needs of this heterogeneous group of immigrants. Their development will be discussed in Chapter 2.

The Development of East Dearborn

By 1976, certain neighborhoods in the south end had reached what is referred to as the concentration phase; that is, 75 to 100 percent of the total population was Arab Muslim.[10] At this point, some of the Muslims began moving northward. These were mostly Shi'i Lebanese. In his 1980 demographic study of Arabs living in northeastern Dearborn, Katarsky found that almost half of his sample had moved from the south end. The other half had arrived directly from Lebanon.[11]

As mentioned earlier, this process continues today. Northeast Dearborn still attracts both new immigrants from Lebanon and Lebanese leaving the south end for the more attractive conditions of the northern corner of the city. They also seek to escape life among the Palestinians and the Yemenis. The Palestinians, of course, became enemies in Lebanon, so this partially explains the aversion to living with them. But there are other factors as well. Many of the Palestinians in the south end tend to wear village dress, for example. Also, their customs are seen as being those of peasants. The Yemenis are perceived as even worse. They generally live in quite poor conditions, and the Lebanese consider them to be backward and dirty. The Yemenis are quite conscious of the fact that the Lebanese look down upon them.[12]

The Lebanese aspire to the middle-class life. Like the earliest immigrants, the more recent arrivals frequently come to America virtually penniless and begin by working in a factory, whether it be Ford or perhaps Thorn Apple Valley. They will save everything they possibly can, living under the most frugal conditions. When enough savings are amassed, they will turn to a relative or two who have undergone the same process and pool their resources to buy income property, a store or a restaurant or, if very fortunate, a gas station.

Speaking of the early "Syrian" immigrants, Khalaf writes:

Their success is not difficult to account for. First, it must be kept in mind that although the bulk of the early immigrants were drawn from villages and towns, a fairly large number were engaged in trade as small merchants and shopkeepers and were quite familiar with urban life and occupations. For example, of the ten thousand adult males with identifiable occupations who entered the United States between 1899 and 1907, nearly 15 percent indicated that they had been merchants in the old country. More important, perhaps, they carried with them the frugal and austere lifestyles they were accustomed to in Lebanon. . . . Even when they were in the lower income brackets, the "Syrians" had, in fact . . . displayed many of the social characteristics of the middle classes in urban centers in America. A score of studies of several "Syrian" communities, conducted in the mid-1930s and early 1940s, all revealed a common pattern: low incidence of deviance and crime, better health, higher IQs among the children, more regular school attendance, and few intermarriages and divorce.[13]

This description seems completely appropriate when discussing the majority of the Lebanese living in East Dearborn. Hard work, frugality, and stability in marriage and family life still characterize the Lebanese, at least the Lebanese Shi'a who are the focus of this study.

Their road to success involves the purchase of one of the solid brick homes in East Dearborn. It is interesting to watch the process of movement to this part of town. Many Lebanese have told me that they don't want to live in an all-Arab neighborhood. Several have told me that they don't like the street on which I lived because "there are too many Arabs." Yet they continue to bring their kinsmen, finding housing for them close by. Furthermore, they continue to socialize almost exclusively with other Arabs, and generally only other Lebanese. Also, few thus far have made the move to West Dearborn or to the other suburbs. This reflects much of the ambivalence that the Lebanese feel about life in America and about their homeland. On the one hand, they want to escape the gossip and jealousies of their fellow countrymen. They don't want to have their every movement observed, a situation that is typical of village life. Many of the women don't want to be tied down to a steady flow of visitors all day, either. If they live in an all-American neighborhood, this can be avoided to some degree. On the other hand, living in an all-American neighborhood is lonely. And Americans don't understand Arabs. Furthermore, there is often a language problem. The compromise is for newcomers to the area to seek out housing on those remaining streets in northeast Dearborn that still have relatively few Arabs. They can thereby have easy access to relatives and friends but can avoid their intense scrutiny.

Neighborhoods are not inhabited along village lines. On a single block, one is likely to find Lebanese from the south, from the Bekaa, and from Beirut. The largest number of immigrants are from a village named Bint Jubeil, now occupied by the Israelis, who are eager for these villagers to receive visas to America. Therefore, there are usually people from Bint Jubeil on most streets. Regardless of where they are from, the women all tend to visit one another, especially in the summer when they gather on freshly swept and hosed porches, drinking coffee until late in the evening. The men are less likely to do this kind of casual socializing since they often work long hours. Their visiting will tend to be more with relatives on their days and evenings off, a carryover from visiting patterns found in Lebanon.[14]

Who visits whom continues to be of great importance. It is still considered an insult when a visit is not promptly reciprocated. But now visiting is done with people with whom one may never have felt any obligations back home. For example, one quite sophisticated woman friend from the Bekaa expressed surprise and dismay when a distant relative, who was uneducated and generally recognized as being overbearing, insisted on telephoning her and paying visits. "She never bothered with my family back home," my friend complained to me. "Why does she want to see me now?" In the village, it seems, my friend's family was seen as different and perhaps a bit uppity. But here such differences tend to be put aside in order to keep contacts with the old country alive.

It is also expected that when someone plans a visit back to Lebanon, he or she will inform all Dearborn friends and acquaintances from that village of the trip. The traveler is expected to carry not only letters, tape-recorded messages, and photographs but also gifts of all sizes to the families back home. On the return trip, the traveler will be laden with goods coming from the other direction. This is because of the lack of mail service to and from Lebanon. No doubt, one of the reasons to retain village ties is so that this service can be provided. Much ado is made of this service. The person who does not immediately let others know of his or her travel plans can expect a bitter reaction. For example, two middle-aged men from the Bekaa have been lifelong close friends. It was rumored that one was going back to Lebanon for an extended visit. His friend questioned him, but he denied that he was going. However, the friend heard further confirmation of the rumor and went to the man's house saying he'd heard he was leaving the next day. The man could not deny this but said that the arrangements had been made hastily. It was obvious that the man did not want to have to carry goods to Lebanon and was trying to extricate himself from this duty. The breach between these two men never healed in the time I lived in Dearborn. When the man returned from Lebanon, his friend never visited him, which in itself is an unforgivable offense.

A young woman planned to visit her family in southern Lebanon accompanied only by her infant son. She dutifully telephoned everyone from the village now residing in Dearborn but said that she was only willing to carry photos, letters, and tapes because of luggage restrictions. When I visited her, she was very distressed because someone had expressed anger at her for not being willing to carry gifts. Regardless of her objections, she was still expected to transport a hair dryer to Lebanon.

Establishing Roots: Educating the Children

Schools and education are essential for entry into American middle-class life, and the Lebanese are well aware of this. While a vast majority of new immigrants have little education themselves, they are determined that their children be educated. It appears, therefore, that before long there will be a glut of Lebanese-American doctors, engineers, and computer programmers in the area. It should be noted, however, that there are immigrants who attained advanced degrees in Lebanon; their families had moved to the Beirut area so that their children could be educated.

In one generation, families that have perhaps never had a literate member suddenly boast a kinsmen with advanced degrees. The results of this situation can be rather odd.

For months, I associated with one extended family from a village in the Bekaa. All the members of the family whom I knew had received only a limited education in their village, although some of the women in the family had come to the United States in their teens and had completed their high school education. One day I heard about the older brother of a woman who had married into this clan. He has a doctorate, is a professor, and owns various businesses. Such social class stratification within families is not uncommon and does produce stress in family relationships.

The Lebanese tend to have large families, though I do hear young women talking about limiting the number of children they have to three or four. The children have swelled the schools of East Dearborn. Of the children listed in the kindergarten "roundup" for one of the east-end grade schools, 64 percent had Arabic surnames. In my son's fourth-grade classes, approximately 75 percent of the children were of Arabic descent.

The schools in this part of town have an active bilingual program to integrate the children into the classrooms. Teachers have told me that they are impressed with the children's linguistic progress but that problems frequently arise because of the parents' lack of knowledge of English. Still, when I have attended school programs, such as musical performances, the Lebanese parents are present in large numbers, enthusiastically cheering their children on and taking their pictures. In turn, the school administrators, at least at the schools with which I am most familiar, exhibit an impressive degree of knowledge of and sensitivity to the Arab culture and attempt to meet the needs of this population. For example, no pork is allowed in the school lunch program, and girls may be exempt, if their families wish, from wearing gym clothing. At one of the east-end schools, shower curtains were provided (at the request of a Muslim mother) in the gym shower room so that the children could shower in privacy.

Relations with the Non-Arab Community

The city of Dearborn has been accused of trying to prevent African Americans from residing within its confines. If so, they have been largely successful in their endeavors. However, the presence of such a large Arab community should not be misunderstood as part of the city's policy to welcome this particular population. They came in spite of the city's opinions on the matter.

The 1960s and '70s witnessed a struggle between the south end and the city of Dearborn when the city wished to demolish the neighborhoods for an urban renewal project which would have succeeded in displacing a large proportion of the Arab community. The city ultimately lost the battle.[15]

As mentioned earlier, East Dearborn is not a ghetto and, hence, has not faced the same sorts of problems that the far less affluent south end has faced. But intercommunity problems do exist. For example, a January 19, 1984, article in the local newspaper, the *Dearborn Press and Guide,* stated that residents were writing to the paper saying that they can't sell their homes because of the influx of Arabs.[16] They complained that "young people" won't buy in East Dearborn because of the Arabs, and they charged the city council with assisting the Arabs in ruining the town. An August 10, 1978, *Dearborn Press and Guide* article had reported criticisms that the Lebanese do not take care of their homes like past owners had done.[17] One of the usual complaints, made by immigrant Polish and Italian neighbors, was that the Arabs do not tend to their lawns. By 1987, when we moved here, the Lebanese in East Dearborn were taking care of their lawns. Many a time I have heard the Lebanese bitterly reiterate this complaint made against them as they pointed to their freshly mowed grass. It is true that home care is generally focused on the inside of the house, not the outside. This is as it was in Lebanon. In Chiah, where I lived, the streets were terribly unkempt, and garbage often piled up outside buildings. But the interiors of the apartments were well cared for. However, the Lebanese have taken the criticism to heart, and lawn mowers are heard as frequently here as they are in almost any other suburb.

One great source of tension is the issue of schools. While the West Dearborn school population has decreased markedly over the past fifteen years or so, the East Dearborn population has skyrocketed, leaving the schools on the east side overcrowded and the West Dearborn schools with too few students. The city proposed busing children from the east side to the west side schools, causing disgruntlement on both sides. At least some west-siders were heard to object to the proposal simply because they did not want Arab children in their schools. Cries of "Send us all your blue-eyed blond ones" were heard. The Arab parents, for their part, did not want to see their children bused far from home and to an environment that was not Arab and Muslim. However, the plans for busing, at least to some degree, have been carried through without major incident.

Tensions between Arab and American youth are a paramount issue in this community today. Furthermore, there were accusations about police brutality against Lebanese boys in East Dearborn. Some gang activity erupted in 1989, with the young men involved allegedly damaging the mayor's car. The mayor has not had smooth relations with the Arab community and has been accused of especially seeking out Arab youths for prosecution. For the most part,

Lebanese community leaders have been able to contain the problems that arise, but there is no question that tensions are on the rise.[18]

Oddly enough, on the other hand, it is not unusual to see a car driven by a Lebanese person with a bumper sticker saying "I Love [written as a red heart] Dearborn Police." Cars sometimes bear this bumper sticker alongside another one reading "I Love Allah." All this simply underscores the independent-mindedness of the Lebanese. It also reflects the desire of the people to live in a safe, crime-free environment. While the Lebanese may criticize the police for being overly rough with their boys, they are more concerned that the crime so rampant in Detroit not spill over into Dearborn. They recognize that Dearborn is a habitable place largely because the police are notorious for their tough stance on crime.

The Lebanese community, thus far, has been relatively uninvolved in the American political process. The new wave of immigrants, for the most part, still see themselves as Lebanese who just happen to be living in America. It is still news from Lebanon that absorbs them. The 1989 mayoral and city council election may have been a turning point for this community, however. For the first time, a person who openly identified himself as an Arab American ran for city council—a lawyer educated in the Detroit area whose family originated from Bint Jubeil. Though he lost, he did better than many expected and received a surprisingly high number of votes from the west side. A woman of Lebanese descent has been serving on the city council for several years; however, several people have told me that in an earlier election she claimed that her heritage was Italian. During the 1989 election, no such ethnic disclaimers were heard. While she did not emphasize her Arabic roots as did the other Arab American on the ticket, the fact that she acknowledged her Arabic heritage is a sign that the Lebanese are beginning to be recognized as an important part of the community.

What is equally interesting, however, is how Lebanese political life was played out through the election process in Dearborn. This city councilwoman is a daughter of the village of Tibnin. Tibnin and the village of Bint Jubeil (from which the other Lebanese candidate originated) are traditional rivals. In spite of the fact that she had previously denied her Lebanese heritage, the Lebanese Americans of Tibnin origin voted for her in the election. Those from Bint Jubeil were with her opponent. I attended a fund-raising dinner for her opponent one evening. Recognizing a fair number of people there whom I knew to be from Bint Jubeil, I asked a friend if all the people present were from that village. She confirmed that this was the case. Obviously, ancient tensions and animosities have not completely died out.

Only the Latest Newcomers

Today, a large Catholic church with school, convent, rectory, and cemetery sits placidly a block away from the Islamic Institute of America. In the cemetery, one finds gravestones with names such as Reuter, Theisen, Esper, Schaeffer—the German Americans after whom East Dearborn streets are named.

The Germans were replaced by Poles and Italians. Today, elderly Polish and Italian couples with their meticulous lawns and gardens are selling their homes and moving to apartments and nursing homes. Their houses are bought by Lebanese immigrants, who in many respects are reenacting the social and religious history of their ethnic Catholic predecessors.

The Shiʿa, and Muslims in general, may face a new set of challenges in the United States, but stories of early Catholic immigrants strike a familiar chord in many respects. The Catholic immigrants pouring into the Detroit area found themselves in a society dominated by long-standing enemies, the Protestants. Here in America, Catholics were met with virulent hatred. As Irving Howe wrote, "the Roman Church was feared as a vessel of medieval superstition, dripping with European decadence."[19]

How and where did these newcomers—these aliens—fit into American society? The words "You shouldn't imagine yourselves as Americans, since you are not that" might have been uttered by a Lebanese Shiʿa.[20] But this statement is actually a quote from a leader of the Finnish Lutheran community in Minnesota addressing the youth of the Hibbing Temperance Societies in 1909. (Ethnic Lutherans often faced the same challenges as did Catholics and had more in common with Catholics than with mainline American Protestants.) In groups such as these Minnesota Finns, religion was the life blood of the community. The fear of being consumed by American protestantism and secularism galvanized people to take action to protect themselves and their heritage.

Throughout this ethnography, we will hear such echoes from our immigrant past. By occasionally showing the problems that many immigrants, particularly Catholics, experienced in America, I hope to convince my readers that at least this particular Islamic community is not really so alien after all.

CHAPTER 1

The Shadow of the Past

THE ISLAMIC CENTER of America, known as the Jamiʿ, is located in northwest Detroit, just over the borderline from the more prosperous city of Dearborn, from which the Jamiʿ draws most of its congregation of Shiʿa of Lebanese extraction. The following is quoted from a booklet produced in 1988 on the twenty-fifth anniversary of the opening of the Islamic Center of America:

The Hijra of Imam Mohammad Jawad Chirri

The community had grown large and they desired to have a learned religious leader serve them and teach their children. After an inquiry and search in Lebanon, they were able to find an exceptional young author and scholar, Muhammad Jawad Chirri. To their delight he was willing to accept their invitation to come to the United States of America. He left Lebanon, where his future notoriety and success were assured, and accepted the challenge of the "New World." Imam Chirri arrived in Dearborn in February of 1949. Almost from the time he arrived factional rivalry erupted within the community. Although Imam Chirri immediately began the work they had contracted him for with zeal, dedication, forthrightness, and progressiveness, he soon was engulfed in the controversy.

This turmoil in the community brought hardship and mental anguish upon the man. False accusations and shameful acts made it impossible for him to remain in Detroit, and, finally, in

December of 1950 he left for Michigan City, Indiana. There a dedicated, small community took him into their lives. He served them well for four years, studying the American life style, and learning the English language. He became proficient in both and was recognized for his ability to teach and convey the meaning of Islam.

During his stay in Michigan City, a group of young people in Detroit had organized themselves into a neo-leadership club. Their goals included gaining more knowledge of Islam, and then teaching the children. Their activities to form a religious school met with some opposition by a select few who considered them a threat to their influence. This time, however, the situation developed differently. The young people allied themselves with a few religious, dedicated, and motivated seniors. This coalition started the community on a difficult, sacrifice-laden road to solidarity and success.

A delegation of the Awlad, as they were called, meaning "children," traveled to Michigan City to meet with Imam Chirri. Armed with sincerity, enthusiasm, and the moral and financial support of the seniors, they requested Imam Chirri return to Detroit. They pledged their unfaltering dedication to him and the community awaited his return. He accepted. And, then, began a fascinating awakening of a group of Muslims that would ultimately lead to the building of the Islamic Center (of America). The "Hijra" was ended.

The Hijra of Imam Chirri resonates in the collective imagination of the Shi'a of Dearborn. For them, it was a reenactment of a great Islamic historical event, an event that reaches back to the earliest days of Islam, when the Prophet Muhammad lived among his followers.[1]

In the year 610, the leaders of the Quraysh tribe of Mecca agreed to kill Muhammad, and the Prophet of Islam was forced to flee to the city of Medina. Among other things, the Meccans had felt threatened by the Prophet's teachings against idol worship, afraid that if the people heeded Muhammad's words, pilgrims to the sanctuary of the ancient Ka'ba would cease to come, thereby destroying one of their sources of income.

The leaders of Medina, an agricultural oasis north of Mecca, had learned of the self-proclaimed Messenger of God and saw in him the ideal man to arbitrate between the fighting factions who dwelt in that city. So, leaving his cousin 'Ali ibn abi Taleb to trick the Meccans by sleeping in his (the Prophet's) bed, he, accompanied by his loyal friend, Abu Bakr, escaped death and began a new phase of his dispensation. The flight to Medina is referred to as the Hijra, and the Islamic calendar dates from this period.

From Medina, Muhammad launched raids against the Meccans who so bitterly opposed the religion he was teaching. Battles were fought with varying results between the Meccans and the followers of the Prophet.

Over the years, the prestige and strength of Muhammad rose to the point where the Meccans felt compelled to accept a truce presented by the Prophet. When the Meccans broke the truce, the Prophet and his army entered Mecca, where they were met with little resistance. The pagan idols in the Ka'ba were smashed, but the Prophet affirmed that the Ka'ba, with its sacred stone associated with the Prophet Abraham, was the central focus of reverence for Muslims for all time. Two years after conquering Mecca, the Prophet died.

Shi'i sources cite statements by the Prophet indicating that it was his desire to have his cousin and son-in-law, 'Ali, succeed him after his death.[2] Sunni sources also acknowledge the privileged position that 'Ali held in the eyes of the Prophet. Statements attributed to the Prophet, such as "This is my brother, my trustee and my successor among you, so listen to him and obey" have been recorded by both Shi'i and Sunni scholars.[3] But when the Prophet died, it was not 'Ali on whom fell the mantle of caliph, or successor, but the elder Abu Bakr, nominated by another close companion of the Prophet, Umar ibn al-Khattab. The majority of Muslims fell behind the leadership of Abu Bakr. The politics of the day influenced the selection. He was from the Quraysh, but Abu Bakr was not from the Hashimite clan of the Prophet. Since many were keen to ensure that power not be monopolized by the Prophet's family (or any other family, for that matter), Abu Bakr seemed a good choice. 'Ali came to accept Abu Bakr's leadership, but only after the death of Fatima, his wife and the daughter of the Prophet; she never ceased to believe that Abu Bakr was a usurper.

On Abu Bakr's deathbed, he appointed the powerful Umar the caliph most responsible for expanding the influence of Islam, both to the east and to the west. Eventually, Umar was struck down by an assassin's knife while leading prayers in the mosque, but as he lay dying, he appointed a committee of five men to elect his successor. 'Ali was one of the five, but chances of his being elected were weighted against him because of the composition of the committee. Again, he waited on the sidelines, serving as an adviser in Medina, as the third caliph, Uthman, ruled.

The caliphate of Uthman differed from those of his two prede-cessors. In the first place, he was from the most powerful of the clans of the Quraysh, the Bani Umayyad clan. Later sources describe him as pious but weak and easily influenced by his clansmen, to whom he gave the most desirable positions in the now large Islamic empire. The most notable of these was the governorship of Syria. This fell to the highly capable but irreligious Muawiyya. Outraged by the growing corruption in the empire, delegations came from Egypt and Iraq to voice their complaints. Uthman agreed to respond to their demands, but a ruthless adviser sent a message ahead of the delegations issuing their death warrants upon their return to their respective lands. Discovering this, the delegations returned to Medina, broke into Uthman's home, and killed him. At that point, ʿAli was declared the caliph of Islam on the streets of Medina. But not everyone agreed to this decision.

While ʿAli played no role in the affair, he was accused by Uth-man's family of having corroborated with the killers. Aisha, Abu Bakr's daughter and the favorite wife of the Prophet, held ʿAli responsible for Uthman's death and led a battle against him, known as the Battle of the Camel. While ʿAli's forces were victorious, and Aisha retired quietly to her home to pursue religious matters, others in the empire were not satisfied. Principally, Muawiyya, governor of Syria, wanted vengeance for his kinsman's death, although his principal motivation, no doubt, was to remove ʿAli from his path to power. Stirring up crowds by displaying the bloodied clothing and severed fingers of the deceased caliph, he declared war against ʿAli and his followers. When it seemed that ʿAli's forces would again win, Muawiyya's side devised a ruse to trick ʿAli's supporters into accepting a truce. Muawiyya announced that he, too, should be con-sidered as a candidate for the caliphate, and confusion reigned in the land until one of ʿAli's former supporters, now a rebellious Kharijite, shot ʿAli in the head with an arrow and killed him.

Muawiyya, with a powerful army to back him, demanded the allegiance of the Muslims. The center of administration then moved from the sacred land of the Hejaz in Arabia, where the Prophet had lived, to Damascus. Muawiyya was able to quell discord, but when he died, those who believed that ʿAli and his descendants were the rightful heirs to the successorship of the Prophet, saw their chance to win their cause. Living under the terror and oppression of ʿUbayd Allah, the governor of Iraq, the supporters of the Prophet's family sent a message to Husayn ibn ʿAli, the grandson of the Prophet. (Husayn's elder brother, Hassan, who would have been next in line before Husayn, was already dead.) They agreed to join forces with Husayn should he come to Iraq and be willing to lead a battle against the Umayyads. With his family and a small group of followers, he embarked on the journey.

What Husayn and his entourage encountered when they reached Iraq, specifically the Plain of Karbala, is a story that has been told as often as the stories of the death of Christ. And just like that earlier event, historical detail is shrouded in wonderful mythology. The facts are that Husayn was met not by those who called themselves friends but by his foes. An army was sent by the governor of Iraq to stop Husayn. Surrounding Husayn and his party of perhaps seventy-two men, along with women and children, the army cut them off from their only source of water. The governor sent his final orders to attack Husayn, and on the tenth of Muharram A.H. 61 (October 10, 680), Husayn's small band of loyal followers who had refused to desert their leader were all slaughtered. Even Husayn's infant son was killed by an arrow while cradled in his father's arms as Husayn begged the enemy for water for the baby. Husayn himself, who fought to the last, was decapitated. The women and children were taken prisoner and led to Kufa in Iraq to face the indignity of seeing Husayn's head brought to ʿUbayd Allah on a platter. The governor taunted them by hitting Husayn's lips with his cane. He then threatened to kill the only remaining son of Husayn, ʿAli, a child who had been too ill to fight. But Husayn's heroic sister, Zaynab, protested that if ʿAli were killed, then she would be killed with him. ʿAli was spared and sent on with the rest of the prisoners to Damascus, where they were ultimately set free because the caliph, Yazid, feared a public outcry. There were many people still alive who remembered the love the Prophet showered upon his grandson Husayn.

Today, those who retell this story are those who call themselves Shiʿa, members of the party of ʿAli. And when they tell this story, each death, each terrible, poignant event, is dwelt upon so that no one having heard it could ever forget it. The events of Karbala are as alive today as they were in the year A.D. 680 when they actually occurred.

The Imamate

ʿAli ibn al-Husayn, who survived Karbala, became the fourth imam of the Shiʿa. His grandfather ʿAli, his uncle Hasan, and his father Husayn preceded him in this role.

The imamate is the crucial point on which the Shiʿa and the Sunnis, who form the majority of Muslims, differ. As Momen states:

"The Sunnis and Shi'is are basically in agreement with each other over the nature and function of prophethood. The two main functions of the Prophet are to reveal God's law to men and to guide men towards God. Of these two functions, the Sunnis believe that both ended with the death of Muhammad, while the Shi'i believe that whereas legislation ended, the function of guiding men and preserving and explaining the Divine Law continued through the line of Imams."[4]

Those who adhere to the belief that there are twelve men who were the divinely guided leaders of the Muslim community are called Twelvers or Imami Shi'a. But after the deaths of several of the imams, there was disagreement over who should be their rightful successors. At those historical points, there were divisions in Shi'ism, and new sects began. Among those sects, the Zaydis and the Isma'ilis are probably the best known.

Throughout the lifetimes of the imams, there was fear of and hostility toward the imams in particular and the Shi'a in general on the part of the Sunni majority. The Sunnis could make no claims to such God-given leadership as the Shi'a had, and it was well remembered that the Imam Husayn had been willing to fight for his right to leadership of the Muslims. The remaining imams, however, did not generally follow Husayn's path but, in general, opted for a depoliticized approach to their duties. During the days of the imams, Shi'ism was not a well-integrated movement and had rather vague religious doctrines that often contradict beliefs that prevail today.

It is commonly believed that the antipathy toward the imamate was the cause of the occultation of the Twelfth Imam about whose life there is much mystery. Some sources say he was born in A.D. 868, but there is confusion on this point. In fact, there were those who questioned whether he had even been born. Much fragmentation occurred among the Shi'a at that time over the issue of leadership. What is important for the purposes of this work is that the Shi'a generally agree that the Twelfth Imam, as a young child, went into occultation, that he never died, and that he is to appear in the "Last Days."

The Growth of Shi'ism

Shi'ism in its various sects grew considerably throughout the Islamic world. In the tenth century, the Buyids, who identified themselves as Shi'a, overcame the Abbasids in Baghdad. The Fatimids of the Isma'ili branch of Shi'ism controlled Egypt and parts of North Africa, the Zaydis were in power in Yemen, and the Shi'i Hamdanid dynasty ruled Syria. But by the eleventh century, all the dynasties were on the wane.

In spite of the fact that they were ruled by leaders identified with Shi'i sects, the majority of people remained Sunni. Nowhere at this time was Shi'ism a majority religion, although there were a few cities that were important Shi'i centers such as Qom and Kufa. Interestingly, though, in the eleventh century, Twelvers began to appear in areas where they apparently had never been before, including Jabal 'Amil in Lebanon.[5] In the next few centuries, the importance of Jabal 'Amil as a center of Shi'i learning increased.

It is not until the sixteenth century, when the Safavids came to power in Iran, that the star of Shi'ism truly rose. Declaring Twelver Shi'ism the official religion, the Safavids set out to educate and convert the majority Sunni population. During the Safavid period, aspects of popular religion, such as visits to the shrines of the imams and elaborate Muharram rituals commemorating Imam Husayn's death, were developed. The Safavids at first sent Iranian 'ulama to study in Jabal 'Amil in Lebanon, but in the reign of Shah Abbas, who built theological colleges in Isphahan, the scholars of Jabal 'Amil went to Iran to teach. At that point, the center of Shi'i learning moved from the Arab world to Iran.

The breach between Sunni and Shi'i Islam deepened during the Safavid period. Also during that time, we see a strengthening of the position of the 'ulama whose main interest became law and the observance of external aspects of religion. The mystical and philosophical aspects of Islam became neglected. The 'ulama under the Safavids also become politically powerful enough to challenge the state.

In Shi'i Islam, the 'ulama act as representatives of the Hidden Imam, that is, the Twelfth Imam who went into occultation. This role often places the religious leaders in direct conflict with the government, whom the 'ulama see as usurping their rightful role to leadership. (However, it should be noted that the 'ulama have also been aligned with various political leaders and, also, that the 'ulama are not a homogeneous group by any means. For example, under the Pahlavis of Iran, there were both 'ulama who supported the shahs and those, like Ayatollah Khomeini, who opposed them.)

The role of the 'ulama has become increasingly complex over the last few centuries. By the eighteenth century, there was a definite hierarchy of clerical leadership based on superiority of learning. A religious elite emerged at the time, referred to as *mujtahids*, who could practice *ijtihad*, that is, make religious decisions based on reason. Eventually, a hierarchy of *mujtahids* came into being,[6] and the concept of *marjiʿiyat taqlid tamm* (complete authority of one *mujtahid* over the entire community) became institutionalized.[7] Superiority in learning is generally held to be the primary prerequisite for the selection of a *marjiʿ*, though there is no clear-cut set of criteria that governs the choice. Ideally, it is the followers (those who are *muqallid* to the *marjiʿ*) who decide which *marjiʿ* to follow.

The Shiʿa of Lebanon

Mikhayil Mishaqa, a fiscal manager to the emirs of the house of Shihab in the nineteenth century, has left us a history of Lebanon in the eighteenth and nineteenth centuries.[8] The following passage gives a taste of what life was like in Mount Lebanon and its environs before the days of the French mandate and Western-style administration:

> During one of his [the author's grandfather, Ibrahim] visits to al-Jazzar [the infamous eighteenth-century Ottoman governor], the deputies had brought in nearly forty of the displaced who were disturbing the peace of the countryside. Al-Jazzar ordered them executed by the stake, one through the buttocks, another through the side, another through the shoulder, when Ibrahim Mishaqa chanced to pass by. They were just finishing this barbaric deed, with only four youths remaining. He asked the officials to refrain from killing the four youths until he should go in to the vizier and send them word whether to release them or to execute them. As the officials were from Sheikh Taha's people and knew of Ibrahim's frequent visits to their sheikh and of the friendly relations between them, they obeyed him. Fortunately al-Jazzar happened to be present, sitting at the palace entrance near the city gate. [Ibrahim] went over to al-Jazzar, who greeted him warmly, and forthwith sought pardon for the four, [promising] to pay a ransom for them to the treasury. He granted his request and issued an order to turn them over. They were sent to them, and he told them of the vizier's compassionate pardon of them, provided they would forswear their former conduct and stay peacefully in their homes. They replied, "We were to be slain, as were our comrades, in a most hideous fashion. Our deliverance was through your intervention. Therefore it is you who have bought us, and we are your slaves for the rest of our lives. We will never leave you, and we will serve you with our very lives. If you drive us away we will sit at your gate. Count us among your followers." He gave them garments [to cover

themselves, as they had] been stripped for execution, and on completing his business in Acre he took them to Sur and Bshara as his escort.

This deed made a good name for Ibrahim Mishaqa, not only among the Christians, but more particularly among the Muslims, and especially among the Shiʿites of Bshara, of whom those who had been rescued from death were. These four promoted Ibrahim's interests the most energetically of all of his followers, who exceeded forty mounted men, Shiʿites and Christians, for it is the custom among clansmen to distinguish followers not with regard to sect, but rather with regard to allegiance and loyalty.[9]

There are few other references to the Shiʿa in Mishaqa's account. He does mention a group of Shiʿa who were "fanatically eager to resist the authorities," but, by and large, they were an impoverished and quiescent lot.

David Urquhart, a mid-nineteenth-century European traveler, described the Shiʿa in the following terms:

They are all in rags, except some of the Sheiks, and are all mendicants. They will come and stand round the cooking which goes on in the open air, and if one is asked to go and get some eggs, he will shrug his shoulders and when told he will be paid for his trouble, he answers, "there is none." If another is asked to sell a sheep or a fowl, he answers, "it is not mine." The filth is revolting. It would seem as if they took a particular pride in exhibiting their rebellion against the law, originally proclaimed from Horeb and afterwards from Mecca, both in regard to their persons and the cleanliness of their villages.[10]

Urquhart went on to call them "unclassifiable" men because they were both Shiʿa and Arab in a time when Shiʿism had become identifiable with Iran.

Over the centuries, the Shiʿa have shared the region today known as Lebanon with the Maronites who became a branch of Roman Catholicism, the Greek Catholics, the Greek Orthodox from whom the Greek Catholics split, the Druze who branched off from Ismaʿili Islam, as well as with Sunnis who constitute the majority religious group in the Arab world. Minority groups have been able to persist in Lebanon largely because of its inaccessible mountainous terrain. Many writers have commented that sectarian differences among these groups were not of paramount importance until intervention by Western powers made them so in the nineteenth century. By backing and protecting the rights of one group or another, the Western powers—British, France, Austrian, and Russian—helped provoke the antipathy of one religious sect toward the others. By the time of the French mandate in 1920, the political system, the Ottoman Millet system, was based on sectarian identity, and the prospects for conflict were only enhanced when France redrew the boundaries of Lebanon, so as to add to Mount Lebanon, the original "Lebanon," the coastal cities, the south, and the Bekaa with all of their diverse populations.

Lebanon is unique among the Middle Eastern countries in that it is home to a very large Christian population. Inclined to emulate the West in many ways, the Christians set a tone for the areas in which they predominated or were found in significant numbers. Hence, the extreme symbols of Islam were often lacking in Lebanon. Certainly in the cosmopolitan city of Beirut, one was not likely to find veiled women or to see shops closing in response to a muezzin's call to prayer. Even in villages with large Shi'a populations, the Christians left their mark. Churches and mosques frequently coexisted, and generally some accommodations were made between the two religious groups.

Aside from the Christians, the Sunnis also influenced the lives of the Shi'a. As a majority, the Sunnis persecuted the Shi'a, forcing the latter to practice *taqiya* (concealing one's faith) and to live in remote areas so as to remain undisturbed. Thus, the Shi'a could be ignored by the government which was dominated by Christians (mainly Maronites) and Sunnis.[11]

That the Shi'a were the poorest and least powerful of the confessional groups in Lebanon seems undisputed. The economic success that Lebanon experienced in the nineteenth and twentieth centuries certainly was not evenly distributed among all groups and regions of the country.[12] Richard Norton states that "even as recently as the 1950s, the Shi'a seemed most notable for their invisibility and irrelevance in Lebanese politics."[13] He cites studies indicating that the Shi'a had the lowest per capita income, were the most poorly educated, and were the least represented in professions and businesses. In 1961, Bint Jubeil, a capital in a district in the south with a population of 10,000, had only two doctors, no pharmacy, no electricity, and only eleven telephones.

However, there were some powerful families among the Shi'a. How they achieved this position depended largely on which part of Lebanon they came from. In the south, these families became influential through their services to the Ottomans. The *zu'ama* in Ba'albek have been the traditional clan or tribal leaders. As Albert Hourani explains, the *zu'ama* of the Shi'i population were feudal lords whose power rested on "their position as landowners, often of ancient lineage, their use of strong-arm men, and their ability to give protection and patronage."[14] These were the men who, after independence from France in 1943, gained political power but failed to produce results for the impoverished masses they were supposedly representing.

Fouad Ajami cites the story of a Shiʿi *zaʿim* who believed that he quite literally owned the peasants who worked for him and denied a bright young man the chance of fulfilling his dream of becoming a lawyer.[15] Yet some young men did escape the grinding poverty of their villages and prospered in other lands, primarily in West Africa. After obtaining university degrees and prospering in business, some returned to Lebanon, hoping to find a place in the Lebanese political system. But they had to buy their way into the process and face the humiliation of the *zuʿama* who maintained a stranglehold on the parliamentary system. Thus, a struggle existed between the old and new strata of society. Furthermore, the peripheral regions of Lebanon, such as the south and the Bekaa, were "dominated by the past" while Beirut was "gripped by the future." As anthropologist Eric Wolf has pointed out, this combination of factors "spells trouble for society as a whole."[16]

Essentially, elections were petty rivalries between competing clans in a region and had little to do with any goals for improving the conditions of the people. Ajami writes: "in the district of Bint Jubeil, the Bezzis, one clan whose leader was willing to do anything to get himself elected to Parliament, either defeated their rivals, the Beydouns, or were defeated by them. . . . What mattered was the intangible honor, the feeling, as the Bezzis of Bint Jubeil put it, that they themselves went to bed satiated while their rivals went to sleep on an empty stomach."[17]

The increasing poverty of agricultural villages of the south in the 1960s forced huge migrations of poorly educated Shiʿa to the Beirut slums, where they lived in miserable conditions. As latecomers to the city arriving in large numbers with great needs, they could not be absorbed into the client-patron system that was the basis of political life in Lebanon. Furthermore, the electoral system worked against them in that their voting privileges were based on the village of their origin and not on where they happened to be living at the time when they cast their votes. The *zuʿama* in the Beirut area who could not anticipate votes from this constituency simply did not provide services for them.[18]

On the other hand, the *zuʿama* were very actively involved in ensuring that working-class families were totally dependent on them and not on the state for their needs. Interested in building their own personal followings, they often stirred up conflicts, many times violent ones, in the process. All forces in areas such as Borj Hammoud, a suburb of Beirut, worked against a unification of the masses, even within a given confessional group.[19] One factor that determined internal division among the Shiʿa was whether people originated from the south or the Bekaa.

Nor were the clergy a source of support for the masses. Afraid of the *zuʿama*, the clergy did nothing to challenge their role. Fouad Ajami calls them "obscurants" who "told fantastic tales about the twelve imams, about their valor and their eloquence—tales that the mind, even the believing mind, had trouble taking in. They were timid and conservative."[20]

It was to this scene that Sayyid Musa Sadr, an Iranian-born cleric from an illustrious clerical family that traced its ancestry to Lebanon and to the seventh imam, arrived. Religiously learned but also a man of action and pragmatism, he pitted himself against the Lebanese Shiʿi *zuʿama* and the quiescent clergy, who had long been cut off from the centers of Shiʿi learning in southern Iraq and in Iran. Imam Musa, as he is called among the Lebanese Shiʿa, was the spokesman of the "oppressed" in Lebanon. Although he actively sought to bridge gaps among sectarian groups, he ultimately saw that the Shiʿa would need to fight on their own. He eventually established Harakat Amal (the Movement of Hope), which began as a social movement but in 1974 became an armed militia, one of many in Lebanon.

The 1970s saw a dramatic change in the political life of the Shiʿa. Musa Sadr's movement competed with other organizations, particularly Communist ones, for the hearts of the Shiʿa. Many youth joined with the Palestinians in their struggle and with other confessional parties and militias in the 1975–76 Civil War.

It was after the disappearance of Musa Sadr, during a visit to Libya in 1978, that the strength of his Harakat Amal grew. The Shiʿa by then saw themselves as being used and betrayed by their erstwhile Palestinian comrades. The Shiʿa in the south suffered most from the retaliatory raids of Israel against the Palestinians who launched attacks from Shiʿi villages. Furthermore, the 1979 Iranian revolution which led to the establishment of an Islamic republic dominated by religious clerics served as an inspiration to the Lebanese Shiʿa: through religion, they, too, could be victorious. Revolt against tyranny, as played out by the Imam Husayn on the Plain of Karbala, became the focus of this community. It was politically activated through religious revival.

Yet Musa Sadr's successor as leader of Harakat Amal was not a cleric but a French-educated attorney who, with his family, lived for some time in Dearborn, Michigan. A man with centrist views, Nabih Berri supports the idea of a multiconfessional Lebanon with the Shiʿa having a larger voice in its running and does not express a desire for an Iranian-style theocracy.

After the invasion of Lebanon in 1982, however, Berri's moderate and secularist position lost its appeal with some of the Shiʿi population. New radical groups emerged but are generally considered to be under the umbrella of the Hizb Allah movement which is Iranian-based and aspires to transform Lebanon into an Islamic republic modeled after the revolutionary government of Iran. For the past several years, Harakat Amal and Hizb Allah have fought bitter battles for regions with large Shiʿi populations. Hizb Allah has been largely successful in the Beirut suburbs and has made deep inroads into the Bekaa, while Harakat Amal has held a tenuous control over the south. But it is a mistake to see these organizations as highly structured and orderly. Furthermore, villagers may have strong sympathies with one or another group but never fight under either banner. Or they may have sympathies with neither.[21]

Life has changed drastically for the Shiʿa of Lebanon since the Lebanese civil war and the Iranian Revolution. The world tends to view them now solely in political terms. They are "radical" and "militant." And they are important only in terms of what they have done to disrupt the West.

It is forgotten that Musa Sadr wanted to awaken his people religiously as well as politically. It might be argued that in Islam, religion and politics are so inextricably linked that they cannot be separated. For some, this is true. Yet the lives and the words of many of the Shiʿa of Dearborn do not bear out this contention. Exactly what religion means today is very much open to debate. We find this debate occurring in Iran, Egypt, Algeria, Pakistan, Indonesia, and wherever we find Islamic communities, including Dearborn. In many ways, the Shiʿa (and their Sunni brethren) have their own language of discourse. However, they also share many of the same concerns that Catholic immigrants from Europe found themselves grappling with in the last century and the earlier part of this century.

CHAPTER 2

The Life of the Mosques

The History

Sheikh Chirri and the Development of the Islamic Center of America

IN 1988, on the twenty-fifth anniversary of the opening of the Islamic Center of America, a booklet was distributed to the Shiʿi Muslims of the Detroit and Dearborn area recounting the tale of how the Islamic Center, the Jamiʿ, came into being. It is a tale of frustration, fortitude, and sacrifice. The story says that because of the guidance of "the ever present, beloved Imam, Muhammad Jawad Chirri, the community united for the most part." It further states that "the people contributed to the new Center with a humble zeal reminiscent of the first Muslims." The community underwent a "metamorphosis."

In the 1940s, Shiʿism in Dearborn needed a heroic figure if it was to survive as an independent faith and not be subsumed by Sunnism, something it has resisted in the rest of the world for centuries. Before the arrival of Sheikh Chirri, there was no "real imam" in the area.

A true sheikh in Shiʿi terms is one who has been trained at one or more of the holy cities such as Najaf in Iraq or Qom in Iran. Aside from the Koran and the Traditions of the Prophet, he will study such subjects as Islamic law, theology, logic, and Koran commen-

41

taries. It will be his main teacher at the theological school who decides when the man's studies should be concluded. He will then either go off to a village in need of a preacher or find a more prestigious appointment. Each sheikh tends to function quite independently. A hierarchy like that found in Catholicism, with its bishops, archbishops, monsignors, and so on, is not found in Islam. The word *imam* (from the Arabic root *amm*, "to be in front") is used in a variety of ways. The twelve "rightful successors" (those descendants of Fatima and ʿAli who were the religious leaders of the Shiʿa in the early centuries of Islam) are always referred to as imams. There is also the term *imam jumʿa*, which means "leader of the Friday prayers," and a person hired to lead the prayers could then be called an imam. However, some Muslims feel it is not appropriate for their local clerics to refer to themselves with this title, as it indicates a sense of self-importance. Regardless of this sentiment, the clerics in this community are frequently called imams. I will generally refer to the clerics as sheikhs to lessen the confusion between the Twelve Imams, (the great religious leaders of early Shiʿism) and the local preachers. However, if one is a *sayyid* (a descendant of the Prophet) and a sheikh as well, he prefers to be called by the former term, and I will refer to him as Sayyid So-and-so.

Returning to the discussion of Dearborn, in the 1940s, this community that had "grown large" consisted of about two hundred Muslim families. These were mostly Lebanese, Syrians, and Palestinians. They were both Shiʿa and Sunni. At least for the Shiʿa, ceremonial and spiritual needs were met by a Shiʿi Lebanese from the village of Bint Jubeil, Sheikh Khalil Bezzi. But informants tell me that Sheikh Bezzi took care of the religious needs for all Muslims, "not only in Dearborn but all over the country and regardless of whether they were Shiʿites, not Shiʿites, or whatever." Illiterate when he came to the United States, he went briefly to Najaf to study Arabic and the Koran, then returned to America to serve as religious leader, but not in a full-time capacity. My informants describe Bezzi in saintly and heroic terms, although he is a far different kind of hero from Chirri. Rather than being revered for his learning and ambitions for the community, it is his humble and almost anticlerical behavior that distinguishes him. Shiʿi clergy in Lebanon are in a class apart from the rest of society. They do not labor but simply perform clerical duties: preaching, giving eulogies, contracting weddings and divorces, and so on. But Bezzi did something no self-respecting sheikh in Dearborn would do today: he made a living driving a truck from store to store selling vegetables. He refused payment for his religious services. In the 1950s, one of my informants and a small group of other believers pooled their money to buy him a car and left it in front of his home, giving the keys to his wife. When he arrived home and found the car, Bezzi telephoned one of the men responsible and told him that he had half an hour to come get the car. If he did not come by then, Bezzi said he would divorce his wife for having accepted the gift. The car was picked up and returned to the dealer.

Michael Gilsenen, writing about the *ulama* of south Lebanon in the 1950s, presents a picture of the clerics as being "the local socially prominent group."[1] Landowners with a monopoly on knowledge and literacy, they formed an elite group that did not question the status quo and did not fight for the rights of the Shi'a. In the 1960s, Musa Sadr, the founder of Harakat Amal, found himself at odds with this style of cleric and helped to revolutionize the role of the *ulama* in Lebanon. Sheikh Bezzi was no revolutionary, but neither was he a quiescent religious leader content to make a living by performing ritual services. From all accounts, he seems to have been an idealistic missionary out not to convert new souls to Islam but to save those already in the flock.

The early Shi'a in this area like to stress that there was a lack of Shi'i/Sunni division in the community, and there is actually strong resistance to discussing this topic. But, obviously, there was a distinction being made between the two sects even in the earliest days. I find it interesting, for example, that it is Sheikh Bezzi who is seen as the religious leader of this community, even though Sunni preachers were also active in the area. The development of mosques and communities in the Detroit area is complicated, but always there has existed some distinction between the Shi'a and other Islamic sects.[2]

In fact, the earliest accounts of Islamic activity in the Detroit area are of Sunni-dominated activities. Muslims gravitated to the highly industrialized area of Highland Park, where Ford Motor Company had a plant, and it is there, according to historian Alixa Naff, that the first mosque in America seems to have been built.[3] A *Detroit News* article dated July 29, 1927, recounts the history of this first mosque, which opened in June 1921 under the direction of a Sunni Lebanese preacher, Muhammad Karoub. The mosque was short-lived, though it apparently had support from a variety of Muslim countries. The article reports that there was a difference of opinion regarding the failure of the mosque. Karoub had brought a religious leader, a mufti, from Lebanon whose ideas were too progressive for the Muslims, who were far from being a homogeneous group. The article says that they were from Persia, Turkey, Spain,

Morocco, Siberia, Arabia and Syria. Others, apparently, were not happy with Karoub's financing of the mosque. The greatest controversy came when a coffeehouse proprietor who had usurped Karoub's leadership and popularity was killed. While Karoub was acquitted of any wrongdoing, his name was tarnished. But, contrary to the expectations of the journalist, Islamic aspirations did not die in the area. Sunnis and Shiʿa both continued to rent buildings and meet in homes for religious and social functions. All my sources state that members of both sects would attend each other's events.

The real growth of Islam in this area actually coincides with the growth of the Ford Motor Company in Dearborn. It was to the crowded southeast side of the town, where the Rouge plant dominates the landscape, that large numbers of Muslims, primarily Arab Muslims, migrated and continue to migrate to this day. On the major street of this quarter of Dearborn stands what is now the Yemeni Zaydi Dearborn Mosque. Opened in the 1930s, it was dominated by Sunnis until recently. A year or so after the establishment of this mosque, the Shiʿa rented a hall only a few blocks away. They named it the Hashimite Hall, in honor of the family of the Prophet. It was to the Hashimite Club that Sheikh Chirri came to teach. He states that he also was involved with the Sunni mosque, which at that time had a large Lebanese congregation, when he arrived in Dearborn in 1949. He, too, resists discussing Sunni/Shiʿi differences, at least with outsiders.

In 1966, Abdo Elkholy wrote a book comparing the histories of the Detroit-Dearborn and the Toledo Muslim communities. He describes the situation in Dearborn in far different terms from the Shiʿi version quoted above:

> He [Chirri] came to America ... where he found the sectarian conflict dying in the Detroit community. He decided to revive it, chiefly, according to several respondents, as a means of increasing his own power. He encouraged the physical as well as the spiritual separation between the two sects in the Detroit community. Now the community has two separate religious institutions, the mosque for the Sunnis and the Arabian Hashimite Club for the Shiʿahs. The Shiʿahs in Detroit have ceased to participate in any religious activities with the Sunnis. ... The division has almost resulted in two separate denominations with completely distinct religious and social activities.[4]

Elkholy's information is not entirely correct. The Hashimite Club existed before Chirri's arrival. The earliest history of Islam in the Detroit area reflects that there was always a consciousness that the Shiʿa had to remain somewhat distinct, though obviously the line between these two major sects had grown fuzzy in comparison to what one finds in the Middle East. Asked if the early believers in the Hashimite Club celebrated such Shiʿi holidays as the birthdays of the imams (the line of successors after the Prophet) and that of the Prophet's daughter, my informants who were there at the time report that these holidays were not celebrated. There were parties and dances and classes for children. But the very fact that there was an institution that took the name of the Prophet's family suggests that this community grasped the significance of keeping their separateness alive. Elkholy remarks that he found the Shiʿa in the Detroit area in the 1950s far more zealous about their religion than the Sunnis, whom he describes as being resentful of Shiʿa success. The Sunnis, Elkholy reports, accused the Shiʿa of having caused a rift between the two sects.

What is most significant about Elkholy's account is that he tells the story of the community from a Sunni perspective. His history of the community is only one history. And one might even go so far as to say it is a dead history. The Lebanese Shiʿa—those refugees from the impoverished regions of Jabal ʿAmil and the Bekaa—have prevailed in Dearborn. They are the most numerous group of Muslims in the area and the most conspicuous. They have, at this writing, one mosque in the fullest sense of the word and two institutes that for all intents and purposes serve as mosques. The Shiʿa are on the way to building an elementary school in Dearborn and have expanded their properties and goals outside the Detroit-Dearborn limits. In the meantime, the Sunnis, organizing themselves as the Bekaa League, have been displaced by the Yemeni Zaydis at the mosque in the south end and now occupy a small building in East Dearborn. What is more, the Shiʿa tend to be the most prosperous group of Muslims in the area. For the victorious Shiʿa of Dearborn, Sheikh Chirri was not a man of selfish designs. He was a self-sacrificing hero who braved all odds to establish Islam (in its Shiʿi form) in America. It is this image that prevails and probably will continue to do so.

When Chirri arrived in America, he found an immigrant community of primarily Ford factory workers who clung to their Islamic identity, perhaps praying, avoiding pork if possible, and asking for the services of a sheikh on ceremonial occasions. This is a community whose gatherings were more of a social than a religious nature. He also found a community that was not book-oriented and that had given in to many of the easier paths offered by American life.

Women felt pressured to give up the scarf so as not to look strange in their new setting. The temptations of alcohol also drove some to compromise their principles. Certainly, the intricacies of Imami Shiʿism eluded this group. Chirri, with his scholarly credentials, taught his people reverence for the saints and the symbols of Shiʿism. "Without Sheikh Chirri, there would be no Islam in America" is a commonly heard expression of gratitude toward this man who is now quite aged. As for the Shiʿi/Sunni split, Chirri is not considered to blame at all. One informant told me that it was visiting sheikhs from Lebanon who encouraged this division, not Chirri. Before this interference, she said, there were Sunnis who attended the Jamiʿ's services.

My informants tell me that from the beginning, it was Chirri's aim to build a mosque. He ran into resistance in the community and left for Michigan City, Indiana. The story is now recounted in religious terms. Just as the Prophet Muhammad was hounded out of Mecca, so, too, was Chirri forced to leave the city in which he had placed so much hope. But, just as there had been with the Prophet, there was also with Chirri a small band of loyalists who stood by him and believed in his mission from the beginning. They must have given him sufficient encouragement; Chirri returned to Lebanon, befriended someone who had access to President Gamal Abdel Nasser of Egypt, and solicited from Nasser enough money to motivate the fledgling band of Shiʿi to begin the task of actually constructing a mosque.

The history of the building of the Islamic Center of America is replete with stories of sacrificial giving. Each fund-raising dinner reaped greater rewards, and I am told these funds sometimes came from remortgaging of individuals' homes. Finally, in 1963, the center at 15571 Joy Road in Detroit was completed and its doors opened. While its domed exterior and minaret give it a mosquelike appearance, its interior is lacking in the lushness and mystery that one associates with Middle Eastern mosques. It is plain in the extreme, with its arid rectangles of rooms filled with folding chairs and Formica-topped tables. In the receiving area is a receptionist's desk in front of the sheikh's office. And on either side of the room are bookshelves. Among the books are those written over the years by its director, Imam Muhammad Jawad Chirri, books entitled *The Shiites under Attack* and *The Brother of the Prophet*. There is no mistaking this for a Sunni mosque.

In *The Shiites under Attack,* in which he makes distinctions between Shiʿi and Sunni attitudes and beliefs, he also calls for the "unity of the Muslims" and reports on his own "humble efforts" in this endeavor: "In 1959, I attempted to begin a campaign in this direction [overcoming Sunni/Shiʿi differences]. I visited Egypt and met the late President Gamal Abdel Nasser. I discussed with him and separately with the late Sheikh Al Azhar[5] . . . the matter of reconciliation between the Sunnite and the Shiite schools. I spoke to each of the two leaders about the necessity of solving the problem and about the way through which it can be solved."[6] He continues by saying that it was his goal to persuade Sheikh Al Azhar to issue a "verdict of equality between the Jaafari Math-hab [the school of thought of the Shiʿi Imam Jaafar as-Sedeq] and the four Math-habs [the four schools accepted in Sunni Islam]." Chirri was successful: "The Grand Sheikh responded to this suggestion immediately. On the following day his son-in-law and secretary . . . visited me and brought the good tidings; the Grand Sheikh had responded to my suggestion and issued a verdict about the subject. I went with him to the Grand Sheikh, thanking him for his historical achievement. The Sheikh read to me the text of the verdict before publishing it."[7]

A picture of Chirri with Sheikh Al Azhar appears in another of Chirri's texts, *Inquiries about Islam*. Such an achievement helped ensure Chirri's success among his American Muslim constituents.

The Jamiʿ over the Years

If the mosque has changed over the years, it is primarily in terms of the appearance and behaviors of those who frequent it. A photograph of a children's class in 1965 shows a group of school-aged children dressed in their "Sunday best." The girls, sitting among the boys, wear crisp, frilly dresses and, except for one little girl in an "Easter bonnet," no head coverings at all.

The older members of this community now laugh at themselves when they look back to this earlier era. "The women used to wear curlers in their hair to the mosque!" one woman told me. Such a thing would be inconceivable today. The earlier community did not think about wearing Islamic dress. Even simple traditional scarves were a rarity. Furthermore, a photograph of Chirri dating from the 1960s shows him in a business suit rather than clerical robes, though he was wearing a turban. However, I am told that he would even forgo the turban at times when in public.

Styles of clothing are not the only things to have changed. One informant who was still a young girl when the Jamiʿ opened remembers going there for parties and dances. It was common to hold weddings at the Jamiʿ, traditional Lebanese weddings with music and singing and dancing. Apparently, the Islamic Center was not the only mosque in North America to experience such events. Orfalea reports that the mosque in Michigan City, Indiana, was also "misused."[8] The son of one of the mosque's founders complained that the people would remove the carpets for weddings and funerals, asserting that it should have been used only for prayer.

Traditional-type weddings occur today in rented halls, certainly not in the local Shi'i mosques. A woman who came here from Jabal 'Amil in the 1950s said that a few people had even started sneaking alcohol "under the table" at the weddings. That she should have told me such a thing horrified her thirty-year-old son. I had to assure him that I realized this had occurred in the distant past, that only a few people would have done such a thing, and that I knew things had changed drastically since then. Indeed they have. Chirri is responsible for some of these changes. He reportedly weaned people slowly to the ways of Islam. "He never pushed us too hard," said one of his admiring early followers, who went on to say that Chirri did not want to scare away the youth by being too strict. He feared that if they appeared to look and behave too differently from the larger society, it would make them uncomfortable and would drive them away from Islam.

Once the Islamic Center of America was built and open, it appears that the Shi'i community developed in a fairly predictable fashion. The membership became largely assimilated into American society. Small in numbers, they found it necessary to learn English as soon as possible. Their children may have grown up speaking Arabic, but few received instruction in reading and writing the language.

Certainly the leadership, hand-chosen by Sheikh Chirri himself, became quite prosperous. The community appeared to be concerned with remaining distinctively Muslim but in a way that also fit with American society. Sheikh Chirri became known among his constituents as someone who understood America and Christianity. Members of this community who remember the Sunday school programs at the Hashimite Club and later at the Islamic Center have told me that they learned a great deal about Christianity from Chirri. One man said that on Christian holidays, there would be lessons at the mosque explaining these religious occasions to the Muslim children, although they would not celebrate the holidays themselves (at least not at the mosque).

Chirri, throughout the years, was interested in teaching Islam to Americans. The books he wrote in English testify to this. Indeed, during the first few moments of an interview I had with him, he insisted on explaining the station of Christ to me. The lecture probably would have continued had I not been able to interject some words that showed him that I had some knowledge of Shiʿism. Those he led expected such missionary activities from him. The earlier immigrants and their children wanted to be understood. They wanted someone who could speak to Christians. However, one gets a strong sense from talking to Sheikh Chirri, and to non-Muslim Americans who have been acquainted with him, that he never did truly grasp American culture. Perhaps he confused "Christian theology" with American viewpoints on religion. This impression is substantiated by his sermons (see "Sermons and Speakers" in this chapter). It is also true, though, that by the time I had spoken to him, he was a very elderly gentlemen facing problems that had more to do with Middle Eastern politics than with American society.

Over the years, Sheikh Chirri has been the spokesman for the Shiʿa of Dearborn and Detroit. On the radio and in newspapers, his opinion has been sought on current events involving the Arab world and Islam. According to his secretary, he feels he has not always been represented fairly by the press and has become more reluctant to speak to outsiders.

The issues that Chirri has addressed to his followers and in public reflect how strongly he has been affected by world events. Having grown up in the south end in the 1950s when Chirri was preaching there, one man recalls that Chirri did not advocate a political struggle for Palestine. He told his listeners, some of whom were Palestinian, that they must resign themselves to the reality of Israel. No doubt, this message was meant to encourage the immigrants to get on with their lives in America. But it also suggests that he was very sensitive to Islam's image in this country. I believe he did not want Islam to be seen as anti-American.

In spite of America's anti-Nasser stance, however, Chirri obviously remained grateful to the Egyptian leader for his support of the building of the Jamiʿ. Nasser's death in 1970 evoked the following words from Chirri, quoted in the *Garden City Guide-Journal* on October 1, 1970: "Every person in our community is deeply saddened. The Arab nation will survive, and perhaps the relations of Arab countries will actually improve because of the tragedy, but the American people will find the west has lost the last big chance for peace there. He was a barrier between communism and the Arab people. And now that barrier is gone." The anti-Communist sentiments again reflect his pro-American stance.

Within a decade after the death of Nasser, the Middle East and Imam Chirri's world had changed profoundly. A revolution, a civil war, hijackings, and kidnappings were daily news, and Chirri's opinions were sought by the press. After the hijacking of a TWA plane in Beirut, on June 23, 1985, the *Detroit Free Press* reported that Chirri "does not condone the hijacking but that it did not surprise him." Chirri was further quoted as saying, "It is like the cat that is sleeping. If you tread on it, should you be amazed that it bites you? If two or three people hijack an airplane because Israel is holding their brothers, should you be amazed?" By the 1980s, Israel could be counted openly as an enemy. Politically speaking, it is the "safest" enemy, as Israel is universally scorned by Arab Muslims. By the 1980s, the number of Muslims in Dearborn was so great that consideration of their feelings was paramount in the mind of any cleric.

But what to say about the Iranians? This was and is an obvious problem. Iran and the Lebanese kidnappings and bombings obviously have been a thorn in the side of Imam Chirri and those closest to him. There is a lengthy article in the *Dearborn Times-Herald* of July 25, 1985, relating to the kidnapping of Americans in Lebanon. Chirri's comment on this issue: "The Shiites are good people who should not be judged for the actions of a few." Although not directly quoted regarding his opinions about Iran, Chirri seems to have left the interviewer with the message he wanted heard. The journalist wrote that the Shiʿa of Dearborn "should not be confused with Iranian Moslems who advocate fiery revolution in the name of Islam. On the contrary, most Shiite sects are moderate and seek only an improved lot in life."

The press wanted Chirri's views again when the *Satanic Verses* issue erupted. Interviewed on television, Chirri felt the need to condemn novelist Salman Rushdie as "a dog that should be killed."

Thus, Chirri found that the challenges facing him and his community had grown and intensified. Old and new immigrants had differing views of what it meant to be Muslims or Shiʿa, on whether they were Lebanese or Americans. Questions such as whether Khomeini was a villain or a hero have the potential of splitting the community as well. By and large, however, the Jamiʿ has remained a house of worship large enough for a variety of viewpoints. In spite of points of contention, the people who frequent this mosque mostly wish to leave behind divisive politics.

"In New Haven, Connecticut, the Irish had built a small church in the 1830s; in 1848 it was destroyed by fire. Within six months the community of Irish laborers had raised thirteen thousand dollars to buy and furnish a former Congregational church. Such commitment to the church was not uncommon. In the poorest of Irish neighborhoods, the people invariably found the means to build the parish church and support it through both good and bad times."[9]

Church building was of the highest priority among the majority of ethnic Catholic groups entering America during the century of massive immigration. Simple, plain structures at first, they bore no resemblance to their fine monuments in the old country or to the grand churches and cathedrals that would become part of the urban American landscape later. But who would take the initiative to build the churches? Among the Germans, it was the lay people who built and ran the churches; the priests served in their ritual capacity only. Among the Irish, clerics reigned supreme, which is the way the Irish wanted it. For them, clergy and church were completely intertwined, and they begged for more and more priests from abroad. The Irish were shocked by the anticlericalism of the Italian Catholics who saw the papacy as exploitative and who, back home, experienced the village priest as a "money-grasping intruder."[10] They were also perplexed by the Poles' demands for lay ownership of church property.

Immigrant groups rarely had to share their churches with one another. If they did, it was usually only a temporary arrangement. Quarrels over language and clergy and dislike of each other's customs and ritual styles drove wedges between ethnic groups. People preferred to worship in their own ways and in their own languages. Dolan quotes a Ukrainian immigrant as saying, "We are not entirely the same as we were in our country because we are missing something. What we miss is God Whom we could understand, Whom we could adore in our own way."[11] Thus, each Catholic ethnic group was driven to build its own churches and its own parishes reminiscent of their old countries.

The people of Dearborn, being both Lebanese and Shi'a, faced the same dilemma. Unaccustomed though they may have been back home to building their own mosques, they recognized that if Shi'ism were to survive in America, they had to act. Under the leadership of Chirri, many of them made significant financial sacrifices to build a structure, not grand and elegant by any means, but one that met the needs of the community at the time and sent the message that Shi'ism had been established in America.

The Islamic Institute (the Majma')

By the mid-1980s, Sheikh Chirri could no longer claim to speak for all Shi'a in America. This fact was underscored by the establishment in 1985 of the Islamic Institute of Knowledge under the direction of Sheikh ʿAbd al-Latif Berri, a relatively young, soft-spoken sheikh from Tibnin in south Lebanon. Situated on Warren Avenue, in the very heart of Dearborn's Shiʿi Lebanese community, the Islamic Institute was not built as a mosque but was converted from a business building and revamped so that various social, educational, and spiritual needs of the community could be met. The interior of the Majmaʿ, as it is known, is lacking in visual reminders of Middle Eastern mosques, as is the Jamiʿ. The main meeting room, the *husayniya*, is generally lined with collapsible tables and folding chairs. During social occasions where food is to be served, the tables bear paper tablecloths, Styrofoam cups, and plastic utensils. For various occasions, the walls will be adorned with plaques of locally produced calligraphy, and occasionally one finds a large photograph of Khomeini dominating the room. But during Ramadan and holy day observances, the aura of the building changes. At those times, the *husayniya* will be strewn with prayer rugs. While some of the believers (the brothers and sisters, as members of the core group call themselves at this mosque) will be engaged in prayer, others, clusters of both men and heavily veiled women, usually with toddlers and infants in tow, will be visiting among themselves in various corners of the room. This room is not where *salat* (obligatory prayer) is performed. Sheikh Berri leads *salat* upstairs in a room that faces the main street.

Sheikh Berri told me, during my first meeting with him, that the Majmaʿ was not a mosque per se but was meant for more educational purposes. He did not want me to think that it had begun as an open breach with the Jamiʿ. Yet it is common knowledge that its opening was in reaction to the Jamiʿ. As one well-informed woman stated, "Sheikh Berri was divorced from Sheikh Chirri." She states that Berri started out as a preacher in the Jamiʿ but left after a short time because of disagreements with Chirri and the Jamiʿ's board of directors. Unpleasant relations between the two sheikhs has not abated. When Wafa, who contributes financially to both the Jamiʿ and the Majmaʿ, telephoned Chirri to make an appointment for me to speak with him, he expressed to her his annoyance that I had already spoken to Berri. She told me quite bluntly that the two men dislike each other. Yet it is apparent that there is communication between the two mosques and that there is at least no public animosity. However, toward the end of my stay in Dearborn, an attempt to unify the clerics during a fundraising event for the Iraqi Shiʿa led to public embarrassment. Sheikh Chirri had been led into the Majmaʿ but was quite disoriented, as senility was rapidly advancing. When he realized where he was, he immediately demanded to be taken away.

The Muslims who supported Berri's establishment of the Majmaᶜ were a people who had been deeply affected by the revolutionary form of Islam advocated by the Islamic Republic of Iran. For this group, the Jamiᶜ, which had been established nearly twenty-five years ago, had become too tolerant of Western ways. Several people have told me that the Jamiᶜ has become "like a church."

During my first days in Dearborn, in 1987, I was given a tour of the eastern part of the city, the part that a short while later would become my neighborhood. My guide was a young Lebanese man whose family I had befriended quickly since I had known some of their relatives when I lived in Lebanon. He drove me by the Majmaᶜ but did not want me to walk by it. He was afraid that if I looked too interested, the people inside would think I was "FBI." How shocked he was to learn somewhat later that I had visited the Majmaᶜ on several occasions and was on friendly terms with a number of the people who regularly attended it. Sometime after that, he and his brother, who both attend the Jamiᶜ, conceded that they had heard "some good things" about the Majmaᶜ but would not go there themselves.

While it is commonly said that the Jamiᶜ is more sympathetic to Harakat Amal, the Majmaᶜ is seen as being closely linked with the Hizb Allah movement. People such as my young friend have frequently seen the Majmaᶜ only in political terms. However, in the five years or so that it has been open, the Majmaᶜ has obviously undergone some changes. When one goes for events such as Ramadan, Id al-Fitr, and ᶜAshura and for purely social occasions, a broad spectrum of the community appears in full force. It is only at times when things Iranian become the centerpiece of the occasion—the death of Khomeini or even the Iranian earthquake—or for special educational programs that one becomes very conscious of the Hizb Allah approach to Islam.

Most people in this community are not actively involved in either Harakat Amal or Hizb Allah. They will say that they came here to escape the fighting which they do not understand. More than a few people have told me that they did not attend any regular services at the mosques because both were too political, yet I also found people who actively shunned the Amal/Hizb Allah dispute, attending both the Jamiᶜ and the Majmaᶜ to show that they are not "prejudiced."

The Islamic Council of America (the Majlis)

The Islamic Council of America, the Majlis, is another story. After it opened in the winter of 1989, some months went by before it was even noticed by some members of the community. Situated in a row of two-story brick commercial buildings, the structure served as a store before its recent transformation to a house of worship and study. Immediately off the street on the north side of this rather narrow structure is a room used for *salat* and for preaching. The south side, again with a door entering from the street, is the *husayniya* where one might go for *iftar* (suppers during Ramadan) or for a general type of meeting. During Ramadan, this room is for the women and children, while the men congregate in the prayer room to hear Sheikh Muhammad Ali Burro, the director of the Majlis, speak. It does not differ from the Jami῾ or the Majma῾ in its simplicity.

But there are certain features that do differentiate it from the other two institutions, the most striking being that no one attends it who is not in strict conformity with the rules of Islam, at least in their outward appearance. This is a mosque not only for the type of *hijab* that has lately become so prevalent in Arab cities but also for the Iranian *chador* and the ῾abaya worn by Iraqi women from Najaf and Karbala. The *chador* or ῾abaya may also be seen at the Majma῾, but usually there will be some lacy scarves to counteract the effect. Not so at the Majlis. One does not find a trace of women's hair (or arms or legs) showing here. The men are often bearded, dress in open-collared shirts, and maintain a serious demeanor. Again, one finds this same sort of men in the halls and prayer room of the Majma῾, but they may be sitting next to persons whose approach to Islam differs significantly from theirs. The other striking feature about the Majlis is the office of the director, Sheikh Burro. It is not only the new carpeting and long, sumptuous sofa that is remarkable but also the fact that before entering this room, one must remove one's shoes, as I did when I interviewed Sheikh Burro. This is an Iranian custom, not Lebanese. Indeed, this is not the only aspect of Iranian life that Burro brought back from Iran, specifically Qom, where he lived for about seventeen years. His obvious pleasure in speaking Persian and his *chador*-covered wife's taste for Persian food suggest how favorably disposed he is toward Iranian culture. Far more important, however, is the extent to which his approach to Islam has been marked by the ῾ulama of Qom.

Burro had begun his work in this community at the Jami῾, but he found it lacking. He disapproved of women who tied scarves on their heads, much as Catholic women did before the 1960s, and sat at tables with men. Men could be seen greeting women with a handshake, something that an observant Muslim, concerned with following the letter of the law, should not do. I am told that he expressed his astonishment that even men who had made their *hajj*, their pilgrimage to Mecca, would do such a thing. His final break with the Jami' came, though, over a more substantial issue, which will be discussed later.

"The Catholic church must fit herself to a constantly changing environment, to the character of every people, and to the wants of each age."[12] These sentiments, stated by John L. Spalding (appointed first bishop of the diocese of Peoria, Illinois, in 1876), were shared by a handful of U.S. bishops, but certainly they had many opponents, including the pope. The bitter dispute over whether to unite church and age or to view the church as incompatible with modern culture was fought among all strata of Catholic society in America over many decades. In the last fifteen years of the nineteenth century, the major question was: "Is there 'American Catholicity'?" By the 1930s, Catholics in America tended to agree that there was, but it was not until Vatican II that the question could truly be put to rest. (Or could it?)

Sheikh Chirri, though determined to sustain Shi'ism in America, was obviously affected by the trends occurring in the larger society. He saw the necessity of Americanizing his religion. In the 1940s, '50s, and '60s, a person could reasonably ask how else a religion could be sustained in America. This was a time when barriers among previously contentious religious groups and nationalities were breaking down. Catholics were mingling increasingly with non-Catholics. Committees were formed to combat prejudice. A diffuse set of values based on Protestantism were inculcated in schoolchildren, and, to use Will Herberg's term, "an American way of life" was developing that transcended confessional barriers. Sheikh Chirri could not have helped but be influenced by these social trends.[13]

But new Shi'i clerics from the Middle East had experienced a different religious and political history from that of Sheikh Chirri. Religion, in their view, should define society, not the other way around. And they could bring evidence to prove that religion in its most absolute and uncompromising form could be viable in today's world; witness the situation in the Islamic Republic of Iran. And so the old dispute, the one that Catholics had fought over with such bitterness decades earlier, would be played out again in Dearborn: whether to fit religion to a changing environment or to take a defensive posture and isolate it from social forces.

Differences in Style among the Mosques

As indicated above, there are some apparent differences among the congregations of the three institutions. When I have visited the Jami', I have never seen a *chador*, although I have seen women in *hijab*. But just as frequently, I will see women with gauzy, almost doily-like cloths on their heads, not even tied under the chin. There is also the occasional broad-brimmed hat complementing a stylish, perhaps even tightly fitting, dress. One finds a wide range of fashion at the Jami'.

It is not possible for me to say exactly what would happen if a woman appeared at the Majlis in fashionable Western-style clothes and a hat. I cannot imagine a woman attempting such a thing. I have never seen a woman, except for myself, at the Majlis who does not normally wear a *chador*, an *'abaya*, or *hijab*. Nor have I seen more than twenty or thirty women there at a time (with approximately an equal number of men). I have been told of an occasion when Sheikh Burro (currently of the Majlis but at the time of this incident at the Jami') publicly and emphatically reprimanded a woman for not wearing a head covering at a memorial service. She was a Lebanese Christian friend of the deceased. The people who told me about this incident obviously disapproved of Burro's behavior.

As for the Majma', while originally it may have appealed to those with a strict notion of how a Muslim must appear in public, the doors have been opened more widely so that for social occasions and major holidays, there will be as great a variety of participants as one finds at the Jami'—actually, even greater, since a *chador*-covered woman or two and her male equivalent can almost always be found at the Majma'. Still, the core membership, those who are very active at the Majma', tend to be very observant in following the laws of Islam. My scholarly Najafi woman friend approvingly calls the Majma' the most balanced and moderate of the mosques.

These differences reflect tensions between "activist" and "traditional" approaches to Islam. How to categorize and name such approaches has been the subject of much discussion recently. Terms such as *modernist, Islamist, Islamicist, fundamentalist, neo-fundamentalist, political,* and the like have been used to describe various activist approaches to Islam. The categories proposed by John Bowen and Olivier Roy illustrate the difficulties.[14]

Bowen, who studied Muslims in the Gayo Highlands of Sumatra, defines modernists as those who believe that only the Koran and *hadith* (the sayings of the Prophet) have absolute authority. For them, commentaries on scripture are useful only for clarification and cannot add or subtract from scripture. But for the Shiʿi leadership in the Islamic Republic of Iran, who also see themselves taking a modernist position, the guidance given beyond the Koran and *hadith* is essential. This continuous and legitimate guidance is based on the reasoned opinions of the ʿulama.

In his critique of political Islam, Olivier Roy has developed various categories. For him, the Islamists are anticlerical and believe themselves capable of interpreting scripture for themselves. In Egypt, some of these Islamists, often recruited from the over-crowded schools and universities of Cairo, have even set up their own political and social organizations.[15] Such Muslims are strongly attracted to the technological advances of modern society. The leading modern-day Islamists that Roy and others describe are often engineers and computer scientists, or are students in such fields. Women, while covered and kept separate from men, are expected to be socially and politically involved in the world. In contrast with the Islamists, Roy's neo-fundamentalists are more concerned with implementing religious law and purifying morals than they are with igniting revolution. Neo-fundamentalists, according to Roy, do not involve themselves with economic and political restructuring but focus on issues such as removing women from the public sphere.

Such classifications do not fit the Shiʿa of Dearborn. More important, the Dearborn Shiʿa do not draw distinctions corresponding to classifications such as Roy's. I have chosen, therefore, to use the term *Shariʿa-minded,* which was coined by Marshall Hodgson in the 1970s; it is a more neutral term and seems better fitted to the circumstances I am describing. In using this term, Hodgson was referring to the program for private and public living centered on religious law (the Shariʿa) that had been worked out over the centuries by both Sunni and Shiʿi ʿulama.[16] I believe this term is applicable to the Shiʿa because the greatest gap in the community tends to be between those who are attempting to apply the law in their lives very carefully and those whose religiosity is less tied to the Shariʿa.

In observing the mosques, I have looked at how much emphasis is placed on the careful application of the Shariʿa. All of the Shiʿi sheikhs in Dearborn would say that the Shariʿa is important, yet there are variations to their approach to following the law. The approach will differ depending on whether they feel it is appropriate to consider the cultural context in which people currently live. In this case, the cultural context is not just American but also Lebanese. The Lebanese Shiʿa, far away from Najaf and other centers of learning and frequently sharing their environment with Christians, inevitably developed a religious identity uniquely their own. The Lebanese, while maintaining the central elements of Shi'i Islam, adapted the religion to their special surroundings, which, as we have seen, have been in the process of drastic change during the latter part of this century.

The Lebanese Shi'a living in Dearborn are at an interesting crossroads. Those who are Shari'a-minded, whether of the political or nonpolitical variety, would like to see a "pure Islam" established in America. They wish to deny that the society in which they live has any bearing on the religion they practice. In other words, they seek to deculturalize Islam. Those with a more traditional approach would like to see their Lebanese culture, including their approach to Islam, maintained, often recognizing that some accommodations have to be made to American society. However, the situation is more complex than this, as reflected in the dynamics of the Jami'.

For the most part, the leadership at the Jami' has been very conscious of cultural context, which, up until the large influx of recent immigration, has meant making accommodations to American society. The earlier immigrants were very concerned that they not be viewed as oddities in the new society. They saw the value of mastering English, they took on American dress, and they assimilated many American values. The later immigrants, on the other hand, who are far more numerous, have been able to maintain many of the traditions and attitudes brought with them from Lebanon. A struggle exists at the Jami' between those who have been thoroughly Americanized and those who see their religion tied to the village and the family dynamics with which they grew up. Religion for this latter group was simply embedded in their whole way of life, not something that it was necessary to examine and analyze. One question I asked people was "How is it different being a Muslim here and being a Muslim back in Lebanon?" An overwhelming majority said that it was much more difficult here because here one has to work at being a Muslim. Back home, everyone was Muslim and no one had to do anything special. For these people, religion was culture. These same people said that it was not possible to do everything religion demanded; some compromises had to be made. These tended to be people either affiliated with the Jami' or affiliated with no mosque at all.

The Majlis presents a very different view. According to Sheikh Burro, there should be no compromise at all with society. Societal norms should play no role in deciding how to live one's life as a Muslim. Burro insisted that I make a distinction between Islam and the way Muslims behave, whether here or in the Middle East. He said there were two types of Muslims: the ones who are very strict and those who call themselves Muslims but do not observe the rules. He stated that he felt there was no reason for Muslims not to follow all the teachings of Islam.

The Majma᷐ also officially teaches a rigorous form of Islam. Classes held at the Majma᷐ teach that one must follow an exemplar, a *marji᷐ taqlid* (see "The Role of the *Marji᷐ Taqlid* in a New Shi᷐i Community" later in this chapter), and precisely follow what he prescribes in his writings. Those who regularly attend the Majma᷐ (there is no formal membership as there is in churches) are keenly concerned with knowing and following the laws of religion. Strict interpretation and application of religious law are paramount. Sheikh Berri does advocate this approach. Yet he also shows some flexibility, recognizing that not all the Muslims in his flock are going to be so rigorous in their application of the law. A case in point involves my friend Wafa, who grew up in Beirut and developed a taste for Italian clothing. Never one to leave her house without wearing makeup and jewelry, she told me that she asked Sheikh Berri if makeup were permissible for women. According to her account of the interview, he told her that she must remove her makeup for prayer. Apparently knowing full well that it was hopeless to ask this woman to throw away her mascara and eyeliner, he instead opted to encourage her to pray and to follow the rules regarding prayer. In this way, he did not alienate her, yet gave her religious advice. The leadership at the Majma᷐ has appeared to come to terms with the fact that too rigid an insistence on strict Islamic behavior would alienate too many of the Lebanese Muslims in the area.

The Majma᷐ is beginning to shed its image of being an exclusively "Hizb Allahi" mosque, that is, a mosque with the aim of forming the Lebanese Shi᷐a of Dearborn in the Khomeini mold. But it now faces the difficult challenge of being strict enough for the core congregation and flexible enough for those who simply want a mosque that will meet their ceremonial and spiritual needs.

Effects of Village Ties

Because loyalties in Lebanon are often strongly drawn along village lines, I had at first anticipated that the mosques would have drawn their congregations according to village or region.

Indeed, when I have asked people what they cared for more, their village or their country, they have said they valued their village more. But the mosques in the Dearborn area draw people from all regions and villages and cities. No mosque can be termed a Bint Jubeili mosque or a Beiruti mosque, for example. Region of origin simply seems to play no role in determining which mosque a person will select.

Elections versus Appointments on the Boards of the Mosques

When the Jamiᶜ was first established, Sheikh Chirri asked Mr. B., a prominent and prosperous member of the community and a person who had spent most of his life in the United States, to serve on the board of directors, whose decisions the sheikh had the power to veto. Mr. B refused on the grounds that such an arrangement was totally undemocratic. Chirri, though, found other men in the community willing to serve on his board. These were mostly men who were being rewarded for their loyalty to him in the early days of his struggle to build the mosque. When there is a resignation or a death of a member, the board, which consists of about twenty-five members, selects a replacement. Chirri justifies the appointments on the grounds that general elections would be "too chaotic" for the community.

When Sheikh Burro, now the director of the Majlis, departed from the Jamiᶜ, one of the complaints he expressed concerned the lack of democratic elections for the board of directors. He saw that it was hopeless to change the direction of the Jamiᶜ so long as it consisted of men with a different agenda for the mosque from his own. Burro is not the only one to complain about this matter. The board and the selection process at the Jamiᶜ are common targets of criticism. One woman said disgustedly that only rich people could be on the board. (I thought it interesting that she and her husband are far more prosperous than some of the board members I have met.) Another criticism was that the board members were all *hajjis* (pilgrims to Mecca) and therefore expected to be treated as though they were very important.

The situation at the Majmaᶜ is quite different. In December 1989, a notice was posted inviting the community members to "elect twenty new members to the administration of the Islamic Institute of Knowledge for the next two years." Those who could vote had to be at least eighteen years old and show "devotion to the great Prophet Muhammad and to his blessed descendants and companions." This indicates that the person must be a Shiᶜa. Candidates had to be twenty-five years of age, "not affiliated with any movement or ideology that contradicts the principles of Islam" and an active participant in the Majmaʿ's activities. The aspiring candidate was asked to submit a written application that would need the approval of the "religious head at the Institute." The notice included the following statement: "Elections and Consultative Councils are a modern Islamic phenomenon that helps to determine the general trend and will of the society, and not meant to score personal victories and create divisive factions. Therefore, it behooves every Moslem to maintain a spirit of calmness and propriety, and to show an attitude of nobleness—away from the recriminations, disputes and divisions that contradict the true spirit of brotherhood and high character of Islam."

The statement that elections and consultative councils are a "modern Islamic phenomenon" shows the influence of the Islamic Republic of Iran. Very early in the establishment of the republic, elections were held, with Khomeini deciding, as does the Majmaʿ's director, who was eligible to run for political positions. The consultative council is, quite obviously, modeled after the Iranian Majlis. For the Shiʿa of Dearborn who align themselves with this modern Iranian model of Shiʿism, the lack of elections at the Jamiʿ is considered both "non-democratic and non-Islamic."

Admonitions to maintain "an attitude of nobleness" and to avoid divisions in the community are apparently a matter of great concern to Berri. While the case can be made that he broke away from the Jamiʿ, thereby causing a rift in the community, it can also be argued that he has attempted to draw the Muslims to his more elevated approach to Islam, rather than simply exclude those who don't already share his philosophy. In other words, while he believes that the Shiʿa should conform to the Shariʿa and objects to a popular interpretation of Islam, he realizes that it is his job to educate the masses to bring them to this "higher understanding." There is far more outreach to the community by the Majmaʿ than there is by the Majlis, which is very much "the home" of those whom Burro has dubbed "true Muslims," that is, those who follow the rules.

The elections at the Majmaʿ do not totally escape criticism. One of my informants complained that the election process was arranged so that the "moderates" were forced out and replaced by "Hizb Allah types." This may be true. A younger man with a more activist approach to Islam replaced as chairman a middle-aged physician known for his moderate tendencies. However, since the December 1989 elections, I have detected no exclusionist trends at the Majmaʿ. It remains a place that draws the ardent, serious student of Shariʿa while it leaves room for those who desire to have their traditional social and spiritual needs met.

Early on the cold morning of Wednesday, December 2, 1885, a crowd began to gather in the forecourt of a handsome brick church on the outskirts of Detroit. The church, only recently blessed, was the Polish Roman Catholic church of Saint Albertus; the crowd, eventually numbering perhaps eight hundred, were Polish immigrants. Most them were women. Shortly after 6:00, seven policemen marched into the convent opposite the church and soon emerged escorting two Polish priests. The group moved toward the church, but at the church steps the crowd—"the women," according to witnesses—began to jeer at and jostle the priests, and even pelted them with gravel. The police responded vigorously, but they and the priests were pushed from the door several times before they were finally able to enter.

There were too few officers to bar the crowd from the church; the pews filled rapidly with agitated parishioners. And when a priest vested for mass appeared at the altar, the sanctuary rang with cries of anger and denunciation. The mass proceeded, but as the police began to remove the loudest protesters, the din intensified. Women clung to the pews and to each other and even struck policemen in their efforts to remain in the church. The service was hurried to its conclusion, at which most of the crowd left to mill outside. Then at 7:30, the two priests reappeared at the altar to say a second scheduled mass.[17]

Leslie Woodcock Tentler, who has written about the conflict in St. Albertus parish, goes on to say that the scuffle did not end with that mass. It continued through the next mass until the priests were forced to abandon the altar, after which a woman ascended the altar stairs and called for a prayer of redress against the bishop who had removed the well-loved (though controversial) priest who had built St. Albertus.

I recount this story because it allows us to compare and contrast the situation prevailing among the Shiʿa in Dearborn with what occurred among these earlier Catholic immigrants. The immediate concern of the Catholics of St. Albertus was to reestablish the priest of their choice as pastor of the parish. It was not as if they were accustomed to appointing their own priests back home in Poland. However, in making this demand, they were, unknowingly, following the pattern of Protestant communities in America. Though poor and not socially powerful, they had a sense that their traditions and old forms of patriarchal control were weakening. Life in America had given many of them the belief that they were free to assert themselves and to demand more say in who would lead them and how they would be led.

The Shi‘a appear to have embarked on a similar journey. While they do not have a bishop or his equivalent to impose a cleric on a mosque, they do have the Jami‘'s board of trustees. The board members are typically assimilated into American society and are very different from the more recent immigrants. Several times, a group under the leadership of a disgruntled sheikh has broken with the Jami‘ and its board and has founded a new mosque following principles more to its members' liking. Such schisms have resulted in turmoil but have not caused divisions in the community since most people feel no need to support a single mosque exclusively.

Conflict between lay leadership and clergy has been an important feature of American religion, among both Protestants and Catholics. In an essay on popular religion, Robert Wuthnow notes that a secularized society poses particular problems for clergy because they don't have great opportunities for advancement except through clerical hierarchies.[18] They therefore develop such measures as high professional standards of merit to distance and protect themselves from encroachment by the laity. The laity, on the other hand, has tended to be successful in gaining control by demanding representation on church boards and by promoting the employment of lay preachers. In Dearborn, the people want erudite, formally trained sheikhs, while they also want a greater voice in mosque affairs. Clergy/laity tensions are therefore inevitable.

I will refer again to the case of St. Albertus. It is not that the violent demonstration was typical of the American Catholic experience—or of the experience of the Shi‘i Lebanese in America—but the issues at stake were very much in the forefront of Catholic debate in America during the immigrant period and are similar to those being debated today among Dearborn's Shi‘a.

The Role of the *Marji‘ Taqlid* in a New Shi‘i Community

In the summer of 1989, Sayyid Imam Abu‘l Kasim Khu‘i, a *marji‘ taqlid* residing in Najaf, made an offer of several million dollars to the Islamic Center of America, the Jami‘, to build an Islamic school in the greater Detroit area. The offer was delivered by Sheikh Burro, the Lebanese preacher who had been employed at the Jami‘ for a year or so. The school was to be under the jurisdiction of the

Khu'i Foundation. The Jami' turned down the offer on the grounds that any school it built would be controlled locally by the board of trustees of the Jami'.

Burro, who had received much of his religious training in Qom, expressed his outrage at the refusal and left his employment at the Jami', eventually starting his own mosque, the Islamic Council (the Majlis). First, though, he took Khu'i's offer to the Islamic Institute in Dearborn (the Majma'). They accepted the offer and began the process of negotiating the purchase of a piece of land with the city of Dearborn.

That the Majma' would accept such an offer and the Jami' would not underscores some of the basic differences between these two mosques and demonstrates the diversity of viewpoints that exists among this Shi'i community. (At this writing, the Majlis is new and not yet well established; therefore, it will not be included in this discussion.)

As mentioned earlier, the Majma' became essentially a home for new immigrants who objected to the lack of rigor found at the Jami' in such matters as women's dress and sexual segregation. Innovations such as Sunday services also drew criticism.

The core membership of the Majma' opts for a strict interpretation of Islamic law: women's hair, arms, and legs must be covered; men and women should not shake hands (there are even some young men who would prefer not to shake hands with *kafir*, unbelievers); men and women should not sit together at the services; women are not to join men during *salat*; men and women should not wear gold jewelry; women should save their makeup only for their husbands' eyes; and *mut'a* (pleasure) marriage, a temporary type of marriage sanctioned only by Shi'ism, should at least be considered an acceptable practice.

These strict attitudes are not totally lacking at the Jami', but there are more people attending the Majma' who believe in such a conservative interpretation. These Shari'a-minded individuals almost invariably will admit to liking the Majma' more because it is stricter than the Jami'. Some are reluctant to admit this at first because they want to give the impression of being a unified community, but usually in the course of a conversation or interview, there will be an admission of preference. At the same time, there are those who are far more liberal in their approach who find the obvious camaraderie and enthusiasm of the Majma' appealing. Frequent dinners during Ramadan, regular classes and lectures, and an atmosphere of "a meeting place" draw the devout together, giving them a refuge from a society that often seems very sinful.

The Islamic Center of America (the Jamiʿ) on Warren Avenue was founded in 1962 under the leadership of the late Sheikh Mohammad Jawad Chirri. (1996, photograph courtesy of Haajar Mitchell.)

The Islamic Institute of Knowledge (the Majmaʿ) on the corner of Warren and Jonathan Avenues in Dearborn was opened in 1985 under the direction of Sheikh Abdu'l Latif Berri. Commonly in the U.S. commercial buildings are transformed into religious centers, as was the case with the Majmaʿ. (1995, photograph by author.)

Amidst the buildings on Warren Avenue being converted into Islamic centers is the complex of St. Alphonsis Church, with its school, rectory, convent and cemetery. The cemetery, shown in this picture, contains the remains of many of the people after whom streets in Dearborn had been named, such as Reuter, Theisen, and Schaeffer. These German Catholics were replaced by Poles and Italians. (1995, photograph by author.)

Laylat al-Qadr, the Night of Power, the holiest night during Ramadan, at the Islamic Center of America. (1995, photograph courtesy of Bruce Harkness.)

At the Islamic Mosque of America, Muslims attend mosque to pray all night long on Laylat al-Qadr, the Night of Power, during Ramadan. (1996, photograph courtesy of Haajar Mitchell.)

Praying at the Islamic Mosque of America on Laylat al-Qadr, the Night of Power, during Ramadan. (1996, photograph courtesy of Haajar Mitchell.)

During the holy month of Ramadan, people attend mosque to listen to nightly lectures at the Islamic Center of America. (1995, photograph courtesy of Bruce Harkness.)

As a young Muslim recites poetry about the martyrdom of Imam Hussein, the audience expresses emotion as they remember the suffering and sacrifice of Imam Hussein. (1996, photograph courtesy of Haajar Mitchell.)

At the newest Islamic center in Dearborn, Dar al Hikmat (House of Wisdom), youth listen to the recitation of the story of Imam Hussein at Karbala. This picture, in which some of the young men are weeping, shows the emotional intensity of this event. (1996, photograph courtesy of Haajar Mitchell.)

The Islamic Mosque of America on Warren Avenue is another example of a commercial building transformed into an Islamic Center. (1995, photograph by author.)

These young Muslim men practice Latmieh, a tradition of beating the chest
to express emotion and sorrow, while special poetry is recited about Imam
Hussein. (1996, photograph courtesy of Haajar Mitchell.)

Buying sweets at Shatila Food Products one evening during Ramadan. Ramadan, Christmas, and Easter are the busiest times of the year for Shatila, which ships pastries nationwide. (1995, photograph courtesy of Bruce Harkness.)

Women and men sit in groups, side by side, at Dar al Hikmat as they listen to Sheikh Elahi lecture about the Prince of Martyrs, Imam Hussein. (1996, photograph courtesy of Haajar Mitchell.)

At the Majmaʿ, Arabic is by far the preferred language, although the need for Sheikh Berri to learn English has not escaped him and his progress in the language has been impressive. But there is not the linguistic tension at the Majmaʿ that one finds at the Jamiʿ, where lengthy speeches are given in both English and Arabic.

Unlike the Jamiʿ, the Majmaʿ has not experienced in its brief history a period of assimilation into mainstream society. Therefore, there is not the American/Lebanese divide as is found at the Jamiʿ. Assimilated Muslims hoping for a dialogue with Christian Americans are lacking at the Majmaʿ. Keeping the Lebanese Muslims on the straight path is the main emphasis for both the Majmaʿ and the Jamiʿ. Yet for the Jamiʿ there is still a longing among some members to continue what had been started before the refugees descended on them: the building of a community that was at once truly Islamic and truly American.

I believe that one of the factors influencing the directions the two mosques take will be the role of the *marjiʿ taqlid*.

The Institution of the *Marjiʿiyat*

In Shiʿi Islam, there is a hierarchy of clerical leadership based on superiority of learning. By the eighteenth century, there was a religious elite referred to as *mujtahids* who could practice *ijtihad*, that is, make religious decisions based on reason. Eventually, a hierarchy of *mujtahids* was instituted, which, as Juan Cole suggests, could have been a means of controlling rebellious lower-level *ulama*, many of whom had become members of the messianic Babi movement of the nineteenth century.[19] Whatever the reason, the concept of *Marjiʿiyat taqlid tamm* (complete authority of one *mujtahid* over the entire community) became institutionalized at that time.[20] Superiority in learning is generally held to be the primary prerequisite for the selection of a *marjiʿ*, though there is no clear-cut set of criteria that governs the choice. Ultimately, it is the followers (those who are *muqallid* to the *marjiʿ*) who decide which *marjiʿ* to follow.[21]

In the nineteenth century, Mortaza Ansari, who was responsible for much of the institutional and ideological elaboration of the concept of *marjiʿ taqlid*, stated that it was not permissible to change from one living *marjiʿ* to another except on the grounds that a second one is more learned than the first one. He further stated that if two were found to be equally knowledgeable, it was permissible to emulate either one. However, once a follower has elected to follow a particular ruling, he should remain with that ruling and not change at will. Also, it is necessary for a person to follow a living *marjiʿ;* this issue became important when Khomeini died in 1989.

The relationship between a *marjiʿ* and a sheikh is complex. While there is a hierarchical nature to this relationship, it is not such that a *mujtahid* can demand the obedience of the sheikhs, as the Pope or a bishop can do. Rather, the *marjiʿ* and the lower-ranking clerics tend to give credence to one another's position in the eyes of the people. The *marjiʿ* can patronize the sheikh and provide him with financial backing, much like what is occurring in Dearborn regarding the school. The sheikh can serve as the *marjiʿ's* representative and through his sermons reinforce the position of the *marjiʿ.* By giving recognition to the *marjiʿ's* position, the sheikh is also elevating his own rank; through his relationship with this religious elite, he gains a kind of charisma.

Several clerics were recognized as *marjiʿ* when the Ayatollah Khomeini came to power in Iran, including Khomeini himself. After his rise to political leadership, he rapidly established himself as the leader of all the other *marjiʿiya.* Those who resisted his authority, such as the well-known ayatollahs Shariatmadari and Teleqani, came to unpleasant ends. Khomeini saw himself as both political and spiritual leader of the people, and, in that capacity (i.e., as the *wilayat al-faqih*), he took unprecedented measures in exercising his power. The vast majority of *ʿulama* who reach the rank of *mujtahid,* including those who are recognized as *marjiʿ,* live their lives far from the centers of political power and are far more concerned with issues relating to, say, ritual purity than the national debt.

Ayatollah Khuʿi in Iraq is an example of the latter type of *marjiʿ.* Khuʿi, whose objections to Khomeini's political activities were well known, continues to have the largest following, his influence extending to Pakistan, India, and East Africa,[22] and, as I have found, to some extent in Lebanon and now in America.

Khomeini's rise to power in revolutionary Iran is a major watershed in Shiʿi history. He made it respectable to be a religious Muslim after years of what Iranians call *gharbzadegi,* literally "Westtoxication."[23] Yet the effect he had on the actual lives of people is extremely varied. For some, he became the catalyst and guide for a total change of life, a life in which only religion sets the standard. Others saw him primarily as a political leader who taught the West that the Islamic world has to be taken into account. Some hate him or consider him to be an embarrassment to Islam, but, judging from the Lebanese community in Dearborn, these are a minority. Most feel that Khomeini is deserving of respect, if not absolute and complete obedience. The Lebanese I interviewed reflect this wide range of attitudes, as will be shown below.

Musa Sadr also must be taken into account. He is for the Lebanese Shiʿa a major heroic figure. This heroic dimension has a role in shaping the Lebanese attitude toward the *marjiʿ*. As stated earlier, Musa Sadr was the spokesman of the "oppressed" in Lebanon, whom the political establishment, on both a national and a village level, considered a threat to the status quo. Although he actively sought to bridge gaps among sectarian groups, he ultimately saw that the Shiʿa would need to fight on their own. He eventually established Harakat Amal (the Movement of Hope), which began as a social movement but in 1974 became an armed militia. Musa Sadr "vanished" in 1978 on a trip to Libya. Because disappearance or occultation is a major theme in Shiʿism, this only added to his prestige. His memory and his militia live on. Harakat Amal's greatest foe at the present time is the Hizb Allah movement, whose members look to the government of the Islamic Republic of Iran as a model of what they hope to achieve. Norton has summarized the difference between the two groups: Amal has a "commitment to Lebanon as a distinct and definite homeland. This position clearly distinguishes Amal from its radical Shiʿi opponents, who have viewed Lebanon as a compartment in the Islamic *umma* that they seek to transform into an Islamic republic."[24] Sympathizers of both groups are found in Dearborn. However, among this community, an admirer of Musa Sadr is not necessarily a detractor of Khomeini, and vice versa. It is not unusual to find portraits of both men in a home or mosque.

Claims that Musa Sadr was truly a *mujtahid* and, therefore, eligible to be a *marjiʿ* are currently being made by adherents of the Amal movement both here and in Lebanon, though this did not appear to be an issue in his lifetime. The new American representative of Amal gave a speech at the Jamiʿ one evening in which he argued for Sadr's *mujtahid* position quite strenuously. This can be viewed as Amal's attempt to present itself as "religiously legitimate," as Hizb Allah members often accuse Amal members of being lax in their religious duties. But, at best, this situation is ambiguous, and, as we shall see, very few view Musa Sadr as a *marjiʿ*.

One of the questions that arose in the process of this research was whether one's political-ideological position affected, first, one's decision to emulate a *marjiʿ* and, second, one's selection of a *marjiʿ*. I found that the Lebanese chose to be as unpredictable in this matter as they were in so many others.

Teachings of the *Marji*ᶜ

Scholars agree that the *maraji*ᶜ do not significantly differ with one another in their opinions. Khuᶜi does teach that women should cover their faces as well as the rest of their bodies, while Khomeini is more liberal and has decreed that the oval of the woman's face may show. But even in this instance, Khuᶜi has left open the possibility for a woman to seek the opinion of another *marji*ᶜ as this is considered an "area of doubt." The most significant difference between the two *marji*ᶜ is in the area of politics, as mentioned above.

As a brief example of Khuᶜi's opinions, I have chosen the issue of *mut*ᶜ*a* (temporary marriage or, more correctly, pleasure marriage), because this is a topic on which people of this community are very divided and because it is of relevance to other aspects of this study.

Temporary marriage is, according to Haeri, "a contract between a man and an unmarried woman, be she a virgin, divorced, or widowed, in which both the period the marriage shall last and the amount of money to be exchanged must be specified."[25] Witnesses are not required for such a union, nor is the union usually registered. A Shiᶜi man may contract as many temporary marriages as he wishes; there is no limit whatsoever. The unions can be formed consecutively or simultaneously. For a woman, however, the rules are quite different. She may form only one union at a time and after each marriage must abstain sexually for a period of time to ascertain whether or not she is pregnant.

In Khuᶜi's book, *Minhaj al-Salihin* (*The Way of the Righteous*), he gives the following instructions for a temporary marriage:

> The contract of temporary marriage has as a necessary condition that the woman say, "I myself take you in marriage of pleasure," or "I wed you," or "I marry you." The acceptance on his part is of the form "I accept." The contract is conditioned on specifying the dowry and also by custom on specifying a set period no longer than the lifetimes of the two parties, since otherwise the contract would manifestly be a contract of permanent marriage. If no dowry is mentioned, the contract is invalid. . . .
>
> Just as in the case of concubines, there is no set limit to the number of women whom a man may choose to take as temporary wives. The dowry may be as large or small as desired.[26]

Haeri states that Khomeini, after the revolution, issued a *fatwa* stating that a virgin must have her father's permission for a first marriage, be it permanent or temporary. Issues such as parental consent for a virgin to enter into a *mut'a* marriage might be under dispute among the Shi'i *'ulama*, but the legitimacy of *mut'a* is not. While Khomeini may have encouraged the practice more strongly than Khu'i has, both men are in favor of this kind of marriage. It should hold that a person who is attempting to follow the teachings of a *marji'* will, at least in principle, believe in the practice of *mut'a*.

Marji' as a New Idea among the Lebanese

Through formal interviews and less formal conversations, I found certain trends arising. It is apparent that the issue of the *marji'* did not loom large in the lives of the Lebanese Shi'a before the Iranian revolution, and for many it still does not. Several people I spoke with, some of whom considered themselves very religious, did not recognize the term *marji'* and needed to have it explained. They understood the concept if I explained that the *marji'* was one of the "big imams in Najaf or Iran." One highly educated man from Baalbek who is around forty years of age said that he had never known anyone who followed a *marji'*. In fact, he had not become aware of this concept until he lived in Dearborn. As I interviewed a young college student from the Bekaa, his sister, who was visiting from Saudi Arabia, interjected that it was only in the past year that she had learned that the people were supposed to follow a *marji'*. Her husband had come back from his pilgrimage to Mecca with this piece of information. Another immigrant from the Bekaa said in a derogatory manner that "this business with the *marji'* is Hizb Allah stuff," implying that it is a recent innovation imported from Iran.

The perception of the *marji'* as an outside interference is illustrated by the following example. Throughout the Muslim world, there is always some question about the exact day that the Id al-Fitr (the holiday following Ramadan) falls on since it is supposed to occur the day after the new moon is spotted. In this community, however, the sheikhs announce the day ahead of time, no doubt to help people plan work and school schedules. During Ramadan in 1988, letters went out to the Shi'i families in the area from the Jami' and the Majma' stating when the Id would be that year. The two mosques disagreed. The Jami's date coincided with that of Iran, and the Majma's date conformed to the rest of the Muslim world's calculations. (This was extremely interesting since the Majma' is the mosque that is supposed to be so highly influenced by Iran.) I asked both sheikhs, Chirri and Berri, why there was this discrepancy, and they simply said that the experts they consulted had given them these dates. However, at a community level, there was great consternation about the matter, and at least some people were convinced that politics was at the root of the problem. A friend from southern Lebanon who has considerable contact with people through her business expressed the anger of many when she said that the Jamiʿ was letting Khomeini dictate to them when the Id would be. "We are Lebanese," she said. "We respect Khomeini, but we don't want him telling us what to do." Her comment reflects both the Arab/Iranian tension that is found among Shiʿa and the fact that she has limits on how much influence she believes anyone outside the community, even a *marjiʿ taqlid*, should be permitted to have.

People from the south of Lebanon are more likely to have at least heard of the *marjiʿ* than those from the Bekaa, although they are not necessarily more likely to follow one. This finding is not surprising in view of the religious history of Lebanon's south in comparison to that of the Bekaa. From the fifteenth century, the south (Jabal ʿAmil) was the cite of the most important teaching work in Lebanon. It was to Jabal ʿAmil that the Iranian Safavids looked when they needed to import scholars to teach the people of Iran, who had been mostly Sunnis, about Shiʿism.

Chibli Mallat documents the activities in Jabal ʿAmil of Muhammad Jawad Mughniyya, who in 1948 was appointed judge in the Shariʿa court in Beirut and throughout his career had close contact with the major figures in the Shiʿi world.[27] An activist who wrote several books on Shiʿism as well as on the deplorable conditions of the south, he was ultimately overshadowed by the charismatic Imam Musa Sadr, whose leadership was more strongly felt in the south than in the Bekaa.[28] It was also in Jabal ʿAmil that the scholarly Shiʿi journal *Al-ʿIrfan* had been published since 1909. Mallat states that this journal, "protected by the Lebanese freedom of the press, became the point of convergence of Arabic speaking Shiʿi writers throughout the century."[29] Nothing comparable came from the Bekaa region. My informants and respondents from the Bekaa generally mention the fact that they shared their villages with Christians, and a few have said that they even went to their churches. A young neighbor from a village in the Bekaa went to a Christian school and said that when her father found her and her sister as young schoolgirls praying in the Christian style, he decided that it was time to teach them to do *salat* (obligatory prayer). However, he evidently was not a very effective teacher; she came to my husband (a scholar of Islam but not a Muslim) for a book to help teach her how to pray.

Ajami characterizes the people of the south as "patient, sub-dued peasants, their villages within the reach of authority. The Shiʿa of the Bekaa Valley were wild and assertive clansmen who resisted the encroachment of outside power. A few gendarmes could terror-ize entire villages in the south; the Bekaa was a place into which government troops ventured with great reluctance. The beys of the south lorded it over cowed men. The beys of the Bekaa operated in a more egalitarian world."[30]

The Jabal ʿAmil/Bekaa difference was weaker but still appar-ent even among the assimilated Muslims. Men and women who had originated from Bint Jubeil and who regularly attend mosque ser-vices were generally likely to say that they followed a *marjiʿ* and always had.

For these earlier immigrants, though, it is usually their reac-tions to current Middle Eastern events that determine their feelings about the *marjiʿ*. Certainly there was a great deal of ambivalence expressed among this group about the role of the *marjiʿ*. One man who is second-generation American but spent some of his school years in the south of Lebanon was at first not sure of the term, but when I clarified it, he leaned over the desk in his enormous, plush business office and burst out, "I hate Khomeini." He added that his loyalty was to America, about which he could find no fault. An active member of the Jamiʿ, Hajj C., also second-generation but whose father originated from the Bekaa, said that he was "theoreti-cally in agreement with the concept of *marjiʿiya*" but does not know who his *marjiʿ* should be. An admirer of Khomeini's achievements, he still is ardently opposed to any sort of outside control of Islam in America. This is not the case for Layla, a woman in her thirties who refers to herself as "born again." Born in America, though she also lived for some years in the Bekaa, she only recently learned of the principle of following a *marjiʿ* but has embraced the idea whole-heartedly as her Islamic duty. Khomeini was her choice.

Those Who Follow a *Marjiʿ*

When a devout and learned young Iraqi, a descendent of sev-eral ayatollahs, heard that I was interested in the role of the *marjiʿ* in Dearborn, his sarcastic reply was "What role?" In his eyes, the Lebanese are so thoroughly independent, so very casual and unorthodox about their religion, that they could not possibly be affected by the teachings of the *marjiʿ*.

Yet about half of my respondents did claim to follow a *marjiʿ*, so I was not able to dismiss the matter as easily as my young friend.

The following case studies exemplify the sort, or sorts, of new immigrant Lebanese who follow a *marjiʿ*.

Issa

Issa, a young man with a serious demeanor, is an engineering student at a local college. Originally from the Jabal ʿAmil, he lived most of his life in one of the southern Beirut suburbs to which many Shiʿa gravitated during the 1970s.

Issa became "very religious" about seven years ago when he started reading Islamic books. He now deplores a traditional attitude toward religion and is irritated that members of his family have been content to take a less serious view toward religion. He believes a person should not take religion for granted: "He must search for the truth. After one has decided on that truth, then he must follow the rules exactly." When asked what he would do if there were a rule he objected to, he responded that he would follow it anyway, because it is the devil who tempts him to go against his religion.

Issa fasts, prays, and is so often at the Majmaʿ that his family teases him about it being his home. He will eat only *halal* meat, believes women should wear the full *hijab* and not wear makeup in public, and will not shake hands with women. In fact, when I first spoke with him on the telephone to set up an interview, he warned me by saying, "I don't shake hands." He prefers the Majmaʿ over the Jamiʿ because "true Muslims" are more often found there. By this, he meant those aligned with Hizb Allah. He will not go to weddings outside the mosque because he is convinced (incorrectly, from my experience) that there is alcohol at the wedding receptions in the reception halls.

Following the orthodox line, he thinks *mutʿa* is "the perfect solution for a social problem" but that *mutʿis* should be only divorced or widowed women, not virgins. When I replied that Khomeini permitted virgins to be *mutʿis*, he corrected himself by saying that it was all right for virgins but they needed their fathers' consent. He added that since no father would consent to such a thing, a virgin *mutʿi* isn't a possibility. He qualified this statement by saying that *mutʿa* is occurring with virgins in Lebanon because people don't understand the rules properly.

He turns to Khuʿi for his *fatwas* or legal opinions on religious matters, but since Khuʿi "cannot speak out on political subjects" because of the oppression of the Iraqi government which had Khuʿi under house arrest, he turns to Khomeini (whom he calls his greatest hero) for political answers.

Issa expressed a desire to live in Iran, but should he stay here and have children, he would send them to the Khu'i school.

Husayn

The same age as Issa, Husayn presents a strikingly different image. A supporter of Amal and a dapper dresser who wears expensive suits and drives a flashy sports car, Husayn reflects the influence of the free-wheeling life of Beirut. He was born in Bint Jubeil in Jabal 'Amil, the village that has provided a majority of immigrants to America from Lebanon. He and his family also lived in the Beirut area. He has a high school education and has been trying to set up his own business as a tailor.

It was at the Jami' that I met Husayn, who was attending Sunday services. He goes there more often than to the Majma' because that is where his friends go.

Husayn prays and has fasted since he was a young child. He does not wear jewelry, eats only *halal* meat, and reads the Koran. He will shake hands with women, and, in fact, he likes to go to nightclubs to dance. He never said directly that he drinks, but he did say that "if a person drinks a little, this is not harmful."

Mut'a is "better than committing adultery," he feels. He approves of it for widows and divorced women and for any man, whether married or not.

Husayn says that he follows Imam Khu'i and always has. He does not keep referring to Khu'i's writings but stated, "I know his way." He added that his family followed Ayatollah Hakim before he passed away in 1970. Husayn said that it was necessary to follow the *marji'* "for important things" but added that everything the *marji'* teaches is not relevant to all times and places: "In America, we can't do everything the *marji'* says. For example, in America, men and women sit together at weddings. Islam must adapt to the surroundings."

Husayn believes that when he has children, he will send them to the Khu'i school.

Fatme

A young wife expecting her first child, Fatme looks older than her years dressed in a modest loose-fitting dress with a scarf that reveals only the slightest trace of hair and is fastened, not tied, under her chin. She has worn the scarf since she was eight years old and wears it in the manner of Shi'i heroines Sitt Zahra and Sitt Zeinab.

From a village in the Bekaa, she attended school through the ninth grade before coming to the United States, where she married. To Fatme, being religious means wearing *hijab*, doing *salat*, fasting, and following all the rules of religion, which she believes she does.

Fatme said that she knew that according to the Shari'a it was all right to practice *mut'a*, but she still does not approve of it. (At this point in the interview, a neighbor whom I knew slightly came into the house. This woman is quite serious about religion and argued with Fatme that *mut'a* is against religion and that "a regular marriage is the only kind of marriage allowed." Fatme tentatively repeated what she knew about the Shari'a but did not argue forcefully, obviously because she hated the institution so much.)

Khomeini is her *marji'*, and she believes he should be followed in everything. She said that he has a special position, "not like one of the Twelve Imams but something close. He paved the road for Imam Mahdi [the messianic figure in Islam] to come."

She, too, hopes to send her children to the Khu'i school.

Ghalia

About the same age as Fatme, Ghalia is young and vivacious in her short-sleeve blouses and flared skirts. Her pretty hair, of which she is proud, is worn long or tied up on her head, never covered by a scarf. The mother of a toddler and an infant, she came from the same village as Fatme about five years ago, attended Fordson High School, and worked in her brother's store. Her marriage to her first cousin was arranged by her brother.

Ghalia considers herself to be religious but had difficulty defining what a religious person is. She knows a Muslim is supposed to follow rules, and during Ramadan she fasted and began to try to pray regularly, something she doesn't do the rest of the year. She occasionally eats hamburgers from fast-food restaurants but usually eats *halal* meat. She shakes hands only with men she knows.

She likes the Jami' better than the Majma' because she feels "more comfortable" there. Even so, she does not go to the Jami' for the regular services but mostly for engagements, weddings, and 'Ashura commemorations. She finds memorials too upsetting.

Her response to *mut'a*: "I don't like it." She thinks it should never be allowed.

She claims to follow Khomeini as her *marji'*. She explained that she tries to understand what he has to say, though she does not actually consult his works. Parts of the Koran are the only religious text she has read at all.

She does not think she will be sending her children to the Khuʿi school.

The Meaning of the *Marjiʿ* in This Community

While the cases presented give some indication of the variety of opinions found among the Shiʿa in this area, they should not be interpreted as being representative of the total community's viewpoints. Consistency of opinion is most likely to be found among a minority who have aligned themselves with the Hizb Allah movement; these individuals are extremely concerned with following the *fatwas* of the *marjiʿ* and "following the rules exactly," as they often say. Among this group are those who felt insecure about their religious education and expressed concern that they might give me "a wrong opinion." Samira, a young woman who had gone from blue jeans and rock music to full *hijab* within the last few years, emphatically stated that she did not have any opinions about religion. Everything that I needed to know was "written in the books," which she kept in front of her for reference during the interview. Samira, like Issa, believes that Iran is a model the world should follow and leaves no room for any other interpretation of Islam.

Among the Lebanese, the Samiras and the Issas are a new breed. Prior to the Iranian Revolution, the Islam of the books was primarily the domain of those relatively few men who went off to Najaf to study at the feet of the learned ʿulama. Most of these men returned to their villages to minister to the needs of the people, who relied on these preachers for their religious knowledge. As mentioned above, if one was raised in Jabal ʿAmil, one was more likely to be exposed to these teachings. Exposed to, but little else. This is essentially not a community of readers.

In the vast majority of homes I have visited, there have been few, if any, books. There is a respect for books—at least religious ones—but books are perceived as being for the sheikhs. In fact, my husband, with his Ph.D. in Islamic studies and his innumerable Arabic books, is sometimes referred to, only half-jokingly, as Sheikh John.

The poverty and deplorable conditions of the Shiʿa of Lebanon are now well documented. For the most part, people's education has been limited to a few years of schooling in the villages. Reading all but the most elementary Arabic is very difficult for them. In my sample, virtually all who were attending or had attended college were of the first generation in their families to have done so.

It is interesting to examine the books read in this community. A majority of people said that they had read parts of the Koran, several said they had read "some *hadith*" (sayings attributed to the Prophet) and "some *tafsir*" (commentaries on the Koran). Of all the books, the one mentioned most, after the Koran, was *Nahjul Balagha (Peak of Eloquence)*, a work of the Imam ʿAli ibn abi Taleb, whom the Shiʿa believe to be the Prophet's rightful successor. I mentioned this fact to the wife of the owner of a local bookstore who often tends the shop. She smiled and shook her head. She confirmed that the Lebanese of Dearborn bought few books and that *Nahjul Balagha* was the one they asked for the most. But she did not believe they read it. "It is very difficult," she said. The store carries a reference book to assist the reader who wishes to understand the points Imam ʿAli is making. She suggested to one customer that he purchase this text, but he seemed to have taken the suggestion as an insult. "We all know what Imam ʿAli says," he retorted.

The Issas, Samiras, and others I interviewed who believed that one must follow the rules exactly place great emphasis on "the books." Often fairly young with some college education (but not always), these serious-minded Muslims like to refer to texts they have read. A few actually brought out books during interviews to read to me an official position on a given subject. But even with this group, the type and degree of reading they are doing are limited. Avoiding philosophical works and anything that might be at all controversial in Islam, they are concerned mainly with learning the laws. However, what is important to this discussion is that they are generally referring to the opinions of a *marjiʿ*.

There is another category of people who emphasize the importance of knowing and following the rules and reading the religious literature. Hajj Youssef represents this group. Meticulous in his obedience to the laws of Islam and a follower of Khomeini until his death, he nevertheless did not approve of *mutʿa* except perhaps for very special circumstances, but certainly not for married men. His even more bookish wife came down far more strongly against the practice. Upon meeting Hajj Youssef and his wife, I had made the assumption that these were Hizb Allah supporters. Certainly their dress and demeanor lent themselves to this interpretation (though later I came to realize that Hajj Youssef's wife's style of dress was actually not completely in conformity to Hizb Allah). An hour or so into the interview, I realized that Hajj Youssef could not be easily pigeonholed and that the dynamics of the community were even more complex than I had thought.

His rejection of *mutʿa* and an offhand remark about the "Hizb Allahis at the Majmaʿ who want to talk to me all the time" suggested that Hajj Youssef and his wife may be "modern," as he put it, but they are not political. Hajj Youssef also commented that in following the laws, one must do so from the heart. Issa, Samira, and others who aligned themselves with Hizb Allah are concerned with following the *fatwas* of their *marji* regardless of any other consideration. Hajj Youssef, on the other hand, is willing to temper his *marji's* opinions, at least in some matters, with his own judgment. In this respect, Hajj Youssef is more representative of the community than are the "Hizb Allah" types.

I see the difference in attitudes between these two types as the distinction between religious devotion and religious fanaticism. The difference can be ever so subtle. Two women discuss proper Islamic attire. Both are immersed in the life of the *'ulama*, through birth or marriage or both. They both follow the teachings of the *marja'* carefully. Yet one insists that the only proper Islamic dress is the *chador* or *'abaya* (the all-encompassing black gown that leaves only the eyes, nose, and mouth revealed). The other woman feels that the *'abaya* is far too extreme to wear in America. Her coatlike dress reaching just above the ankle (and usually worn over slacks) and her scarf hiding her neck, her hair, and part of her forehead are modest enough under the circumstances. She believes that Americans would not understand the *'abaya* and that it would cause a negative reaction. (Indeed, a woman's *'abaya* swishing through the aisles of stores at the shopping mall is quite a spectacle, even for one who lives in multiethnic Dearborn.) The woman in the *'abaya* is simply interested in the most "careful" interpretation of the law. One woman is capable of seeing another point of view and reacting to it in a reasonable fashion; the other is not.

But what about Ghalia in her short-sleeved blouses and flowing hair? And Husayn spending his Saturday evenings in nightclubs? What does it mean to people like them to follow a *marji'*?

There is probably not a single answer to this question. Husayn is from Bint Jubeil. He claims that his family follows Khu'i and before Khu'i they followed Hakim. Husayn's father came to the United States some years before the rest of the family. Husayn, who has been fasting since he was eight years old, was raised by a mother who wears a scarf and for whom prayer and fasting are part of life. Life alone in America caused his father, on the other hand, to be less observant of the rules. The rest of the family continued to fast and pray after arriving three years ago, and now Husayn's father has begun fasting again. For Husayn, following the *marji'* is part of the tradition learned from his mother and his Muslim surroundings in Lebanon. Yet his father's more cavalier response to religion has opened the way for Husayn's "compromises" with American life. It should be noted, though, that Husayn justifies these compromises on the grounds that Islam is an adaptable religion. He never suggests that his forays into American nightlife are the result of a lack of concern about his religion. Furthermore, he uses a religiously sanctioned means of having relations with women, relations that would otherwise be forbidden.

Ghalia, on the other hand, grew up in a village in the Bekaa and attended a Christian school before coming to Dearborn, where she went to the public schools. She, too, follows a more traditional religious path. Her parents are both *hajjis* (pilgrims), and her mother, on a recent visit, was chagrined to find that most of her daughters and daughters-in-law had stopped wearing the scarf. While Ghalia lives a relatively isolated life with her children and husband, she has been affected by the world to some extent. She may not conform to standards of Islamic dress, but she is aware of the influence of the Hizb Allah movement, which now dominates her village, on her countrymen. And she is very ambivalent about this. One evening, she joined me and some other women on a neighbor's porch. She called my attention to some sheikhs who were going inside another neighbor's house. "Linda," she said, "look, Hizb Allah," and, of all things, she made a sign of the cross and laughed. On the other hand, Khomeini, the ultimate leader of the Hizb Allah movement, is, even to someone like Ghalia, someone to be admired. He has forced the world, particularly the West, to take heed of the Shi'a as no one else has ever done. While she pays no attention to Khomeini's *fatwas* and carries out only the most basic of Islamic obligations, she does, as she says, "like to hear what he says." In other words, Ghalia doesn't really have a *marji'*, she simply has a hero.

And what of young Fatme from the Bekaa, who reads religious books, rigorously follows all the laws as she understands them, and claims to follow Khomeini as her *marji'*? She does not fall into the exact category of any of the other individuals presented here. Her religiosity is very much the result of the Lebanese civil war and the impact of Hizb Allah in her village. Like Samira, she claims to follow Khomeini as her *marji'* in spite of the fact that, properly speaking, she should have transferred her allegiance to a living *marji'* after Khomeini's death. Like Hajj Youssef and unlike Samira, she expresses some misgivings about the practice of *mut'a* in spite of the fact that her *marji'* was an avid supporter of this type of marriage. Some of the differences are, of course, just the result of different personalities, but I found that each of these individuals represents a certain type of Shi'a. For Fatme, as for Issa and Samira, Khomeini is both a charismatic leader and her *marji'*. On the other hand, Fatme did not feel obliged to consult books throughout the interview, nor did she share Issa's or Samira's sense of obligation to convince me of the perfection of Islam. While Fatme may be sympathetic to Hizb Allah, she lacks the politicization found with those who identify with this movement.

Which *Marji'* to Follow

One of the Dearborn sheikhs claimed that 95 percent of the local Shi'a follow Khu'i as their *marji'*. This should probably be amended to state that 95 percent of those who claim to follow a *marji'* follow Imam Khu'i." This is not surprising in view of the fact that Khu'i's influence has extended farther afield than any other *maraji'* in the history of the institution.

At the Majma', Sheikh Berri instructs the people that they may choose between Khomeini and Khu'i, as these were the two most learned *maraji'* in the world. Perhaps, again, it should come as no surprise that the only other *marji'* mentioned during the course of my interviewing was Khomeini, although certainly not everyone in this community is following the instructions of Sheikh Berri, or any other sheikh, for that matter. A few people did mention being followers of Musa Sadr. One elderly woman explained that she chose Musa Sadr as her *marji'* because he was a sayyid (a descendent of the Prophet) like herself. Another person, a young student, claimed Musa Sadr as his *marji'* because he was the founder of Harakat Amal which his family supported. But in most cases, people who had any concept of what the *marji' taqlid* was believed they had a choice between Khomeini and Khu'i and either accepted or rejected such leadership.

In the Persian Gulf, evidently, choosing between these two men was a weighty matter. Several of my contacts have lived in the Gulf region and have told me that fighting broke out on occasion between those who followed Khomeini and those who followed Khu'i. One young man told me that the Khu'i followers were being called *kuffar* (infidels) by the followers of Khomeini.

I expected that in Dearborn, too, one would find a clear-cut distinction between those who followed Khu'i and those who chose Khomeini as their *marji'* and that there might be tensions between the two factions. However, Khomeini's death during the course of this research made predictions more difficult. Had Khomeini survived, I would have predicted that only those who believed in the establishment of an Islamic government with a member of the clergy as the guardian of that government would look to him as their leader. This essentially constitutes those who align themselves with Hizb Allah. On the other hand, I predicted that Amal supporters, if they followed a *marjiʿ* at all, would follow Khuʿi, if only as a response against the Iranian-backed Hizb Allah. I initially expected that, aside from avowed Amal supporters, strictly religious but apolitical types would follow Khuʿi. However, as I have shown, one does not have to be very strict about following the decrees of a *marjiʿ* to claim to be a follower of one.

Predictions about the pro-Amal faction following Khuʿi generally received some support. Khalil, well known in the community for his efforts in behalf of Harakat Amal, claims always to have followed Khuʿi, yet he also states that it has only been in the past several years (since coming to America) that he has become more religious. A man who despises Hizb Allah, he rejects Khomeini for his political views. On the other hand, Muhammad, a young student who claims that he and his family are Amal supporters, also mentioned that he saw Khomeini as one of his leaders. Wafa, a cousin of Harakat Amal leader Nabih Berri, believes, at least sometimes, that Berri and Amal are a major part of the solution to Lebanon's problems, while she also believes, at least sometimes, that Khomeini's *fatwas* should be followed.

How can these seemingly opposing points of view exist simultaneously? There may be multiple answers. In listening to people speak, I came to realize that Khomeini was viewed as "the Teflon ayatollah." A majority of people either believed that the Western media distorted his image or that, if they believed injustices and atrocities had been committed by his regime, these were the doings of his followers unbeknownst to him. They simply denied that he had any responsibility for kidnappings, murders of dissidents, or, for that matter, the formation and support of the Hizb Allah movement. The other answer, again, is that Khomeini, regardless of what else he has done, stood up to the West, made the world take notice of Islam, and carried out a war against the "Yazid of the Age," Saddam Hussein of Iraq. Norton states that even Nabih Berri, the current leader of Amal, speaks respectfully of the ayatollah in public, though he is ardently opposed to Lebanon becoming another Islamic republic modeled on Iran.[31]

I expected politically militant Shiʿa to claim Khomeini as their *marjiʿ* for as long as Khomeini lived. After a *marjiʿ* dies, a person is supposed to turn to another learned person. Whom would this group follow now? In November 1989, I met some Iranian students who were active in asserting the righteousness of the Islamic Republic. I asked whom they followed now that Khomeini was dead. They told me that their *marji* was the Ayatollah Araki, who was in charge of issuing opinions on Islamic law for the Islamic Republic during the time of Khomeini. There were other, higher-ranking *maraji* in Iran, but Araki had endorsed Khomeini's program and thus became the leader of this young, activist set. I assumed that at least some of the more militant Lebanese would follow suit.

My predictions were completely mistaken. No one volunteered the name of Araki. During conversations with two local sheikhs, I inquired about this man. Both men politely and in veiled terms led me to believe that they considered him merely a government functionary. My learned young Iraqi friend (who is looked up to by the young, ardent Lebanese set) frankly said that Araki merely rubber-stamps the *fatwas* of Khomeini and makes no new decisions. He characterized him as weak and senile. Some of the Lebanese may have opted to make Khomeini their leader, but they are not going to follow blindly the Islamic Republic come what may. As far as this Shi'i community is concerned, the past ten years or so have presented the world with two *maraji* they could potentially follow: Khu'i or Khomeini.

Did those who aligned themselves with Hizb Allah, or at least with the movement's interpretation of Islam, transfer their allegiance from Khomeini to Khu'i when Khomeini died? First, did they consistently agree that Khomeini was their *marji* and, second, did they follow the admonition that they must turn to a living *marji* after the death of the *marji* they had been following?

My data can only provide the range one finds in attitudes in this community. Suad, whose attire (all-covering black gown, scarf draped under the chin so as to hide the neck and then fastened with a pin near the ear) identifies her as an advocate of Hizb Allah, claims she has always followed Khu'i. Muhsin, a middle-aged man who has become serious about religion since the Iranian Revolution, was a follower of Khomeini but now follows Khu'i. However, he still believes in the doctrine of *wilayat al faqih*, Khomeini's highly controversial doctrine of guardianship by the highest-ranking *ulama*.

Muhsin's comment (similar to Issa's reported above) brings up one of the most controversial aspects of the concept of the *marji taqlid* that I have encountered. There is a minority, but a vocal and active one, that advocates following Khu'i religiously but following Khomeini politically. This decision is justified on the grounds that

Khuʿi does not speak out on political matters; they believe he is kept from doing so by the oppressive Iraqi government. Because Khuʿi is prevented from addressing political issues, these people feel that they have no recourse but to adhere to Khomeini's opinions.

This belief elicits harsh criticisms from a variety of fronts, ranging from Harakat Amal supporters to very religious and legalistic but apolitical types, on the grounds that one can follow only one *marjiʿ* at a time. The intensity of feeling that this issue evokes must be examined. Why is it that in a community of such diversity in religious opinion and behavior, we find that the seemingly innocuous practice of following both Khuʿi and Khomeini simultaneously arouses such ire, at least among those who are familiar with the rules? My learned young Iraqi friend gave me some insight into this matter. He said that people who claim to follow both *marajiʿ* simultaneously are only interested in politics. In other words, stating that one still follows Khomeini even after his death suggests that one's overriding concerns are essentially political and not religious. Otherwise, one would simply turn to Khuʿi. Whether or not this is true, it is perceived as true. And for those who are devoted to Islam as a religion (albeit a religion that addresses the realms of government and politics), transforming Islam into a political movement is not acceptable. It is particularly offensive in this case because politicization of Islam implies a forceful establishment of an Islamic regime, specifically in Lebanon, something the majority of Lebanese Shiʿa (at least those living in the Dearborn area) are opposed to.

Only those who say they follow both Khuʿi and Khomeini at the same time are considered true "politicos," as one man put it. Following Khomeini alone does not necessarily put one in this category. Um Mousa, for example, would hardly count as a "politico." She arrived in the United States in the early 1950s. Her fashionable clothes show off her still-slim figure. She expresses resentment toward the recent emphasis on Islamic dress; she herself has never worn a scarf and does not intend to. Yet Khomeini was her *marjiʿ* until his death. She now follows Khuʿi, obviously being selective about the points on which she is willing to be a follower. Hajj Youssef also followed Khomeini while he lived but transferred to Khuʿi after the Iranian leader's death. His serious endeavor to follow the laws of Islam exactly in no way implies that he wishes to impose an Islamic regime on Lebanon or anywhere else. While he admires what Khomeini did for Iran, he still expresses a great affection for America, finding nothing about it that meets with his disapproval: "Khomeini said that if you have made a country your home, do not bad-mouth it."

Turning to the *Marjiᶜ* in Everyday Life

A *marjiᶜ* has an opinion on a great many matters. Khomeini, in his *Clarification of Questions*, has given his imitators 2,897 opinions on questions such as ablutions, the bathing of the dead, obligatory prayers, sexual matters, and so on. These opinions are highly detailed and specific. For example, he has entitled one category of opinions "Precepts of Undue Bleeding." Opinion 394 reads, "With small bleeding the woman must, for each prayer, practice one ablution and change or rinse the cotton and rinse the exterior of the vulva in case blood has reached it." Opinion 395 reads, "If she sees moderate undue bleeding before or during the prayer she must practice bathing for the prayer." Opinion 396 explains what she must do for "large undue bleeding."

I chose to quote from the section on prayer and menstruation because this is a concern of women I know who are striving to follow the rules of religion. At least one of the sheikhs conducts classes only for women in which he addresses matters of proper ways of bathing after menstruation or sexual intercourse before one prays. This sheikh ascertains who one's *marjiᶜ* is before answering questions of an individual and, when teaching a class, gives the opinions of both Khomeini and Khuᶜi. Women who are eager to know how they must care for themselves and conduct their prayers so that they are ritually correct discuss these matters among themselves. But, again, this is a select group. And even very religious women, while talking over a cup of coffee, are much more likely to be concerned with who is marrying whom than whether the couple is following all the intricacies of the marriage contract as stipulated by their *marjiᶜ*.

The *marjiᶜ* gains much more prominence in this community when issues such as the end of Ramadan and the direction of the *qibla* are concerned. The end of Ramadan, of course, affects the community as a whole. When does the community end the fast and conduct its holiday? The emphasis on the direction of the *qibla* is a little more difficult to analyze. If a person is religious at all, he or she usually tends to pray at least occasionally, and performing *salat* involves turning toward Mecca, the *qibla*. The exact direction in which a person should face seems to arouse interest in this community as other matters do not. Furthermore, at least one of the sheikhs is not entirely clear about the exact direction Muslims living in the Dearborn area should face and asked Khuᶜi to address this matter for him. Interesting here is that these are not issues that would seem to an outsider as being of great moment. They are certainly traditional, religious concerns, and not the concerns of militant fanatics.

The Role of the *Marji*ᶜ in Extraordinary Cases

The Lebanese, if they follow a *marji*ᶜ at all, usually follow Khuᶜi. Yet when the Ayatollah Khomeini issued a death warrant for Salman Rushdie, the Lebanese in Dearborn joined millions of Muslims worldwide in expressions of support for Khomeini's *fatwa*. In fact, this issue united the community as none other that I have witnessed. Sheikh Chirri was interviewed by the media shortly after the *fatwa* was proclaimed. He agreed totally with Khomeini's position. Quiet, apolitical people mainly concerned with getting on peacefully with their lives were convinced of the wisdom of Khomeini's decree. None of them having read the book, they were convinced that Rushdie, in their eyes a Muslim who had become heretical, had insulted the Prophet and the religion of Islam.

After the news of Khomeini's *fatwa* came out, I visited my friend Wafa. I naively asked her if people were talking about Rushdie. She replied, "What is there to talk about? The man is dirt. He should be killed. That's all there is to say." When I proposed that perhaps Khomeini's death threat was a bit drastic, she asked how I would feel if someone killed my mother. Wouldn't I want to kill that person? She equated the book *Satanic Verses* with the movie *The Last Temptation of Christ;* because Christians had been offended by it, the movie had not yet been produced on video cassette. I suggested that preventing the sale of video cassettes and the issuing of a death warrant by a national leader were not quite in the same league, but she did not see the distinction. In her eyes, Rushdie is like a murderer and should die.

An elderly, uneducated woman paid me a visit one night. As she sipped coffee, she brought up the topic of Rushdie. "The man is no good," she said, but I noticed that the young woman she had come with wished to change the subject. Not everyone was eager to discuss it. When I encouraged Ali, a college student, to talk about his opinions, he brought out a magazine article. The author, a respected Muslim, believed in censoring Rushdie's book but was "more moderate" than Khomeini. Ali felt more comfortable with this approach.

So, while not everyone was prepared to load a gun just in case he or she should run into Rushdie, there was certainly no one in this community whom I had met who was defending Rushdie's right to free speech. And there was general agreement that somehow the man should pay for his crime.

A year after the Rushdie episode, a professor at a local college, a person of Middle Eastern Muslim descent but known for his liberal views, announced that he was giving a lecture on the reaction to *Satanic Verses*. He hoped to show that Muslims were not a monolithic group of blind fanatics and that fanatical opinions were found even among liberals in our own open society. No sooner did the flyer appear announcing the topic and the speaker than a petition was circulated to prevent the lecture. A threatening letter was placed under the professor's door. Not wishing to appear intimidated, he gave the talk anyway but was jeered and insulted through most of it. The situation became unpleasant enough that the major hecklers had to be removed from the audience. Chants of *"Allahu Akbar"* and blessings on the Prophet and the family of the Prophet punctuated their heckling. Though the loudest of the protesters were removed from the auditorium, many remained who were in complete sympathy with the view that Khomeini's *fatwa* should not be questioned and that even discussing the Rushdie book was intolerable. For a Muslim (or one who was at least born a Muslim) to question Khomeini on this matter was tantamount to announcing one's atheism. And "atheist" was one of the insults hurled at this professor.

When the sheikh of the mosque attended by the young male hecklers learned of the incident, he expressed embarrassment to my husband. The matter was dropped as kinsmen, eager to avoid trouble, intervened, bringing the rabble-rousers under control.

In summary, the Rushdie incident shows that, while a small minority may be willing to follow Khomeini on the intricacies of ablutions, a vast majority are willing to throw themselves behind Khomeini on an issue involving the protection of Islam. This they see as his main function.

The Mosques and the *Marji*ᶜ

If this research had been conducted as few as ten years ago, I probably would not have dedicated an entire chapter to the issue of the *marjiᶜ taqlid*. I might never have heard this term uttered in the community. By all accounts, the early (pre-civil war) Dearborn Shiᶜi community was pleased to be carrying out the basic tenets of Islam. The fine points of, say, ritual purity were apparently not foremost on their minds. As two of my informants stated, when Sheikh Chirri weaned the women away from wearing hair curlers to the Jamiᶜ, this was seen as a major accomplishment. Yet to come were long-sleeved blouses and any sort of head coverings.

Sheikh Chirri did not see his congregation at the Jamiᶜ (and it does seem to have been very much a churchlike congregation) as being under the control of Najaf or Qom. Though he was trained in

Najaf, he did not turn to a *marji'* for financial assistance when seeking funds to build the Jami'. Rather, he turned to Egypt. This is not surprising; the sole *marja'* from 1947 until 1961, Ayatollah Borujerdi, was hardly an activist and would not have seen mosque building in America as part of his role. After his death, there was no ayatollah prominent enough to assume leadership. Also, the shrine cities of Iraq were suffering financially and could barely take care of local needs, let alone finance projects elsewhere.[32] As a consequence, the *marji''s* prestige was limited, while that of Egypt and Nasser was on the rise. From all accounts that I have received, Sheikh Chirri did not teach the necessity of following a *marji'*. The Islamic Center of America was to be an American mosque with Sheikh Chirri as its spiritual leader.

The role of the Middle Eastern *'ulama* was bound to be enhanced as Lebanon became increasingly influenced by the Islamic Republic of Iran. New immigrants pouring into the Dearborn-Detroit area were far more likely than the older immigrants to have been taught that it was imperative to follow a *marji'*. Sheikh Chirri could not ignore these newcomers, many of whom now crowd the meeting rooms of his mosque. New, younger Lebanese sheikhs, fresh from Najaf or Qom, do not hide their disapproval at seeing men and women shaking hands in the mosque or women in non-Islamic garb. Two teenage girls, one who grew up in the United States, the other a recent newcomer from the Bekaa, were helping out with some clerical work at the Jami'. As they worked, their scarves slipped back on their heads. Sheikh Burro, newly arrived from Qom, was about to enter the room, but, seeing the girls improperly covered, he backed out of the room, sending a messenger to tell the girls to prepare for his entrance. Such incidents produce tension not only between newcomers and more assimilated Muslims but also between those who wish for a stricter interpretation of Shi'ism and those who do not. The days of curlers in the hair, sleeveless blouses, and dances at the *Jami'* are probably forever a part of history. A sign at the main entrance reminds women to cover their hair. A photograph of Khomeini occasionally hovers over one or another of the rooms of the *Jami'* as a further reminder to observe Islamic propriety. On the other hand, the Jami''s refusal to act as an agent for the Khu'i Foundation on the grounds that it wanted control of its facilities suggests that, at least at the board level, the role of the *marji'* will remain limited.

The Majma', on the other hand, was established with the purpose of guiding people to a stricter interpretation of Shi'ism, which involves following a *marji'*. The involvement in Dearborn affairs by scholars from Najaf is far less likely to be perceived as interference. Indeed, the Majmaᶜ now serves as a representative for the Khuᶜi Foundation. Its role vis-à-vis the *marjiᶜ taqlid* is largely cut out for it.

While the violence at St. Albertus Church, as described earlier, was triggered by the dismissal of a popular priest, the issue at stake, the authority of the church, was being debated in many Catholic parishes. Bishops were accustomed to demanding complete obedience from their flocks in all matters of morality, faith, and church life. The position of most bishops in America was that "the American Church might grow and thrive in a democracy, but it could not be a democratic institution."[33]

In Catholicism, church hierarchy is extremely pronounced, with the bishop being only a middle man who is expected to obey archbishops, cardinals, and, ultimately, the pope. In the nineteenth century, the Church acted decisively in its attempt to squelch dissent. Feeling a threat to his authority, not the least being from Catholics in America, the Pope pronounced his infallibility in 1870. The faithful were expected to accept his pronouncements without question. In the eyes of their American Protestant neighbors, Catholics were highly suspect. To whom do they pay their ultimate allegiance, the United States or the Pope?

Muslims will argue readily that no such system exists in Islam, stating that there are no clergy and that certainly there is no Pope. It is true that Muslim clerics are not ordained and do not administer sacraments, but they do act as upholders and interpreters of the sacred scripture. And in America, their roles have developed so that they are nearly indistinguishable from Christian clergy. As for the *marjiᶜ*, this institution is becoming increasingly important. In fact, high-level *ᶜulama* are debating whether to model it after the Vatican for the sake of uniformity in the Shiᶜi world. The Lebanese Shiᶜa realized the tension that existed between following a "foreign" *marjiᶜ* and being American. And, much like Catholics before them, most compartmentalize their lives so as to reduce this tension.

The Theme of the Imam Husayn

The Death of Khomeini

The following is quoted from my field notes:

June 3, 1989. Khomeini died last night. All day, people have been filing into the Majma‘ down the street, and I heard from various sources that there were services today at the Jami‘. Arabic school was canceled at the Majma‘.

The neighbors' aunt, Sharifi, was next door this morning when I went to visit. Skineh [Sharifi's niece by marriage] told me that Sharifi's uncle just died. She has lost several relatives, including a daughter, in the past few months. Skineh said there was going to be a memorial service at the Majma‘ this evening and asked if I wanted to go.

In the evening, I walked with Skineh, her brother Husayn, and sister-in-law Nahia and our neighbor, Um Muhammad. I overheard Husayn say something to Nahia about Khomeini. Then Um Muhammad, who has never been one to mince words, asked if I liked Khomeini. I shrugged, and everyone laughed. No one pursued the matter.

We arrived at the Majma‘ about 6:30, before it was very crowded. There were huge pictures of Khomeini on the wall of the meeting room. Tables were lined up as usual. The only decorations were white tablecloths and, besides the pictures of Khomeini, two plaques with calligraphy on the walls.

Sheikh Berri's wife and daughters came in. His wife and one daughter, the teenage one, wore ‘abayas. Mrs. Berri came over to say hello to Skineh and her sister, but mostly, I am sure, to inquire about me. Skineh told her about me and added that my husband has lots of Arabic books and knows Islam very well. She smiled approvingly and went back to her table. She propped her foot up on a chair next to her and seemed relaxed. Her younger daughter, despite the ‘abaya, was quite the teenager. During part of the service, she was giggling and playing with a plastic coffee stirrer. Her demeanor changed later.

One by one, the sheikhs entered and sat at the head table with men of the deceased's family. At first, there was only Sheikh Habhab [who had been with the Jami‘ when I first came to Dearborn but is no longer affiliated with any of the mosques on a permanent basis] and Sheikh Hashim Husayni, whose specialty is recounting of the sufferings of Karbala. Later came Burro, who recently left the Jami‘, but Berri wasn't there. The female relations sat at a table, also at the front of the room, but on the other side of the podium.

From the start of the sermons, the name of the deceased relative was associated with Khomeini. I kept wondering if I had come to a requiem for Khomeini or for Sharifi's uncle. Emphasis kept shifting back and forth. First Habhab spoke, he being the lowest-ranking sheikh. He praised Islam and Khomeini. After he spoke, it was Husayni's turn. I was in for a real treat. He is a wonderful *khatib* [reciter of the tale of Karbala and the suffering of Imam Husayn and his family]. First, he chanted with much passion, then he proceeded to tell the story of Karbala, crying out the names of those who suffered and died. Tears rolled down his cheeks, and the people sobbed. Sheikh Berri's young daughter's head was on the table, her whole body convulsed in grief. There were dry eyes in the place, but not many. How easily one could be carried away by the spell cast by this eloquent storyteller.

This over, the people dried their eyes and then faced a grim talk by Sheikh Burro, who does not spare words. He kept comparing the Imam Husayn with Khomeini. He barely mentioned the uncle. Finally, a relative of the uncle got up and spoke about the deceased relative, and the women relatives cried a bit. But many of the people who had come obviously were there for the sake of Khomeini. I knew for a fact that many in the room were not from Sharifi's village.

For a week afterward, well-attended, intense commemorative gatherings were held at the Majmaᶜ. On June 5, there was a televised broadcast from the Majmaᶜ in which one of the young men spoke of Khomeini in semi-messianic terms. He stated the tradition that says someone will come in every century to renew the Faith (a *mujaddid*), a mystic perhaps. Khomeini was portrayed as one who fit what Michael Fischer has called the "Karbala Paradigm," the emotionally intense story of the martyred grandson of the Prophet with its focus on corruption and tyranny. As Fischer states, the story has an "ever-present, latent, political potential to frame or clothe contemporary discontents."[34]

The Role of the Imam Husayn

The recounting of the tale of Karbala, the story of the martyrdom of the Imam Husayn, was not unique to the funeral memorials of Khomeini. At every Shiᶜi memorial in Dearborn, the mourners are reminded of that ultimate suffering, though the deceased are not usually compared to that great hero. The women and girls, lined up facing each other across the Formica tables, may chat away to one another during the prayers or sermons, but the story of Karbala sets a somber mood among both the men and women. Jocularity can be transformed to sorrow in a matter of seconds.

As stated earlier, the suffering of Imam Husayn, the grandson of the Prophet and, according to the Shiᶜa, part of the line of rightful heirs to the leadership of the Muslim community, is central to Shiᶜi belief. Thus, the ritualized mourning of Imam Husayn reminds the people of their history of heroic resistance to illegitimate authority.[35] In A.D. 680, during ten days of the month of Muharram (these ten days being referred to as ʿAshura), Husayn and his family and a small band of followers were surrounded by an Umayyad army. Virtually defenseless and dying from thirst and hunger in the blistering heat of Karbala, the men, and even Husayn's infant son, were cut down by swords and arrows. Finally, Husayn's head was carried back to Damascus and presented to the infamous caliph, Yazid. The ten days of ʿAshura are, for the Shiʿa, more than any other time, the period when "history reveals itself . . . as a new dimension of the presence of God in the world."[36] ʿAshura is "sacred history."

Mourning ceremonies for ʿAshura were first conducted in A.D. 953. Through the centuries, these ceremonies have allowed Husayn's followers to feel a sense of participation with their martyred saint in the struggle against injustice. Husayn fought against the Umayyads, but over the centuries the Umayyads have been linked with any oppressive regime, usually Sunni. However, after the Safavids came into power in Iran and established Shiʿism as the official religion in the sixteenth century, the commemorative services, called taʿziya, continued to play a role in the religious and sociopolitical lives of the people. After the establishment of the Safavid regime, "there was no longer any conflict between the rites of the Shiʿas and those of their religious opponents or about the Shiʿas holding their mourning ceremonies. In place of former conflicts between opposing sects, the Shiʿa mourning processions now competed with each other, using various fanatical pretexts for hostility, so that each group appeared to the other as its imagined enemy. Real battles were fought, and people were injured and even killed. They participated in a drama partly real and partly fantasy."[37]

But the martyrdom of the Imam Husayn is not always interpreted to mean political struggle. Mary Hegland found two images of the Imam Husayn operating in the Iranian village where she conducted her fieldwork. One was indeed a revolutionary image utilized by Khomeini and the revolutionaries, but also there existed an image of Husayn as an intercessor between God and man, someone a person could turn to for help with personal problems.[38]

Before the Iranian Revolution, the Shiʿa of Lebanon generally had a quiescent view of the martyrdom of Husayn. Michael Gilsenan offers an insightful explanation of the use of the ʿAshura commemoration in Lebanese villages in the 1950s and 1960s. Losing their high status in South Lebanon because of mass migration to the cities and new educational opportunities for the common man, the Learned Families and those who could claim descent from the family of the

Prophet, the sayyids, felt threatened by the changing world. Gilsenan states that these elite groups used the play "as a statement of authority of the sheikhs and sayyids. . . . The play is a confirmation of the social order incarnated by the Learned Families."[39] The elite saw a struggle between themselves and other social groups among the Shiʿa. In Iran, on the other hand, the ʿulama portrayed the battle of Karbala as a battle between all classes of people and an "outside oppressor," the Qajar dynasty. Thus, it was used as a means of revolt.

Before the outbreak of the civil war, the Shiʿa were quite circumspect in their observance of ʿAshura so as not to antagonize their non-Shiʿi neighbors.[40] In fact, true taʿziya, by which I mean the dramatization of events with actors, props, costumes, and so on, seems to have occurred only in the town of Nabatiyeh in southern Lebanon. Those I have interviewed who attended taʿziya in Nabatiyeh have told me that, along with the actors performing and narrating the story of Karbala, there are processions of men beating themselves until blood flows. In other parts of Lebanon, however, it appears that ʿAshura was a quiet affair with prayers, recitations of suffering, and perhaps a bit of chest pounding. But even a quiet ʿAshura commemoration serves as a marker of sect solidarity.

Of all Islamic communities in America, the Twelver Shiʿa are unique in having brought with them their saints. The Sunnis, too, have saints. But they are localized ones, the ones the women go to regularly to ask for their intercession so that they will become pregnant, or the ones the village visits once a year for a day of picnicking, prayer, and socializing. But they have no universally recognized saint such as Imam Husayn, who comes with a ritual that all Twelver Shiʿa participate in. In fact, one could say that this ritual defines Shiʿism. Besides, the Sunnis who have saints are always at least potentially at odds with their more conservative brethren who consider reverence for saints to be the equivalent of polytheism. Not so for the Shiʿa. All, from the most exalted marjiʿ taqlid to the humblest peasant, revere Imam Husayn and remember his story.

That the Shiʿa have brought the ʿAshura rituals with them almost ensures that they will thrive as a religious community in the United States, just as the rituals involving saints have perpetuated Catholicism in America.

Commemorating ʿAshura

The Dearborn mosques are filled to capacity, if not overflowing, during ʿAshura. During ʿAshura in 1989, at the Majmaʿ, in the gathering hall known as the Husayniya, named after the martyred Imam, Khomeini's picture was in the place of honor. The hall was hung with black banners with slogans praising Husayn, such as "God loves the one who loves Husayn." It was what one might call "a Christmas and Easter crowd." There were quite a number of perfunctory scarves, exposing a great deal of hair. Children ran about, as usual, some wearing their "Sunday best" while others wore shorts and wild T-shirts.

Typically, the events of the evening begin about 10:00 P.M. with someone who specializes in dramatic recitations of the Karbala story, the *khatib,* addressing the audience from the podium. The story starts in ordinary prose in pure classical Arabic, contrasting the size and character of the two armies at Karbala. As the story progresses, the *khatib* begins chanting it. Each hero is presented to the Imam Husayn (and to the audience) before he goes out to die, bidding farewell to the Imam and to the women. Each evening, the suffering of a particular individual or of the women in general is emphasized as part of the ritual telling of the story. After about an hour, there is a break when a collection may be taken. After the break, there is about another hour of recitation which becomes increasingly emotional. At this point, there is much weeping by the people, though some sit dry-eyed and looking bored.

The recitation is followed by responsive chanting. The *khatib* chants a verse, and the audience responds with a chorus, an elegy in which the Prophet's daughter Fatima figures prominently. At this point, the chest beating begins with varying degrees of energy.

On one occasion during 'Ashura, I witnessed a sudden shift of gears. Everyone instantly stood up, held hands in the air, and chanted various slogans, such as "There is no God but God," as well as praises of the imams. This continued for a few moments. Then everyone turned to the back of the room, which faces the *gibla,* and chanted "Ya Allah" and other slogans, standing with their palms up in front of them.

On another evening, the chants stopped abruptly, and after a few moments, young men began to rush in with trays full of paper bowls containing a thick porridge of grain, shredded meat, and fat. The porridge eaten, the young men began crowding forward to chant and breast-beat in earnest.

Not everyone is in the Husayniya every night during 'Ashura. There are those who congregate in the lobby and, in the summer, overflow into the cooler street. They are still part of the gathering nonetheless. But an onlooker from the street would not be aware of the emotional drama inside the mosque. There is no breast beating on the streets, no processions.

At the Jami', I witnessed another 'Ashura commemoration, this one just for women. Two women narrators chanted the story of the marriage of the Imam Husayn's daughter to Husayn's brother's son, Qassem. Before the marriage could be culminated, Qassem was struck down. The wedding scene was actually reenacted, with women carrying trays of flowers and candles on their heads. Upon reaching the part of the story in which Qassem was slain and word was brought to his wife, the audience began to sob. At the Jami', there is no breast pounding or self-flagellation. And, again, there are no displays on the streets.

However, during one evening of the 1989 commemoration of 'Ashura, a busload of Shi'a from Toledo came to the Dearborn area, stopping first at the Jami', with the aim of enticing the mourners to have a procession in the streets. Though I never heard the details of this event, I have been told that a brief fight ensued between some of the believers at the Jami' and the out-of-towners. The latter were persuaded to leave and set off for the Majma', where they hoped to find a warmer welcome. Apparently, the leaders at the Majma' were able to persuade their guests to participate in the prepared program.

Feelings about 'Ashura

The emotional commemoration of Karbala, which takes place at both the Jami' and the Majma' (the Majlis had not yet been open by the time of the 1989 'Ashura), indicates the hold that these events still have on the Shi'a in this area. People who do not attend any other services, with the exception of social occasions such as weddings and funerals, will attend the 'Ashura commemorations. A few women I spoke with hired female *khatibaat* to do a recitation of the Karbala story in their homes. These female *khatibaat* come from Lebanon during 'Ashura to provide this service. One nine-year-old boy told me he hoped his mother would have a female *khatibah* come to their home for his birthday. His mother expressed her disapproval of this idea since a happy occasion should not be linked with 'Ashura.

There is some disagreement over how 'Ashura should be commemorated. The ardently anti-Hizb Allah Khalil was taken to a *ta'ziya* in Nabatiyeh as a child and had been very moved by the performance. His feeling that in Lebanon it was "possible to feel closer to the Imam Husayn's sacrifice than it is here" was echoed by others. He would like to see the passion plays performed in the Dearborn mosques. Ebullient Ghalia, she of the long flowing hair and short-sleeved blouses, wishes there were processions of men flagellating themselves on the streets as there had been in South Lebanon. Obviously, the Imam Husayn reaches deeply into the psyches of the Shiʿa, and the remembrance of his martyrdom cannot be easily understood by invoking pat political and sociological explanations.

Not everyone is so eager to participate in the ʿAshura commemoration. Not surprisingly, those few who claim not to be religious at all do not go to the mosque to hear the story of Husayn's martyrdom. But even some very religiously active people avoid the events. Layla, a woman who is very active in the Majmaʿ, expressed the view that she did not really approve of the ʿAshura commemorations because "every day should be a commemoration of ʿAshura." She went on to say that people cry at ʿAshura, then go home and turn on their televisions. Abdo was raised in Dearborn and regularly attends the Jamiʿ but avoids the ʿAshura commemorations because he feels that the people only focus on a narrow meaning of the event: "ʿAshura should not be an occasion for sitting around and weeping." To Abdo, ʿAshura should be a reminder of the religion's social message.

These last two comments were made by individuals who otherwise had very different approaches to religion. Nevertheless, they both reflected the attitude that religion should not be treated as a series of events marking the year. Religion in general and ʿAshura in particular should be a driving force in one's life, very much akin to the idea that the spirit of Christmas should live in one's heart throughout the year.

Saroya offers another opinion of ʿAshura. She is a middle-aged woman who regularly attends the Jamiʿ and may attend an occasional ʿAshura commemoration, but she does not consider it her religious duty to do so: "ʿAshura is a reminder of Husayn's social message, that people are to be treated fairly. But this is not religion in the same way that the Koran is religion. It is not as important as following the Koran." This is certainly a minority view but an important one. Saroya refers to the Koran frequently when she discusses religion, which is a very important topic to her. The Koran, of course, is one element of Islam that is shared by all Muslims. By stressing the Koran, she is downplaying her distinctiveness as a Shiʿa. (I should note that Saroya has a picture of Nasser hanging in her refurbished basement. Hers was the only home in which I saw a picture of the Egyptian leader. This suggests a more pan-Arab philosophy than is usually found in this community. Such an attitude fosters a sense of harmony with Sunni Islam, which also stresses the paramount importance of the Koran.)

Faye expressed a similar idea to Saroya's when she stated that she did not attend ʿAshura commemorations because she does not like "to have the reminder that there is a division and animosity between Sunni and Shiʿa." Again, this was not a view commonly expressed. Even the early immigrants who wanted to impress upon me that there is no Shiʿi/Sunni distinction are at the mosque for ʿAshura.

Because of the civil war in Lebanon and the Iranian Revolution, it is logical to assume that ʿAshura would have become a very political event in the Dearborn area and that the martyrdom of Husayn would be viewed as a paradigm for the community as a whole, much as it has been used in Iran. Also, in Lebanon a very activist view of Husayn prevails. Or, as Hegland puts it, Husayn is viewed as exemplar. I watched a home video (produced in 1990) of a funeral being held in the village of Machghara in the Bekaa valley. It was the funeral of a man who had been killed by Israelis. The emotional level was very high, with men obviously competing with one another as they pounded their chests and heads, weaving through the streets, chanting slogans as they went.

I asked people who was their greatest hero in all of history (not specifying that it be a religious hero). If this community held an image of itself as revolutionary, the Imam Husayn would have been the overwhelming first choice. But, this was not the case. Most people to whom I spoke saw the Imam ʿAli, Husayn's father, as their hero.

The Imam ʿAli was also killed, but not in so dramatic a way as his son. It is not his death that people comment on but rather his knowledge, his wisdom, his leadership skills, and his strength. This finding substantiated my impression that the members of this community are not seeking martyrdom or revolt but, rather, good leadership. This impression was strongly supported by most of my conversations with people. It was also confirmed by the fact that the mourners, even in the throes of sorrow brought on by the recitation of the Imam Husayn's sufferings, refused to act out their feelings in a public procession. Had they done so, they certainly would have risked an unpleasant encounter with the local police and could have aroused fear and anxiety among both non-Muslims and other Muslim groups.

On the other hand, the community still faithfully commemorates the Imam's martyrdom. This event, while not obligatory in Shiʿism, is not to be forgotten in America. It serves as a reminder that the Shiʿa are a people apart from all others.[41] It is a statement that, while they might benefit from the peace and prosperity of

America, they are not truly of this society. They may not want an antagonistic relationship with those outside their group, yet they are eager to maintain their sectarian solidarity. Throughout history, remembering Husayn has shown to be an effective vehicle for maintaining this goal.

By the 1860s, the dominant trait of American Catholicism was devotionalism, the exercise of piety. With the Mass and sacraments insufficient to meet the spiritual needs of the people, Catholics developed other forms of religious rituals. Their devotions centered on the passion of Christ or the suffering of Mary or some other saint, toward whom they developed an intense feeling. The devotions generally took place in a church or a public place over which a priest presided. More popular than the Mass, these devotions became the most important communal ritual in Catholic churches throughout America. First Friday of the month devotions, May processions in honor of Mary, June devotions in honor of the Sacred Heart, October gatherings for saying the rosary—all of these helped nourish a culture of piety that set Catholics apart from other Americans. This movement in Catholicism came with strong papal approval. It also served to strengthen the position of the priesthood: it was priests who led these devotions, which in turn focused lay attention on individual spirituality and away from social movements and church administration.[42]

Like Catholic devotionalism, the ʿAshura commemorations offer a rich, deeply expressive sort of religious experience to the Shiʿa. They are singularly powerful rituals that bring alive a historical moment and draw the people to the mosques as no other religious occasion does. The people of Dearborn, whether traditionalists or Shariʿa-minded, show no signs of abandoning the Muharram commemorations. Most likely, this ritual, more than any other, will fill a spiritual void in the lives of people in a secular, materialistic society. A legalistic, scripturalist approach to Islam will not suffice for most people, if indeed it is attractive at all.

Over the centuries, the ʿAshura commemorations, as is true of rituals in all religions, have undergone various interpretations. It appears that this pattern will continue as the Shiʿa become more established in Dearborn. At this point, it seems unlikely that the Sunnis will find themselves inclined to join the Shiʿa in commemorating the Imam's martyrdom. On the other hand, it seems equally unlikely that the Shiʿa will use ʿAshura as a means of rebellion against their host government. Like Catholic devotionalism, it is a means of strengthening a Shi'i ethos that includes respect for clerical leadership and promotes a sense of piety in the believers.

When Italians came to America in large numbers in the late nineteenth century, they held boisterous street celebrations of the feast of the village patron saint.[43] Today, such dramatic public displays have been replaced by the more decorous practices of the Anglo-Irish tradition. One might have anticipated that the Shi'a would have carried out the 'Ashura commemorations in their more dramatic, physical form, as did the Italians on their holy days. But this has not been the case. There are no raucous public displays of religiosity among the Shi'a in the United States. Prejudice and even open hostility and violence against Catholics were prevalent in America in the nineteenth century. Most Catholics do not seem to have been concerned about winning over the goodwill of their Protestant countrymen. The Shi'a, on the other hand, especially at the leadership level, do care about the sensibilities of their Christian neighbors.

The Day, the Week, and the Year in the Mosques

Defining a Mosque

It is instructive to look back on the evolution of the mosque in the Muslim world. Oleg Grabar outlines four stages in the development of the mosque.[44] Quoting from the Koran, Grabar points out that there are references to a *masjid*, a term that later referred to some mosques, but they do not necessarily refer to a special building just for Muslims. Instead, they refer to a place belonging to God. Two conflicting themes in the early days of Islam would have influenced the development of the mosque. On the one hand, a *masjid* could be simply a place where any individual prayed; no clergy or intermediary was required to act between the people and God. On the other hand, there arose the concept of the community of the faithful and a need for a place of worship large enough for the congregation.

In the Middle Ages, writers such as Ibn Khaldun were interested in defining the role of the mosque. He distinguished between minor ones for specific segments of the population and the great spacious mosques for which the caliph and other authorities were responsible. He felt it was important that the caliph who was serving as temporal leader also have the spiritual leadership of the community and did not wish to see these functions divided.

But very early in the history of the Islamic world, the notion of greater and lesser or public and private mosques simply did not exist. During this time, the *masjid* was basically an open space that served exclusively Muslim purposes such as prayer, collection of taxes, and military recruitment. There was no formal structure or well-defined purpose.

The second stage of mosque development fell between A.D. 650 and 750. While smaller *masjids* operated during this time, the tendency was for the governor of an area to embellish one mosque and make that one of primary importance so that others would be diminished in significance. Mosques were built so that they could be expanded or contracted according to the needs of the community. They were enclosed by walls and did not have exterior facades. This was also when the minaret became a characteristic of the mosque, as did the dome and the *mihrab,* or axial nave. These features acquired a religious meaning and became involved in the ceremony of prayer.

The third period of the mosque began during the second half of the eighth century, which was the time of the great masterpieces of the Islamic world. These mosques were found in the major cities of the Middle East. The sanctuaries increased in size both to accommodate the larger population and to remind people of the glory of their rulers. Also during this period, different mosques became identified with different social groups. Most significantly, the palace and the mosque were no longer necessarily adjacent. No longer was the caliph's visit to the mosque an ordinary occurrence.

The twelfth century marks the beginning of the fourth stage in mosque development. The major architectural monument of this period was the Great Mosque of Isphahan in Iran. It occupies a large space in the city and is significantly different in appearance from earlier mosques. According to Grabar, "the twelfth century mosque replaced an earlier hypostyle mosque and reflected, therefore, a conscious formal change. Instead of the large space of the hypostyle hall with its endless possibilities of movement and growth, there is an interior courtyard (and not merely the open part of a single area), with an interior facade and a division of the covered parts into four separate areas through the creation of large *eyuans* on each side of the courtyard. The earlier internal unity of spatial arrangement is gone, and enlargements become impossible except through the addition of separate buildings attached to the original *masjid.*"[45]

Also important in this era is the construction of a new type of building known as the *madrasa,* which is a religious school. A type of monastery for mystical orders also emerged in the city, as did mausoleums for saintly men and women. The distinction between *masjid* and *jamiᶜ* began in this period as well, the latter term referring to older or larger mosques. These changes reflected changes in society. For example, the mausoleums would have competed with the mosques as places of prayer. With monasteries came the separation of certain individuals from the total community and with the *madrasas* the institution of training individuals to become experts in religious matters. Grabar also suggests that the breakup of the original unity of the building was a result of divided allegiances within the city. The increase in the number of such buildings suggests that there were probably many competing poles of spiritual allegiance in existence. Furthermore, more and more individuals had the means to build such monuments. As a consequence, a greater variety in style arose. Finally, the trend for the separation of secular buildings from the religious sanctuaries became more pronounced during this period.

The mosques in the Dearborn-Detroit area seem rather strange entities. Certainly, the Islamic Center of America is larger than the other Shiᶜi mosques, so that technically it can be designated Jamiᶜ. But it was not built for the glory of some wealthy potentate. Rather, it was built by the Shiᶜi community at large. The Islamic Institute (the Majmaᶜ), with its office building appearance, in no way resembles what one expects a mosque to look like, nor does the Islamic Council (the Majlis). As in many poorer Christian denominations in America, these houses of worship are very humble structures that serve the purpose of acting as both places of worship and civic centers. Perhaps in some ways, they are in keeping with the original *masjid* of the earlier periods of Islam, basically spaces for Muslims to conduct their business. It should be kept in mind that Lebanon was never a land of magnificent mosques built by great potentates the way Iran and Turkey were. In fact, the Husayniya is the most common religious building in Shiᶜi areas of Lebanon. So it is unlikely that the Lebanese Muslims in America would ever aspire to emulate the masterpieces of these lands.

The mosques in the Dearborn-Detroit area, though not differentiated along social class lines, do reflect varying ideological allegiances. They all see their role heavily in terms of education, yet their interpretations of this role differ.

The Jamiᶜ on Sunday Morning

The centerpiece of the Jamiᶜ is the Sunday service held every week. The fact that Sheikh Chirri and his board elected to have a

Sunday service has become controversial over the years. Faced with the reality that in America people usually have to work on Friday, the day set apart for special prayer in Islam, Chirri found it sensible to have a Sunday morning service. In keeping with so many of his other early decisions, it also had the effect of deemphasizing the differences between Muslims and Christians. Younger sheikhs and their more ardent followers are less inclined to be sympathetic with this approach. In their view, Friday should not be replaced by Sunday, even in America. Criticisms notwithstanding, the Sunday service has continued over the years.

The service begins sometime in the late morning. It begins when the speakers think enough people fill the hall to make proceeding worthwhile. People dribble in over a period of at least an hour, obviously undisturbed by having to wait. After all, a major reason for coming is to socialize with friends and family members. People often sit at tables, which facilitates this socializing. There is not a great deal of emphasis on male/female segregation. While there may be some clustering based on gender, this is certainly not uniform. Sunday school classes are conducted consecutively with the adults' program, but there is always an abundance of children of various ages milling around and tugging on their mothers.

A table is set up near the podium for those who preside over the meeting. A banner with a Koranic verse often serves as a backdrop. Otherwise, the room has a definite sense of austerity about it. The chairman of the board of directors is invariably present, as are one or two other board members who may double as lecturers. They are dressed in fine business suits, not the open-necked shirts found at the Majma.[46] Next to them sits Sheikh Chirri, the longtime Jamiᶜ director (who retired during the course of my fieldwork) who generally addresses the congregation in English, and the assistant director, Sheikh Saᶜil Attat.[47] Accompanying this group of men is a young muezzin, often referred to as a sheikh without a turban. A bearded man who wears open-necked shirts, he often dons a cloak over his clothing which distinguishes him as "cleric-like."

The chairman introduces, generally quite lavishly, each speaker, though the congregation is thoroughly familiar with these individuals. The muezzin, who is never a speaker, is always first. With his rich, deep but nasal voice, he chants lengthy prayers as he sits before the microphone at the podium. This over, the chairman again proceeds to the podium. Sheikh Chirri is too elderly to give speeches, but this is a very recent development.[48] As an English speaker, he is now being replaced by a second-generation member of the board. The sermons of Sheikh Attat, the assistant director, are always in Arabic. Language is an important and divisive issue at the Jami⁽ since this mosque is very broad-based in its membership which includes early immigrants and their offspring as well as very recent immigrants.

During the sermons, there is little reduction in noise from the audience. Some people do attend to what is being said, but many continue their conversations with their neighbors. While the buzzing of voices does not appear to bother the rest of the audience, it is apparent that it is annoying to some of the speakers, who might raise their voices or suggest that the children be made to sit down. (The same situation prevails at the Majma⁽. During a solemn occasion, the chairman commented that he had visited a Christian church where everyone sat silently throughout the sermon. He suggested that it would behoove the Muslims to show such decorum. The advice went unheeded.)

The programs for these services do not vary. A meal might be served by the women of the mosque on special occasions, but other than that, the visitor to the Jami⁽ can look forward to the chanting of prayers, announcements, and lengthy speeches. For holy day observances, there may be some chanting of a verse with the congregation doing the chorus.

The presenters and the program tend toward a rigid, formal, and serious style. There is no humor or interchange between the presenter and his audience. On the other hand, the behavior of the audience is otherwise extremely informal. People come and go as they please, they speak to one another freely and a few might even light up cigarettes.[49] It is as if the formality of going to the mosque and sitting in a room during a sermon is sufficient for meeting one's religious duty. A few people have commented to me that they already know what the sheikh is going to say, so why bother to listen?

Certainly, the Sunday service—or any service, for that matter—is a time to meet with friends. This is very much the case for young unmarried men, who cluster in corners of the building. Not always welcome in the homes of one another's parents because of the unmarried sisters who may be present and because they are often perceived as a general nuisance, the mosque is a safe haven for them. Unless they have pretensions to religious sophistication (in which case they are more likely to be at the Majma⁽ or the Majlis), enlightenment by the sheikhs is probably not their primary concern.

For at least some of the speakers, there is serious concern about the inattentiveness of the audience. They feel that their message is extremely important to the community and are frustrated when it seems to fall on deaf ears. They see a need to bring the people to a deeper understanding of Islam now that they live in a predominantly non-Islamic community. For their own sakes but, more importantly, for the sake of the name of Islam in the community, they must know enough about Islamic laws, history, and mores so that they will not be led astray by the myriad temptations of American society.

Perhaps of even more immediate concern to some of the Jami' leaders is that the recent immigrants not confuse Lebanese tradition for Islam.[50] One board member expressed his frustration with the provincialism of the newer immigrants, saying that they even equated Lebanese food with Islam.[51] But people such as this board member are greatly outnumbered by the recently arrived villagers who can manage adequately in Dearborn without ever tasting a hamburger or uttering a word of English.

Whether or not the people are listening to the men at the pulpit, obviously the Sunday program does serve the purpose of giving visibility to the mosque leadership and reinforcing their position in the community. The insistence on flattering introductions of already well-known speakers suggests that the leaders are sensitive to the fact that they are leaders of a relatively small, insignificant group. Under such circumstances, there is a need to elevate one's position, not just for the sake of the individual but also for the sake of enhancing the position of the entire group, at least in their own eyes.

The continued and undeviating presence of Sheikh Chirri at the head table for all mosque functions is also significant. Basically, Sheikh Chirri's presence means that the status quo can continue. Thus far, the Jami' has not had success in finding the proper replacement for Sheikh Chirri. It is still too early to make any definite predictions about the new assistant director, Sheikh Attat. The diversity of opinions and views of the people who run and frequent the Jami', along with the general desire of the sheikhs to function independently of a board, makes filling this position particularly difficult.

Friday Prayers at the Majma'

All mosques are places where people—particularly men—congregate to do *salat*. At the end of the Sunday service at the Jami', men start filing out of the main hall to a room designated for prayer. But there is an interesting significance given to the Friday prayers at the Majma'. First, the Friday prayers at the Majma' are attended exclusively by males. Second, the prayers and the sermon that follows given by Sheikh Berri are faithfully broadcast on cable television, just as the Sunday Jami' services are regularly shown. I believe that the Majma' leadership selects these occasions for public consumption as they so clearly represent the image the Majma' wishes to project. After prayers, Sheikh Berri, usually standing but never at a pulpit, addresses a small group of men seated on the floor. With his voice always calm and never dramatic, he selects a topic on a purely religious subject. Afterward, the men have time to ask questions. The tone is extremely serious and decorous. There is no levity or familiarity.

The men who attend these Friday prayers are of all ages, but there is a core of young men who are regularly in and out of the mosque. One day, while I was interviewing Berri, he telephoned to the front desk of the Majma' to see if there were any *shibab* (youth) present for *salat*. Indeed there were, and the meeting had to come to a close. These *shibab*, usually sporting beards and open-collared shirts, dominate the scene at the Majma'. They come and go at all hours, clustering in groups in the lobby and the various gathering rooms. It is they who arrange the rooms for meetings. It also falls to them to carry and serve the huge platters of food that the women have prepared in the kitchen. They are the ones summoned when another water pitcher or more bread is needed at the table during the frequent dinners served at the Majma'. They have an unmistakably proprietary feeling about their mosque.

On occasion, the *shibab* at the Majma' will organize special events. One example was a memorial meeting for Muhammad-Baqir al-Sadr, a major contemporary political thinker among the Shi'i clergy of Iraq who, along with his sister, was executed by the Iraqi government. This event was highly political, as people spoke openly against the Ba'athist regime of Iraq. Including the chanting of prayers, the formal portion of the program continued for more than four hours, with five sheikhs giving speeches to an audience of about 125 people, almost evenly divided between men and women. The sermons were followed by dinner, served cafeteria-style, with the young men slapping food onto people's plates with the efficiency of army cooks.

Gilsenan discusses the relationship between sheikhs and young men and suggests that sheikhs "are associated informally with what might be viewed as an extended rite of passage for those in transition to full adult male status. That is to say, those who tend to make up the bulk of their followers or attendants, who go to the rituals, and sit in their reception rooms are very often the unmarried (or only recently married) young men."[52] He goes on to say that these young men, by reaching their mothers and sisters, broaden the influence of the sheikh.[53]

While the sheikh-*shibab* relationship may have traditional roots, at the Majma', and now more recently at the Majlis, it seems to have taken on a new meaning but one that is growing on a world scale. These young men take a very active role in the relationship with their sheikhs. They see themselves as knowledgeable and proper representatives of Islam. They are sometimes reminiscent of what Fouad Ajami refers to as the "half-educated urban youth."[54] More often than not, they are attending or have attended college to study engineering or computer science, disciplines that reinforce the idea that there are right and wrong answers to every problem. Their approach to religion reflects this type of thinking. Kepel and Roy both note that the majority of the activists in the Islamic movements in Egypt have been students studying practical and applied sciences. Munson also has noted that students of these disciplines have been the major instigators and proponents of Middle Eastern revolutions and uprisings.[55]

The sheikh, to these young men, is an authority figure and a person to be respected, but not someone seated on an unreachable pedestal. That the sheikh is held in high regard should not be taken for granted. In fact, Kepel reports that the leader of the group that assassinated Sadat was an electrical engineer who had written a manifesto beginning with an attack on the *'ulama*.[56] The Shi'i clergy in Lebanon often were held in contempt by this modern breed of young Muslims. The clergy today often are seen as weak and ineffectual pawns of the elite class. The *shibab* will give their loyalty only to a religious figure who is seen as a defender of the "true Islam," an activist Islam that is also scripturally based.[57] He also must be seen as a man of the people, someone who is accessible, just as the Prophet himself was accessible. Ideally, he should not be hidden behind a pulpit; he should sit or stand among his people. He may have firm control over the running of his mosque, but he should never appear to be autocratic. A mutual need exists between sheikh and *shibab* at both the Majma' and the Majlis. They give each other a sense of legitimacy.

On the other hand, the sheikh needs a broader base than the *shibab* if he is to be an effective leader in such an eclectic community. The *shibab* and their older male counterparts, all of whom refer to themselves as "brothers," and the women, the "sisters" who share their menfolk's religious views, often set the tone for the activities at the Majma'. At such times, the men and women are strictly separated, and the women tend to be more fully covered. Yet a growing number of occasions seem to be outside their control, with a more casual style taking over. Fund-raising dinners are one example, as are the annual commencement ceremonies of the children's Arabic classes. At such occasions, one sees nearly the full gamut of the community.

Donation Dinners at the Majma'

Swelling the throng of well-wishers who will forgo other Sunday afternoon activities in order to attend the occasional donation dinner are individuals who never frequent the mosque for regular services. During one of these occasions, I sat across the table from a woman who fidgeted constantly with her scarf, as did many other women in the room. She wasn't accustomed to attending the mosque, she told me, and wasn't comfortable with wearing a scarf.

There is no abatement of the noise level in the room during opening prayers and speeches. Even on such social occasions, the sheikhs and honored guests see it as their duty to give lengthy and pious speeches, though the audience members do not appear to consider it their duty to pay attention.

The meal consists invariably of roast lamb served with rice and pine nuts, salad, and chickpea dip (*hommos bi tahini*). During the dinner, contributions, above and beyond the ten dollars per person for the meal, are collected, and the names and amounts are read aloud from the podium. During one of these dinners, I calculated that two hundred dollars was the average donation. There were quite a few fifty-dollar contributions, but these were offset by donations of one thousand dollars, and there was even one for two thousand dollars.

At least two objectives are accomplished at the fund-raising dinners, the most obvious being to support the functions of the mosque. (The Jami' also has fund-raising dinners, but they are more elaborate and costly affairs.) The fund-raising dinners also allow for visible displays of generosity. The theme of generosity is well documented in any account of traditional Arabic life. While the exigencies of American life have brought about changes in how generosity is expressed, that it remains important to the Lebanese in American is beyond doubt. What is seen at the fund-raising dinners is a very competitive and ostentatious display of generosity. Contributions allow individuals and families to make the dual statements that they financially support their religion and that they are doing well in earthly matters. While a nice home and car, expensive clothing, and gold jewelry are indicators of prosperity, contributions to the mosques are a means of purifying and justifying newly found wealth, something about which they are ambivalent. While they are proud of their prosperity, they are also aware that their religion admonishes them to beware of the temptations of wealth. Giving to the mosque is a means of alleviating any moral dilemmas they may have about money, especially money that has been made through not altogether lawful means. For example, if a man owns a party store and sells liquor, he is considered to be earning money unlawfully.

The notion of purifying money is built into the purity code of Shi'ism. Paying the one-fifth tax, or *khums*, is an extremely important part of the religion. Half of the *khums* should be paid to the impoverished *sayyids*, the descendants of the Prophet, while the other half goes to the *marji'*. According to Khu'i, "If property is derived in part from forbidden sources and it is not possible to distinguish the lawful from the forbidden or determine the amount of the property from forbidden sources or its rightful owner, then it becomes lawful by paying *khums* on it. . . . It is an obligatory precaution to do this with the permission of the religious judge."[58] After this payment, the assets become lawful. The Iranians have a joke about this procedure: If someone asks whether something is *halal* or *haram* (permitted or forbidden), the response is "Pay the share of the mullah, and it is *halal*."[59]

There is a great deal of discussion at the Dearborn mosques about *khums*, but I have never heard anyone joke about it here. It is clear that in this community, people consider their financial support of religion as an extremely important duty. At the Majlis one night after *iftar* (the breaking of the fast during Ramadan), Sheikh Burro gave a lengthy speech about *khums* that went on until about midnight. (This was after a day of approximately fifteen hours of fasting!) The speech was followed by several questions generally requiring substantial responses regarding the details of paying *khums*.

Children at the Mosques

"Sheikh Chirri taught my children to pray and to fast when they were growing up," one woman told me. Her children were born here in the 1950s and '60s when the community was still small. In those days, the sheikh was seen as the teacher of the entire community, young and old. Today, the children are taught by laypersons, some more knowledgeable than others. One young man, teaching children the basics of Islam—*salat*, the five pillars, and so on—at the Jami' bemoaned the fact that the sheikhs have so little contact with the children and shun the job of teaching them. The Jami', he told me, did ask one of the younger sheikhs to teach Sunday school classes, but he refused. My informant was surprised when Sheikh Attat, as the new assistant director, visited the children's class to address the children and to encourage them in their religious life.

Teaching children is rarely seen as a high-prestige position in either the West or the Islamic world. In America, the teaching of children has never had the status that other professions carry. It is generally viewed as "women's work" and not worthy of a great deal of respect.

In the Middle East, a young man aspiring to a clerical position goes off to the Atabat in Iraq or to Qom in Iran to study with a learned *mujtahid*. The teacher ultimately decides the fate of his scholars. Those who show the least promise are sent to villages to teach the Koran to schoolchildren.

That sheikhs do not come to America with the goal of teaching Sunday school classes is obvious. Freed from the usual constraints of the religious hierarchy, the clergy find themselves in roles that would not have been available to them in Lebanon, and the potential for exercising authority here is tremendous. It also can be argued that the sheikhs who serve as the imams or leaders of the mosques are far too preoccupied with other concerns that leave little time for teaching children. It has been instructive to sit in Sheikh Berri's office where he continuously takes telephone calls and receives messages and visitors. As a sheikh in Dearborn, he has taken on the role of marriage counselor as well as an authority on all matters of religion. The vast majority of people to whom I spoke said that they would feel free to call on the sheikh with matters regarding religion, and I have known many individuals, both men and women, who freely pick up the phone to call the sheikhs with questions. In speaking to Shiʿi sheikhs in other parts of the country as well, I have come to appreciate the burdens they are shouldering. Accustomed to a life of study, they are suddenly confronted with a myriad of social and personal problems that would not have been part of their domain at home. One told me of cases of marital problems and spousal abuse that he was attempting to deal with, another of telephone calls at all hours of the night from people with problems and questions.

In view of these constraints of time and tradition, it is obvious that others will perform the job of religious education of children.

At the Jamiʿ, rows of children, perhaps a hundred in all, crowd into a large room where they are instructed in the intricacies of performing *salat*. A middle-aged man leads the prayer, and the children follow with varying degrees of success and seriousness. At such gatherings, they will learn the basics of their religion. The classes are conducted mostly in English, although they learn their prayers in Arabic.

If children are going to learn to read and write Arabic in Dearborn, they must attend the after-school Arabic lessons given at several public schools in the East Dearborn neighborhoods. These are sponsored by the Islamic Institute, the Majmaᶜ. Each spring, there is a graduation ceremony at the Majmaᶜ for children who have attended the Arabic classes. They also can attend the religious classes given in Arabic on Saturday and Sunday mornings at the Majmaᶜ. I am told that approximately sixty children attend these classes, which are conducted in Arabic.

The fact that "the eloquent Arabic" (as Sheikh Berri calls it) is being taught to children through the mosque is significant. Children, of course, learn colloquial Arabic from their parents, but it is the formal or standard form (also referred to as classical Arabic) of the language that is the Arabic of the Koran. Standard Arabic is extremely difficult, and without serious instruction, these children would be unlikely ever to learn it. Teaching standard Arabic will help ensure that children can read the Koran and other religious texts in the original language, which, in turn, will help ensure the survival of Islam in the community. The cause also will be advanced by the building of the elementary school funded by Ayatollah Khuᶜi's foundation.

That the Majmaᶜ has assumed the task of teaching Arabic and the Jamiᶜ has not reflects, I believe, the differences in attitudes between the two institutions. The leadership at the Jamiᶜ—the Islamic Center of America—has seen the mosque as both in and of America. To study Islam has been considered essential; to study Arabic has been generally regarded as peripheral. I asked Sheikh Attat why Arabic was not taught at the mosque. He had been under the impression that it was. Another person in the room confirmed that it was not directly taught. Sheikh Attat replied that he would see to it that it was taught. Whether Arabic will become part of the Jamiᶜ's curriculum remains to be seen.

Sheikh Berri at the Majmaᶜ uses the word culture frequently. He places a high value on "Arabic culture," the learned aspect of Arabic culture. This attitude is reflected clearly by the fact that he frequently recites poetry during his sermons. He has said that he believes a person must know the language of a people in order to understand their culture. It is obvious that he has placed much weight on the instructing of Arabic to children in the community. Arabic is spoken at the Majmaᶜ almost exclusively, but sometimes one does hear English. On one of these occasions—a "donation dinner"—a group of boys and girls recited a Koranic verse in English. Whether or not the Arabic language can be kept alive in the mosques is debatable. At this point one can only document the efforts being made.[60]

Salat for the Id

About 10:00 A.M. on the holidays, such as 'Id al-Fitr and 'Id al-Adha, one may see a man walking along the street carrying his small child, his *hijab*-covered wife beside him towing along a daughter in a frilly dress and hat. A few minutes later comes another man, followed by a procession of four or five children. Not more than forty-five minutes later, they will return, the children clutching bags of sweets. They have been to the mosque for the special *salat* said at holidays.

The *Husayniya* is strewn with carpets for the occasion so that the believers can prostrate themselves in prayer. The men line up in the front of the room, closest to the sheikh who leads the prayers, and behind them are the women, with children interspersed throughout the room. When the prayers and blessings are over, the men line up to greet and embrace the sheikh. Sometimes a woman may exchange greetings with the sheikh, after the men have had their turn. Meanwhile, the children are given treats and perhaps an opportunity to purchase a gift for their parents in the lobby.

Holiday celebrations at the mosques transcend the ideological differences that exist in the community. On such occasions, there will be no reminders of political divisions. They are certainly not universally attended, but those who do attend represent a wide cross-section of the community. These are occasions when people can take their children to the mosque for brief services. While so many of the mosque functions involve lengthy speeches and are geared toward adults, the holiday prayers do not make undue demands on a child's patience. Furthermore, children can look forward to the treats put out especially for them at the end of the service. Holidays are easy opportunities for parents to reinforce their children's identity as Muslims in the community. And parents who might not utilize the mosque at many other times are likely to want to expose their children to what they see as purely religious rituals.

Engagements and Weddings

Marriage in Islam is not a sacrament. It is essentially a contract between two families. A sum of money is paid by the man or his family to the woman or her family. Provisions are made for the woman to receive part of this amount at the time of the marriage, with the stipulation that in case of divorce, the remainder should be paid. From early times in Shi'ism, it has been the sheikh's role, as a religious and therefore legal expert, to draw up the contract and officiate at the wedding. The early Muslims in this area saw it as a major duty of the sheikhs to perform marriage ceremonies at the mosques. As stated earlier, the mosques and the Hashimite Hall in southeast Dearborn were congregational places where Muslims could share their social lives. The early community used the mosques not only as a place where the sheikh would carry out his duties but also as a place where the people could sing and dance to celebrate the union of a new couple.

In the 1970s, the new wave of immigrants came. Things began to change after that, in interesting ways. To understand the process of change, it is important to explain first what a wedding is in Lebanese terms.

When a couple (invariably with the involvement of the families) decides to marry, they may go to the sheikh and sign a contract. In the Dearborn area, this is commonly done at the mosques. The sheikh officiates at a short ceremony in which the young couple stand together, their fathers at their sides. The sheikh asks if they all agree to the terms of the contract. He may give a short speech about marriage, and the couple will exchange rings. This is referred to as an engagement. At this point, the couple may be seen together in public without provoking criticism. In some cases, the woman may move into her father-in-law's home. According to Islamic law, it is permissible for the couple to have sexual relations at this point, but Lebanese custom rules that the couple is not yet married and therefore may not have sex. On the other hand, if one or the other member of the couple decides that he or she does not wish to be married after this formal engagement has taken place, a religious divorce is required. In the cases I have known of in which such a "divorce" takes place, there is much bitterness, and a woman's reputation is tarnished, even though she has remained a virgin. As one informant said, a woman who has been engaged and divorced is seen as "someone who has been used. Who would want her after that?"

Alternatively, a couple may have an engagement at home without the presence of the sheikh. They simply exchange rings in front of family members and perhaps close friends. Should the engagement end under these circumstances, no divorce is necessary, as there has been no contract signed.

In Lebanese terms, the wedding is the celebration—in American terms, the "reception." If a couple has been before the sheikh for the engagement, the sheikh need not become involved in the matter again. No separate wedding ceremony need take place. On the other hand, if the sheikh was not in attendance for the engagement, he will officiate at another small ceremony just before the wedding reception. After the wedding celebration, a public occasion, the couple is expected to live together and have sexual relations.

In Lebanon, weddings do not occur at the mosques. "People went to the mosques for prayers and funerals, not for weddings and engagements like they do here," one woman told me. When the new immigrants arrived and saw weddings with dancing and music at the mosques, they were shocked. Very recent immigrants who never witnessed such things can hardly believe their ears when they are told that people actually danced in the mosques. One woman, a college student who is quite liberal in her dress and attitudes, was astounded when she learned of this and exclaimed, "That's terrible!" In the old country, weddings and engagements took place in halls, private homes, and gardens but not in mosques. The new immigrants I spoke to who were old enough to remember attending mosques in Lebanon were almost unanimous in their agreement that the mosques are used differently and more frequently here than they were in Lebanon.

The Muslims at the Jamiʿ, which was the only Shiʿi mosque until the mid-1980s, had a dilemma and sought solutions. The leadership, facing accusations of being un-Islamic, put an end to the music and dancing, though I am told this decision met with some resistance by the more Americanized Muslims. Over the years, many in the community have opted to have the engagement at the mosque. Such an engagement is usually a simple affair at which coffee and sweets are served. Then, some months later, there will be a wedding, a large party with music and dancing and dinner at a hall.

Others do still elect to have weddings at the mosque. This is quite a different kind of affair from a wedding at a hall, since in the mosques today there is no music or dancing, and dress is far more modest and conservative.

People may have different motivations for having a wedding at a mosque. One consideration is money. It is much cheaper to hold a wedding at a mosque than at a hall. While the groom is expected to contribute something toward the use of the mosque, it is far more reasonable than it would be to rent a hall, and there is no band to pay. Propriety is another consideration. A friend was invited to a wedding at the Jamiʿ. She expressed disappointment that the wedding would not be held in a hall. I asked her why the couple had decided on the Jamiʿ, and she told me that there had recently been a death in the family and that it would not be proper to have a big celebration at that time.

In the cases I have referred to thus far, the choice of holding a wedding at a mosque has involved practical and personal considerations. But there is a large minority in the community that views popular music and dancing as *haram* under any circumstances. For this group, the most obvious place to conduct a wedding is a mosque.

In Dearborn, there is a new interpretation of the purpose of the mosque. It is actually part of a process that was started in the early part of this century. The mosque initially was used for all social events, many of which had nothing to do with religion. Then an earlier group of the new wave of immigrants came. Steeped in tradition, they tried to bring the mosque in line with what was done in Lebanon, so they moved weddings out of the mosque. A slightly later group, strongly influenced by political changes in the Middle East, arrived, and once again the mosque (particularly the Majmaʿ) became a center for all types of occasions. But all of these occasions have been redefined as religious. For this latest group, the Shariʿa-minded, there simply is no distinction between religion and nonreligion, between sacred and profane. If one's entire life, one's every step, is guided by religion, as one young woman explained to me, how can it be otherwise?

" 'The mid-nineteenth century was *par excellence* the era of the urban parish church, the lodge, the benefit association, the social athletic club, the fire company, and the gang.' In a changing city, people were searching for 'a sense of social place and community,' and many immigrants found this in the parish."[61]

That Catholics centered their lives on the parish church does not mean that core membership in the church was universal or even close to it; in fact, it may have been in the 25 to 30 percent range. But most families appear to have had at least one member involved in a parish society. Dolan explains that the parish meant different things to different people: "For some it was a reference point, a place that helped them to remember who they were in their adopted homeland; for others it was more, a place where a sense of community could be found; for still others it gave life meaning, and it helped them to cope with life in the emerging metropolis or the small town."[62]

One of the important roles of the Catholic parish was religious education, although the emphasis was on developing parochial schools rather than Sunday school, as in Protestantism. Parochial schools gained in importance, especially among certain ethnic groups, as the quest for universal public education grew in America. Catholics viewed parochial schools as the best way to preserve the Church in America, and women religious from the old country served as a ready supply of teachers for these schools.

A Polish-American Catholic I interviewed, Emil Wozniak, the son of immigrants, attended St. Andrew's School in Detroit in the 1920s. He remembered vividly the nuns who taught him. These nuns, along with the priests, dominated much of the behavior of the Catholics of the parish. They placed stringent restrictions on activities that could be carried out on Sundays and during Lent, made confession a monthly obligation, relied heavily on the use of a yardstick for discipline, openly condemned their archrivals, the Polish nationalists, demanded weekly pennies as a contribution from the children, and decided who could be buried in the Catholic cemetery.

Religious education is only one function of many in the Shiʻi mosques. Like the Catholic parish churches of the earlier immigrants, the mosques are utilized for many more types of occasions than was ever found in the old country—prayer services, holy day observances, political meetings, and donation dinners.

The Shiʻa, too, face the challenge of how best to educate their children in a land where their religion is not in the air that they breathe. Most recognize that it is imperative to teach their children the basics of the religion, but there is little agreement about whether this is to be done in the home, in Sunday school, or in a specifically Islamic school. Certainly, if the parents of all the thousands of Shiʻi children in Dearborn were to choose to send their children to some sort of religious school, there would not be enough teachers. What the children learn of their religion, of course, is the key to whether or not Shiʻism will thrive in this community.

Sermons and Speakers

Once under ... a bush, [ʻAli] saw the war of the ants. He instantly knew the cause of the war and the nature of the parties. The red ants, whose bite [he had been told] was slightly poisonous, were Sunnis, the party among the Muslims that rejected the claim of the descendants of ʻAli, and they were attacking the black ants, who were obviously Shiah, since black as well as green was the color worn by people like ʿAli Hashemi's father who claimed descent from [the Imam] ʿAli. He remembers admiring the black ants for the justness of their cause and their individual heroism; but as the battle continued he began to admire the orderliness and steadfastness of the slower-moving red ants. As far as he could tell, neither side won.[63]

The centerpiece of any mosque event, whether spiritual or purely social, is the sermon. Frequently, more than one sermon is delivered at a single event. In Islam, it is customary to think of the sermon as associated with Friday prayers. However, in Dearborn, to neglect the sermons of other occasions would be to deny the importance of the experience of the majority of mosque attendees in the community. Far more people attend Sunday services at the (Jamiʿ than attend the Friday prayer service at any of the mosques. Furthermore, men, women, and children are present for the Sunday sermons, while Friday prayers at the mosques still draw only men (although the Friday sermons from the Majmaʿ are televised). Aside from these regular occasions, sermons are also delivered at memorials, engagements, commemorative occasions, and so on.

Necessarily, then, this section will be only an overview of the types of subjects addressed in the sermons and the different styles used to convey messages.

Those Delivering the Sermons

It is not possible to separate the sermon from its deliverer. Most sermons heard in the mosques are delivered by men who have undergone training in one or more of the holy cities of Shiʿism. All have received some training at Najaf in Iraq, and two also trained in Qom in Iran.

According to Michael Fischer, when a man desires to become a member of the ʿulama, he selects the teacher with whom he wishes to study. The teachers are mujtahids, some at the level of grand ayatollahs such as Golpayegani, Marʿashi, and others whose names became familiar during the early days of the Iranian Revolution. The teacher uses a dialectical style of argument and counterargument, and the student is encouraged to participate. A topic will continue for a period of several days. The teacher will illustrate the fine points of the theological debate and the various ways the argument can be approached. In these theological schools, there is a refusal to deal with any possible scriptural symbolism. The approach to the Koran and the traditions of the Prophet is completely literal.[64]

At the end of his training, the student is qualified to be a teacher of other Muslims himself. His position may be that of a lowly village *mulla* (the Iranian term for *sheikh*), or he may become a specialist on one area of Islamic learning, depending on his talents, capacities, and interests.

In anthropological terms, these men are trained to become "priests" in the fullest sense of the term. As Victor Turner says, "the priest is concerned with the conservation and maintenance of a deposit of beliefs and practices handed down as a sacred trust from the founders of the social and religious system."[65] His power is derived from the knowledge he has received from his elders, and he transmits this knowledge in as pure a form as possible in order to preserve the entire religious heritage. He is a preserver of culture. As mentioned earlier, Muslims often are opposed to using the terms *priest* and *clergy* when referring to the *ulama*, because these men are not ordained and do not administer sacraments as they do in Christianity. However, as we shall see, the term *priest* when defined as a transmitter and preserver of knowledge is very suitable.

Styles of Presentation

One predominant role of the sheikhs in the Dearborn area is to deliver sermons in the mosques, and, as mentioned earlier, the sheikhs are called upon to deliver sermons for a great variety of occasions. To determine the message that is being delivered in these sermons, it is necessary to examine not only the content but also the style and language. By "language," I mean not only the actual tongue used, that is, Arabic or English (although this is certainly an important consideration), but also the formality of the language. In Arabic, this means a choice between the standard form, *fusha* (the language of the Koran, also known as classical Arabic), and the colloquial form. Since *fusha* is the language of the sacred scriptures, it is deemed the only form of Arabic suitable for conveying religious ideas. A sheikh giving a sermon in Arabic is not expected to speak the everyday language of the people. To do so would be inappropriate and tantamount to admitting his ignorance and unsuitability for his position. His knowledge of the sacred texts qualifies him to be a sheikh, and knowledge of the Arabic language is the primary requirement upon which all else is built.

The three sheikhs who have arrived from Lebanon in the past ten years all preach exclusively in standard Arabic. Their style of speech conforms to what Bloch refers to as formalized speech acts. Limitations on loudness, intonation, vocabulary, and sources for illustrations are all apparent, and the speakers all conform to certain stylistic rules.[66]

Steven Caton has illustrated the importance of these stylistic rules among Muslim Arabic speakers. In his fascinating study of Yemeni tribesmen, he has shown that formulaic speech, used even in everyday conversation such as greetings, reflects a Koranic model of language, thereby enhancing its power.[67]

The question arises of whether or not the use of such formalized speech affects the message being conveyed. Bloch argues that it does. Formalized speech, he claims, prevents the speaker from tackling specific issues or dealing with divisive actions. It conveys less information about the world than ordinary speech, but it enhances its "illocutionary" potential, its ability to influence people. What the speaker says is predictable. The constraints of the speaking style make it so. The predictability of the speech is what makes it "coercive." As Boyer puts it, "the actors are 'caught' in a discursive pattern which makes it impossible to disagree or contradict, since the series of utterances is predetermined from the outset. Ritual language can thus serve an ideological purpose in that it is a 'hidden' yet powerful mechanism which reduces drastically the possibility of dissent."[68]

If Bloch's theory is correct, one should find that the topics of sermons are of a purely traditional nature and that subjects reaching outside the realm of conservative Shiʿism are not addressed. Patrick Gaffney studied the sermons given by clerics in contemporary Egypt. He found that the sheikh who used the highest degree of formalization in his sermons was the one who was most aligned with the official religious establishment, supporting traditional values of order and harmony, not dissent.[69] But Antoun found that the preacher in the Jordanian village he studied also conformed to formalized speech yet was able to handle local and divisive issues in his sermons.[70]

It is not possible to draw simple conclusions about sermons in Dearborn. They are given in a variety of circumstances and by a variety of speakers. Furthermore, not all are in Arabic; many are given in English. It is important to compare the messages of the English and Arabic sermons.

The Speeches

Traditional Islamic sermons fall into three separate categories. The *khutba*, given during the Friday collective prayers in the mosque, is a ritual event with strictly defined parts, delivered mostly in very sophisticated Arabic. In the Islamic world the *khutba* traditionally had political implications; the preacher was expected to mention the name of the ruler, the mention being one of the recognized signs of sovereignty. The Friday preacher usually was appointed and paid by the state. The *khutba* would be delivered only in the section of the mosque devoted to collective prayers. The Majalis Husayniya are ritualized retellings of the sufferings of the imams in general and Husayn in particular. The multipurpose room in the Dearborn mosques was officially a *husayniya*, a hall devoted to Majalis Husayniya. More generally, the preaching outside the prayer hall was *waʿz*, or exhortation. The distinction between *khutba* and *waʿz* corresponds roughly to the distinction a Christian might make between the sermon delivered in a church service and the less formal sort of preaching done by an evangelist in another setting such as a revival or a television show. In the Dearborn context—and, I suspect, in Shiʿism in general—there is no real difference between the second and third classes of preaching, apart from occasions such as Muharram when a specialized receptor of the sufferings of the imams would come to perform. The *khutba* do differ somewhat in form from the preaching in the *husayniya*, but since the themes and content are more or less identical, I have not treated the three kinds of preaching separately.

The theme most commonly dwelt on in the sermons from the mosques (whether in Arabic or English) is undoubtedly that of Shiʿism itself. That is, those signs and symbols that are peculiar to Shiʿism are stressed during sermons. ʿAli, Husayn, the other imams, the Prophet's daughter Fatima, and his granddaughter Zaynab are either the main theme or are alluded to regularly in a sermon. These heroes are the models for one's life. The following are some examples of statements made:

"The Imam ʿAli was born in the Kaʿaba itself, and this was a wonderful sign."

"ʿAli is an example to the weak."

"ʿAli is a mystery and a miracle."

"Muhammad called Husayn a nation among nations."

"Anybody who wants to do revolution must learn in the school of Husayn."

"If you want to be saved, you must believe in Hassan and Husayn."

"Fatima Zahra was the best creature, the best lady. You find women today who have learned from her. The [Muslim] women today are proof of the greatness of Fatima."

No other theme is repeated as often. There is continual reminder that these central figures serve as models for the Shi'a of today, as they have done for hundreds of years.

There is never any "interpreting" of the characters into modern-day situations. Their attributes are listed, legends about them retold. But never have I heard a sheikh or any other speaker suggest trying to see, say, the Imam Husayn in the light of a twentieth-century dilemma. Husayn is portrayed as a model of both "patience" and "revolution." It is left to the listener to interpret for himself or herself what Husayn means for modern life. The same holds for Fatima or Zaynab. These were good and virtuous women, models of womanhood. Both displayed courage in times of duress. Both stood behind their men through adversity. They are portrayed as multifaceted: they are mothers and wives on the one hand and, on the other, women who have stepped outside their family role to do heroic acts. Which facet of the life and personality of the heroine the audience wishes to focus on is not specified.

Reverence for and belief in the Koran, the Prophet, and the family of the Prophet (the Ahl al-Bayt) are common threads that weave this community together. All three mosques reinforce this common identity. There is no distinction or dispute at this level. Whether a sermon is delivered in Arabic or in English, the theme of the Ahl al-Bayt prevails.

Furthermore, the "oppressors" of the Shi'a continue to be the Umayyads. Only rarely does a speaker venture out of the historical realm of the early days of Islam to make his point. Occasionally, Israel is mentioned as being an enemy of Islam. But it is usually not railed against as the main theme of a speech.

There are also occasional references to the Sunnis. These differ from other topics in that they are in response to perceived recent attacks on the Shi'a. The killing of Shi'a in Mecca and a negative article in an Egyptian magazine regarding Shi'ism provoked two of these sermons. But these are rare occurrences.

Differences among Arabic Speakers

The differences in sermons given by the three Arabic-speaking preachers of the mosques are generally quite subtle. All three use highly stylized presentations, never deviating from the use of standard Arabic. However, even within the narrow range allowed, there are variations in style of speech.

It is commonplace in this community to hear people speak of one mosque being aligned with a certain Lebanese militia and another with an opposing militia. Yet one would be hard pressed to prove this by the surface content of speeches. Sheikhs do not refer to political groups during their sermons. Particular political figures are not mentioned. Religious leaders who may also be considered political leaders may be alluded to, but always in the context in which there is general agreement. For example, Khomeini is seen as a hero to the Shiʿa because he strengthened the identity of the believers and gave them a new sense of pride. He is not spoken of as the proponent of Hizb Allah. Imam Musa Sadr is also one who brought people "out of materialism and taught them the true Islam." His role as creator of Harakat Amal for a general audience will be ignored.

Only when a political group has organized an event at the mosques and that event is known to be a political one will there be references to the appropriate political organization. For example, at the Jamiʿ there was a memorial for the disappearance of Musa Sadr. It was held in the evening and announced well in advance. At this event, posters and flags associated with the Amal movement were displayed throughout the mosque, and only those sympathetic to Amal were in attendance. Posters and other insignia of Amal would not appear at the Sunday service even if the topic of a sermon was Musa Sadr. Instead, there would have been a sermon most could agree on: Musa Sadr attempted to help the Shiʿa improve their material and spiritual condition.

During sermons, the preachers do not denigrate one another. Each mosque functions quite separately. The leadership of one mosque might heartily disapprove of the actions of another, but each mosque is quite cautious about causing open splits in the community.

The most extreme differences can be found between the speeches of Sheikh Attat (who sympathizes with Amal) at the Jamiʿ and Sheikh Burro (a supporter of Hizb Allah) at the Majlis. Again, these two sheikhs speak only in Arabic.

Both Attat and Burro have given sermons on Islamic ethics. Burro begins his talks with rhymed prose and then launches into a highly abstract, intellectual speech about the different levels of ethical systems. It would appeal to a college-educated, religiously studious sort of audience. Attat's handling of the subject is quite different in terms of its intellectual level, not so abstract and learned, with simpler ideas. His is less the seminary lecture and more the "Sunday church sermon."

Of course, such differences may reflect basic personality styles, but they also reflect different views of Islam and how it should be applied—in other words, political views.

Sheikh Burro follows the style of the great *madrasas* or seminaries of the Shi'i world. He aspires to be noted for his learnedness. He expects the people to come to him. The fact that only those who wish to emulate this very learned approach to Islam would do so does not seem to concern him. In his sermons, Burro has even introduced the concept of *'irfan*, Shi'ite mystical philosophy that gives an esoteric explanation of the exoteric features of Islam.

Mottehedeh states that *'irfan* was instrumental in creating the political style of Khomeini: "the very heart of *erfan* is the destruction of the distinction between subject and object—an experience of this world in which seer and seen are one. And teachers of *erfan* seek to impart to their students a sense of the fearlessness toward everything external, including all the seemingly coercive political powers of the world, which true masters of *erfan* should have."[71]

My young scholarly Iraqi friend has sat through many hours of Burro's sermons. He rejects the idea that there is a political aspect to the sermons on *'irfan*, but, on the other hand, he believes that such sermons are inappropriate in this community because the Lebanese do not have the proper religious training to understand such concepts. He expressed irritation, in fact, that the ideas of *'irfan* were being totally misunderstood by the Lebanese youth. He claimed they were thinking of themselves as enlightened mystics after a couple of lectures on the subject.

It is almost inconceivable that Sheikh Attat would address his audience about mysticism. In his speeches and his demeanor, he is a man of the people. Not at all esoteric in his approach to religion, he is very much the proletariat sheikh. More dramatic and less intellectual in his approach, he indicates a concern to appeal to the majority of the Muslims rather than to a select group. His is not the seminary approach. His behavior is most definitely modeled after the activist Musa Sadr, who presented himself as a man of the people. Attat is also the only preacher who differentiates the Sunday (or regular) sermon from that given at a social occasion. For example, at wedding engagements at the Jami', he interjects humor, and both he and the audience laugh quite heartily. At one such occasion, he persuaded a few of the women who had not covered their hair to do so by speaking jokingly about it.

Sheikh Berri is seen as someone in between the other two. Poetic and eloquent, he speaks with invariable calm. He is distanced without being aloof. His sermons, while completely within the realm of Shi'i topics and ideology, will address issues that concern the everyday lives of a majority of Muslims: prayer, marriage, pilgrimage. Rarely are concrete examples or personal references given;

these are lacking in sermons from all the clerics. But on one occasion, he did allude to his own pilgrimage and how he happened to be able to become a *hajji*. This was alluded to but not dwelt upon. The spiritual significance of the *hajj* was what was important. Berri is very culturally oriented. He loves poetry and language and is a bit more open to seeing Shi'ism as a contribution to world culture than are others in this community.

The purpose of the Arabic sermons delivered in the local mosques is to convey the truth. It is not to challenge the people's thinking about the role of Islam in America. It is not to attempt to modernize Islam for a new and different environment. It is not to make Islam "relevant." And it is most certainly not for advocating revolution. The purpose is to remind people of the essential verities of Islam: Muhammad was the messenger of the one true God, Imam 'Ali was his rightful successor, Imam Husayn suffered cruelly at the hands of the Umayyad oppressors, and other designated members of the Ahl al-Bayt are to be emulated and revered. Thus far, the results corroborate Bloch's theory.

However, even within the very narrow constraints offered by the formalized speeches given in Arabic, one can find significant variations in the message conveyed. Generally speaking, the message from the three mosques is essentially the same, but the listener is being compelled to respond in a different manner, depending on which sheikh is conveying the message. None of the sheikhs is coming up with new or innovative approaches to Islam. They are all reiterating what they have learned from their elders, the teachers at the seminaries. Yet Burro's highly intellectualized speech on ethics conveys a different message from Attat's more homely variation on the same theme. And by introducing a topic such as *'irfan,* Burro is subtly making the statement that the people should approach Islam in such a way as to differentiate themselves drastically from the rest of society.

All three sheikhs stay within "pure" Shi'i theology. All utilize formalized speech acts to convey their message. Yet, through emphasis on particular subjects and through demeanor, they are quite capable of imparting messages so different that they could cause major rifts in the community should that community allow them to do so.

The Audience's Reaction

Bloch claims that the formalized speech act reinforces the hierarchical nature of the relationship between the speaker and the hearer. As he says, "ultimately the power of formalized oratory does not simply spring from its form, it springs from the forces of social power."[72] The relationship between clergy and laymen in the Middle East is very complex. The clergy are an inextricable part of life and indeed have had power throughout the ages. Among the Shiʿa, this power has either been generated from the state as it was in, say, Safavid times, or it has been generated from the people as it was in the 1979 Iranian revolution. But the Shiʿa rank and file have generally shown a certain independent-mindedness about their clergy, who are commonly the butt of jokes and derisive stories. Of course, they also can be devoutly revered. In this community, feelings toward the clergy run the entire gamut.

Answers to questions I posed to people regarding the clergy suggest that the vast majority see these men purely as religious specialists who have expertise in theological matters. Most said that they would turn to the sheikh for a purely religious matter such as prayer or fasting but would not bring other matters to him (though, as mentioned earlier, many people do bring their problems to the sheikh). The sheikh is seen as a person with a job, and that is to remind the people of the truths of Shiʿism and to assist them in following the correct spiritual path.

As mentioned earlier, there is much inattentiveness to speeches at the mosques. At the Majmaʿ and the Jamiʿ, there is nearly as much visiting among the audience during sermons as there is during a dinner. At the Majlis, the situation is a bit different. There the room is usually arranged so that chairs are lined up side by side, and less visiting can occur. However, even at the Majlis, when the people, particularly the women, are sitting at tables, they are likely to talk among themselves during sermons.

In general, it is not expected that the sheikh will say something remarkable or novel. The audience has heard what he says before, in one form or another. There are no interchanges between speaker and hearer except when the audience reiterates the blessing of the Prophet and his family. On some occasions, when the sheikh is addressing a small group of men, he will allow questions at the end of the speech to which he gives lengthy answers. This is commonly found at the Majmaʿ and the Majlis. But, again, this is very formalized, and the questions are expected to be concise and unchallenging.

The audience does not complain, nor do they suggest that the speeches be shorter or that the format be changed to allow more participation. The sheikh is doing what he is hired to do: remind people of the fundamentals of their religion. Consequently, subtle differences of style are generally of little consequence. Nor does it matter particularly that the sermon is delivered in a form of Arabic that may not be totally comprehensible to the listeners. The general idea is grasped, and that is sufficient.

Of course, not all clergy can accept this attitude from their audience. Sheikh Burro, who began his career in America at the Jami', was obviously not content with what he would have seen as fulfilling a functionary's role. He resorted to opening the doors of a new mosque in which he could have complete control, albeit one with a very small and narrow congregation. Sheikh Berri also opened a new mosque but has attempted to appeal to a larger number of his countrymen and has been quite successful. I believe it is because he has been more willing to accept his people as they are than has Burro.

The majority of Shi'a in Dearborn are not willing to allow the sheikhs to play a divisive role. They do not want a community split along strong ideological lines. The aspects of sermons that could be divisive are simply not heard by the majority of people in the community.

Sheikh Chirri's Sermons in English

During Sheikh Chirri's early history in America, he found a totally different community with a different set of needs from what sheikhs Attat, Berri, and Burro found upon their arrivals. A sheikh was needed in Chirri's time who was knowledgeable in Islam but able to relate to the problems of a people for whom the Arabic language and Middle Eastern traditions were rapidly being supplanted by all things American. It was not adequate to deliver sermons that were only half comprehensible. The need was for a preacher who could communicate in the language that was becoming predominant: English. Some clergy would have flatly refused to relinquish the use of the Koranic language to discuss religion. Indeed, today some clergy in the United States (though not in Dearborn) have rejected the idea of learning English, which is considered the language of the *kuffar* (the infidels).[73] Chirri realized that if Islam was to flourish (or remain alive at all), it was incumbent upon him to speak the vernacular.

It is only possible to study the speeches given by Chirri during the last two or three years before his retirement, which may have been affected by the changes occurring in the Middle East and the arrival of the new clergy. However, according to informants, certain topics have always been dear to his heart, and it is unlikely that the general pattern of speech has changed over time.

Sheikh Chirri begins his sermons with the first *sura* of the Koran in Arabic, then proceeds to address the "ladies and gentlemen" of the audience in English. His English is unpolished. He drops the final consonant of a word, giving his speech an uneducated quality. It is apparent that he learned English principally to communicate with a second- and third-generation Arabic community, though he also has written religious texts explaining Islam and Shi'ism to a non-Muslim audience. Still, the utilitarian approach to language appears even in his writing style. For Sheikh Chirri, it is the message, not its means of conveyance, that is of greatest import. There is nothing poetic in his presentations. He wants his listeners to know that there is "only one Almighty God who is the creator of the universe." He tells the Muslims that they should be grateful to have been blessed with eyes and ears and to be the ones chosen to follow God's message for this day. He admonishes the people to follow the teachings of Islam, using the imams and Fatima as exemplars. He is also fond of referring to the Patriarch Abraham, who "was not like other Jews" and obeyed the Almighty God. But it is through the message of Islam that one receives salvation. Certainly, one of his favorite topics is that of the return of the Imam Mahdi. This subject stirs him to some excitement, and I have heard him insist that the congregation, noisily chattering at their tables, listen to him because he feels strongly that they will have to recognize the Mahdi when he appears in the not too distant future. They must be prepared.

In comparison with the sermons of the other sheikhs, Chirri's speeches do not qualify as formal speeches. There is not the same rigor of style. There is more variation in volume and intonation. Yet little else is truly different from the other sheikhs. The scriptures are essentially the only thing invoked. The truths of Shi'ism are reiterated. Even in the forceful and direct appeals to the people to heed his word, there is never any variation from the standard discourse on Islam. It is all within the bounds of Shi'i theology and never deviates from that level.

The greatest difference between the sermons of Chirri and those of the three Arabic-speaking sheikhs concerns the issue of teaching the faith to non-Muslims. Proselytizing for Islam is not a common theme of any, yet Sheikh Chirri is more inclined to refer to this topic than are the other clerics. In one sermon, he instructed his audience about how to teach Islam. "Be friendly, say good morning," he advised. Then, he urged them, "turn the conversation to religion." They are to tell the Christians that there is only one God, that Jesus and Mary are not gods. Mary, he said, was a great lady but not a god.

What is so striking about such a sermon is that Sheikh Chirri has continued to see America throughout these years only in theological terms. To him, America is Christian, and the major difference between Christian and Muslim is the issue of the station of Christ. Rather than approach the issue of teaching Islam from a more social perspective, he still addresses the problem as a purely ideological one. In other words, he does not discuss the fact that Americans may see that Islam's forbidding of drugs and alcohol could have beneficial effects for a society suffering from the ills of substance abuse. Steps are not taken to begin a teaching campaign based on the social principles of Islam. Rather, Chirri suggests that his audience tell the Christians there is only one God. (The fact that the other sheikhs are not stressing the teaching of Islam to non-Muslims suggests that they perceive Islam as still so tied to Middle Eastern culture that it would be nearly impossible to bridge the gulf between East and West.)

How does this relate to Bloch's theory about the effects of formal speech? There is limited use of formality in Chirri's speeches, yet he still seems to operate under the constraints of formalized speech in avoiding divisive or controversial ideas and maintaining his distinct and hierarchical role vis-à-vis his audience.

What this suggests, then, is that it is not the style of speech per se that sets the limits and the type of relationship between speaker and hearer. It is, rather, the entire tradition of clerical training that most defines what message will be conveyed. The Shiʿi cleric is trained in a certain school of thought. His education in law, logic, and philosophy "compels" him to think in a certain way. The style of speech used only reinforces the message; it does not define it.

A Layman's Approach

Even before Chirri's retirement, it became increasingly difficult for him to make sermons. For the most part, it has fallen on one of the members of the center's board of directors, Hajj C., to deliver the English sermon, as Sheikh Attat has not mastered English. The Jamiʿ does not wish to cater only to new immigrants; it also wants to include those who have grown up in America and who are more comfortable in English. To someone like Hajj C., English should be spoken in an American mosque.

Hajj C. is a second-generation immigrant who might be described as a Muslim evangelist. His messages are direct. He admonishes his audience to be good Muslims, not by habit but by conscious decision. He wants the Muslims to set a good example for the larger community. Rather than accepting the socializing that goes on during sermons, he tells his audience to observe silence when the words of the Koran are being read. He wishes them not to take the words for granted or treat them as if they are magical (my concept) but to listen to them for the content and live by them. He refers to the scriptures but also will refer to actual recent happenings to make his points. He grapples with the Sunni/Shiʿi split, explaining that there are political, not religious, differences between the two sects. He gives a specific example of how the split could be downplayed. He alludes to an occasion when Sunnis came to visit the Jamiʿ. The call for prayer was sounded, and the men went to the prayer chamber. One of the Shiʿi men began to pass out prayer stones (pieces of clay from Karbala), and Hajj C. asked that this not be done so as to avoid offending their Sunni guests. Not using the prayer stone would be a controversial act for many Shiʿa, discussion of which would not normally be included in a sermon. But this lay teacher is a man with a message that goes beyond the usual Shiʿi theological subjects. He was not trained in the Attabat or in Qom.

Hajj C. does not conform to the formal speech acts in the highly stylized sermons of the Arabic-speaking sheikhs. He goes outside the usual domain of what is considered appropriate subject matter and appropriate style for a mosque sermon (though his English is quite correct, and he is a very articulate and fine speaker).

That being said, the deviation, when scrutinized, is really not so very great. Hajj C. ultimately gives the same message the other sheikhs do: Shiʿism contains the truth. He expands this to include the need to find ways to share this truth with others. For him, a conservative, card-carrying Republican, the ultimate goal is for as many people as possible to be prepared for the return of the Imam Mahdi and the Judgment Day. He does not advocate any relaxation in the practice of Islamic law to fit American society. His ventures into ecumenicism are still limited. It is one thing not to display prayer stones in the presence of Sunnis. It is quite another not to hold observances for the anniversaries of the family of the Prophet. While Hajj C. is not grounded in the seminary education of Najaf, he is grounded firmly in the teachings of Shiʿism, and any controversy his speeches might generate will be fairly mild. Though the sermons he delivers do not have the highly stylized form of the Arabic-speaking sheikhs and do not reflect the style of *madrasa* education, Hajj C. still operates within the confines of his religious tradition, something that has not been affected greatly by his American upbringing.

Divisiveness among church leaders was commonplace in America, and Catholic priests were generally not reluctant to express their views. The pulpit was a place where opinions about politics, whether of the church or of the nation, were aired. Polish Catholic priests became embroiled in the politics of their homeland, and a group of them formed the Alliance of Polish Priests in America, which worked in cooperation with the Polish National Committee. Some also worked with Polish relief and recruitment organizations on behalf of the Polish legion. Thus far, in Dearborn, the sheikhs have been far more circumspect in broaching divisive matters and far less openly involved in Middle East politics.

But in one regard, there are strong similarities between the sermons and behavior of the sheikhs and those of the immigrant priests. The sheikhs, like the immigrant priests before them, expound what we might loosely refer to as orthodox religion—the religion of learned books, learned clerics, and the distant, senior clergy of the old country. Neither has promoted a religion of folk beliefs, cults, or magic, although in both Islamic and Catholic societies, we find these approaches well represented. In both cases, orthodox beliefs and the high religious culture are preserved through the use of formal, classical languages not characteristically used in everyday speech.

In American Catholicism, the priests were only one source of religious interpretation. Certain folk beliefs continued to thrive. Cults of the saints and, in particular, extreme devotion to the Virgin Mary were vital to the lives of Catholics. Marian mysticism, catechized in the parochial schools by nuns and with its direct link to the divine, was used to challenge the authority of the clergy, though not to the extent of causing schism.[74] Even in the most extreme cases, however, there is not a sharp division between "high" and "low" forms of religion. In Catholicism, the priests were generally wise enough to know that they would be unsuccessful in trying to wean people away from their folk beliefs and that an attempt might very well backfire. Besides, the priests were also raised on these same "superstitions."

As we will see in the following chapters, among the Shiʿa, there are other sources of religious belief besides the sheikhs, the *marajiʿ*, and their texts. And we will see that the distinctions between formal, high religion and folk beliefs are often difficult to discern.

CHAPTER 3

Islam in the Town

The Shariᶜa in Dearborn

Life Outside the Mosque

WHILE THE DEARBORN area mosques increase in number and diversify in their uses, to focus exclusively on their role in this community would be a mistake. A substantial number of Shiᶜa never enter a mosque except perhaps for a wedding, funeral, or occasional holiday. Sermons, congregational prayer, and other group rituals are simply not part of their lives; attending mosque is not a religious obligation as attending mass is for Catholics.

Islam was established as a way of life. Much of the Koran was revealed in response to immediate problems and concerns of the believers. Early followers committed to memory the sayings of the Prophet and his actions (i.e., the Hadith and the Sunna) so that they could serve as a model for future generations of Muslims to follow. While one may attend the mosque to learn from the clergy how a Muslim should live, one is also free to read the Koran and other religious texts on one's own. The believer is expected to turn to a religious expert, a *marjaᶜ*, regarding matters of personal behavior, but he or she can consult a book to obtain answers, or simply ask the sheikh what the *marjaᶜ* says without attending any kind of formal program. In these days, the conscientious person can simply make a telephone call to the sheikh with questions.

When asked "What does it mean to be religious?" it was a rare person who mentioned mosque attendance in his or her answer. Attending mosque could not be equated with the truly important matters of fasting, praying, and following "all the rules of religion." As we shall see, there was little agreement about what "all the rules of religion" actually entailed, but going to the mosque was not considered one of them.

Therefore, to have a fuller picture of Shi'i Islamic life in this area, we must leave the world of the mosque. Certainly, what goes on in the home is at least as important as what is occurring at the Jami' or the Majma'. Prayer and fasting and following dietary laws are principally, although certainly not exclusively, aspects of private religious life.

While I am interested in what religious laws and rules are being followed or neglected, I am also interested in the spirit with which religion is being practiced, what religion actually means to the people. Are people reassessing their religious beliefs and practices now that they find themselves in a new environment? Do the mores of American society affect religiosity, and, if so, how? What aspects of religion are most important to people, and to what lengths will they go to observe their religious obligations under circumstances that make religious observance far more difficult?

Being Shi'a in America

I asked people in what way being a Muslim in America was different from being a Muslim "back home." There were two types of responses. People usually told me that it was easier being a Muslim in Lebanon, essentially because in the old country, "everyone is Muslim." (Oddly, even those who came from villages with a substantial Christian population said the same thing.) Older people and those with little contact outside their immediate family were likely to say that there was no difference because of the large number of Muslims living in Dearborn.

A few said that Islam is the same no matter where one lives. I predicted that this would have been the opinion of the more Shari'a-minded in my sample, because they seem to dismiss cultural influences in so many other ways. But I was mistaken. This group is undergoing the same types of struggle as those who reflected a more traditional approach to Islam.

Zuheir, an engineer in his thirties who was raised in a "traditional" religious atmosphere in Beirut, said, "It is much harder to be a Muslim here because there are so many temptations such as drugs, women, financial things. The religious person here is more praiseworthy because back home there were not all those temptations." In spite of all the "temptations," Zuheir does not see that he has changed in his approach to religion since living in the United States. As he has always done, he selects what aspects of religion are important to him and practices accordingly.

Khalid, also college-educated and somewhat more religiously learned than Zuheir, said, "There are lots of challenges here. You can't practice religion here perfectly. You cannot pray anytime. You make compromises. If you want to be accepted, you must do things like eat non-*halal* meat. You get more rewards from God here. In Lebanon, no one opposes you because you are surrounded by Muslims. You feel like a pioneer here." Making compromises or not, Khalid admitted that he has become more religious since living in America, as a "reaction to a sinful world." He went on to say that he saw religion as "a shelter to shield me from what is going on." But Khalid, too, is selective about what rules he follows.

Mahmoud, around forty years of age and affiliated with the Hizb Allah movement, told me, "Here I get to practice religion more. There are so many bad things around me. I must look into my religion more. Back home, everyone is Muslim, so it is all built in." Mahmoud did not consider himself religious until he was "born again" after the Iranian Revolution. Before this point, he describes his life as being "boring." His life now revolves around his religious activities, and he considers it of utmost importance to "worry only about pleasing God" and to follow all the rules of religion.

About a third of the people to whom I spoke claimed to have become more religious over the years, either as a result of the civil war, the Iranian Revolution, their new surroundings in America, or simply growing older, no one claimed to have lost his or her religion because of American experience per se. I knew two people who had actually come to lose their faith and had replaced it with Marxist ideology but this process was completed while they were still in Lebanon.

Men were twice as likely to speak of becoming more religious in America than were women. I believe this difference can be accounted for partially by considering how much more exposure Lebanese men have to the outside world than do the women. Men are in a position to learn of competing ideologies. Before Musa Sadr assumed leadership in the Shiʻi community, Shiʻism in Lebanon was not seen as a vehicle for advancement in any sense. If the Shiʻa were drawn to an ideology at all, it tended to be communism. The missionary zeal of Musa Sadr and the success of Khomeini turned this around. The women, on the other hand, tied to the home and their traditional religious roots, would not need to undergo a serious revival. Perhaps they came to believe that they must dress more modestly or be a little more conscientious about prayer, but, by and large, they were still, religiously speaking, the same people they had always been, people who believed deeply in God's unwavering presence. The two women I know who underwent the most extreme religious transformation had spent their formative years in America. Both, on their own, decided that a lukewarm attitude toward religion was not sufficient and have thrown themselves into an activist approach to Islam.

As I mentioned, America has not tended to lessen religious zeal, at least not in the past ten to fifteen years. True, there are women who have stopped wearing the scarf, but this was not done either as a gesture of protest against religious "oppression" or as an expression of indifference to religion. Mona, a widow who has been struggling for years to provide for her children, came to America wearing the *hijab*. From South Lebanon, she was strongly influenced by Musa Sadr. Though she wore the *hijab* for a few years after she came to the United States, she finally abandoned it, claiming that someone had assaulted her because he thought she was Iranian and blamed her for the hostage situation in Tehran. But her decision to abandon the scarf probably has more to do with the fact that the *hijab* would interfere with her aspirations to work as a cosmetologist and that she wanted acceptance from American society. It does not appear to reflect a diminishing concern for her religion. While the turmoil in her life does interfere with the demands of prayer and fasting, she certainly considers it her ideal to follow all the rules of religion.

Other women who have removed the scarf justify their action by saying that they don't think their religion demands them to wear it. This is far different from saying that they know their religion demands it but they don't care. Some young women say that they only need to wear the scarf when they are older, which they claim they plan to do. While the woman who removes her scarf may not be making a statement about her religious feelings, the woman who suddenly dons it usually is.

Iman is a quiet, thoughtful woman who was brought to Dearborn as a bride at the age of seventeen. Though she said her mother taught her to pray and fast, she never wore the scarf or studied her religion. About five years ago, after having lived in America for several years and having had three children, she began to wear the scarf, study religion, and follow the teachings of Ayatollah Khu'i.

She claims that she has been "hassled" for wearing the scarf by Americans, but this seems only to have strengthened her resolve to continue to wear it.

While men do not have as obvious a symbol as a head covering to show their religious feelings, they also express an increased interest in and concern for religion. By all appearances, Ashraf seems almost totally assimilated into American society. In his blue jeans and T-shirts and with his easy command of English, he interacts comfortably with Americans. He even admits to being serious about an American woman, which has aroused the anger of his relatives. For most of his life, being religious has meant being ethical, moral, and kind. Up until very recently, he has not concerned himself with the rules of Islam. But he has begun to associate more with a relative who is aligned with the Hizb Allah movement, someone Ashraf considers religious. This, he said, has affected him, and he has started to pray and fast and pay attention to other requirements, though he does not agree with his relative on many points.

Religion and Education

It is generally assumed that a Western-style education will have the effect of causing religious doubt. In 1954, the Orientalist Alfred Guillaume posed the question, "To what extent are modern Muslims affected by modern historical criticism, modern philosophy, and modern science?"[1] The Lebanese civil war and the Iranian Revolution notwithstanding, this is still a relevant question. Approximately half of my sample were either college-educated or attending college at the time of the interview. (Only two of them had parents with any education beyond high school.) As I have said previously, there is a tendency among this population to study practical sciences, such as engineering and computer science, as these majors are likely to lead to promising careers. The fields they choose are also fields that do not challenge their religious and philosophical thought; courses that may do this are generally avoided.

Lebanese Shi'i students particularly avoid any courses dealing with human evolution, which they consider to be against Islamic teaching. Some who had taken a course covering evolution say they are glad to understand the theory but don't believe it. One young woman, who is exceptionally open to American ways, said that her introductory anthropology course only made her believe more than ever in the Koran.

Ahmad is working toward his master's degree in engineering. Very serious about his religion and enamored of the "New Islam" of

WITHOUT FORGETTING THE IMAM / 134

Iran, he considers himself a rationalist and would like to see the mosques serve as "a place of dialogue between Muslims and non-Muslims." At the mosque, "there should be discussion which can lead one or the other parties to change his mind." But he made it clear that he believes everything about Islam is true and correct because intellectually it can be proven. Ahmad even gave a scientific justification for the existence of the *jinn*, the spirits spoken about in the Koran. He explained about the different dimensions and how we could not know the *jinn* because they had more dimensions than we do. (Another engineer also spoke about the *jinn* in "scientific" terms.)

But those few who have pursued studies in the humanities and the behavioral sciences are affected by Western thought. Hisham has a master's degree in economics. His interest in religion was short-lived. As a young student in Lebanon, he became sensitive to the suffering around him and began to blame God for injustice. The idea that there would be a reward for the poor in the next life was unacceptable to him. He became influenced by the writings of Marx and Hegel and now does not concern himself with the question of whether or not there is a God. Fadwa, a woman about thirty years of age, went through a similar experience. She regrets that communism has lost ground among her generation of Lebanese and that Khomeini's Islam has taken its place.

Although he has been subjected to many of the same influences that Hisham and Fadwa have experienced, Ridwan's attitudes have evolved differently. He, too, began to have religious doubts when he was about seventeen, at a time when religion had become unfashionable among university students in Lebanon. With an advanced degree in one of the social sciences, he still maintains doubts about the Koran being the word of God, but, on the other hand, he says that he fears God. Mostly, he thinks of religion as serving communal and psychological needs. "Religion is part of a heritage, and you feel you are part of it," he stated. He enjoys going to pray on Friday at the mosque to experience this communal feeling.

But Hisham, Fadwa, and Ridwan are anomalies in this community. Indeed, Fadwa was so aware of the "oddness" of her views that she sought me out so that her opinions could be represented. She did not want me to think that all Lebanese in the Dearborn area were religious. While not everyone else to whom I spoke would claim to "be religious," it was clear from their other responses that religion—at least at some level—continued to play an important role in their lives.

To Be Religious

Michel Mazzaoui's claim that the Arab Shiʿa have a more "exoteric" approach to religion, as opposed to the Persians' more "esoteric" approach, is supported by the fact that it is, by and large, the Persians who have produced the philosophical and mystical treatises over the century.[2] For a variety of reasons probably involving historical, political, economic, and ecological factors, the Lebanese have not been involved in producing such works. Certainly, in this study, I found much emphasis on the external aspects of religion in this community, but this is not the entire picture.

To the question "What does it mean to be religious?" I received a wide variety of responses. Nearly a third of my respondents did emphasize "following the rules." There was no difference between men and women or between early and late immigrants. Two educated, professional women who grew up in the United States and now have grown children of their own both stated that being religious meant following the rules of religion. One stressed the importance of modesty, though she did not wear Islamic dress.

In contrast to the rule-oriented response was the comment "A religious person is someone who believes in God and that he will leave this life soon and go to the next world. He is grateful to God." And another person said, "A religious person is at peace with himself."

What is so interesting here is that these latter comments were made by people who were emphatic about following the letter of the law. They both consulted the works of their *marjiʿ* and believed that there should be no compromise with society. The rules must be followed.

On the other hand, several people who referred to the importance of following the rules were themselves very lax in doing so. Mr. S. is a case in point. A warm, congenial man from the Bekaa who is employed as an auto mechanic, he does not pray or fast. He told me gleefully that he has even done what is considered almost unthinkable in this community: he has eaten pork. His college student daughter, an admiring devotee of her father, claims that he has always taught her to be kind, loving, and accepting of everyone. She describes him as deeply religious in an "inward" sense. Yet when I asked him what it meant to be religious, he provided a follow-the-rules response.

Why these contradictions exist is fairly obvious. The Shariʿa-minded, whether Hizb Allah-oriented or not, have set the standards for this community. These are the people who are considered to be religious. Their behaviors, attitudes, and style of dress have influenced others. I noted over and over in my interviews that men and women compared themselves to those with a more legalistic view of Islam than their own. They were often reacting to the influence of their more orthodox relatives or friends, either by becoming more rule-conscious themselves or by having to come up with justifications for not following the rules.

Zahra D., a college-educated woman from a politically important family in Lebanon, says that she is religious "almost to the point of being superstitious." Yet fasting and prayer have not been a part of her life. She normally wears jeans and pullovers and dons a scarf only on those rare occasions when she attends mosque. When I interviewed her, she was in a state of transition in her approach to religion. Zahra's sister-in-law and cousin, whom Zahra considers to be very religious, has taken it upon herself to lead Zahra to her more orthodox approach to religion. Zahra has begun to pray and was planning on fasting during Ramadan.

Still, there is considerable ambivalence about what constitutes religiosity. Ali B., a flamboyant entrepreneur with dealings in show business who has been in America for thirty years, responded, "Who would say they are not religious?" He made it clear that his religion meant much to him, though it had little to do with any legal aspects of Islam. He distinguished between those, like himself, who were religious, and those who were "super-religious who follow everything in religion."

Following the Laws: Prayer

One morning, my friend Wafa called to invite me for coffee. As we sat at her kitchen table, she told me about a dream she had the previous night. As dreams often are, this one—to me, anyway—was a disjointed series of scenes. Emotional struggles were evident, and there was an overriding religious sort of theme. But to Wafa, it meant one thing: "God is telling me to pray," she said definitively. Over the years that I have known her, Wafa has struggled with sticking to prayer as American women struggle with diets. Just before Ramadan began in 1990, she told me that she was making an appointment to see the sheikh so that he could help her with her "prayer problem."

Abu Hisham, a factory worker from Bint Jubeil who enjoys attending the services at the mosque but has not wanted to be bothered with prayer and fasting, also had a dream one night. In this one, the Imam ʿAli appeared to him and began to push him. Clearly, the Imam ʿAli wanted him to pray. For a while, he did so, but he has become lax again.

Most Lebanese Shiʿa in Dearborn will say that they pray, that is, perform *salat*, the obligatory prayer. However, they might be exaggerating. *Salat* takes time, not only for the prayers themselves but also for the ablutions that precede them. Mona claimed that she performs her prayers five times a day. Yet I have spent a considerable amount of time with her and can recall no occasion when she has gone off to pray. I do not mean to say that she and others have deliberately lied to me. I do think that if people perform *salat* at all—or if at periods of time they pray regularly—they tend to think they have done their religious duty. Furthermore, there is a strong tendency in this community to want to convince others of one's religious commitment. Religiosity is held in high esteem. Those who are lax in their religious obligations are the ones who are on the defensive these days.

American work schedules certainly interfere with prayers, and many men bemoaned the fact that they could not go to Friday prayers at the mosques. However, this is not as serious a problem for the Shiʿa as it is for the Sunni. In Shiʿism, it is acceptable to condense the noon prayer and the late afternoon prayer into one and to combine the evening and midnight prayers. The Shiʿa can then pray three times a day rather than five and still meet the legal requirements.

It was striking that men such as the social scientist Ridwan and the engineer Zuheir, both of whom are busy with their jobs and have no interest in listening to sermons, try to take time for prayers at the mosque. That prayer is a paramount obligation goes unquestioned among the believers in this community.

Prayer seems even more important here in America than it was in Lebanon. America is seen as a land riddled with sin among the new immigrants in this community. This opinion is held by sheikhs and uneducated factory workers alike. America is a land of free sex, drugs, alcohol, and materialism, and prayer is seen as a means of protection from these evils. The fact that more people do not pray is indicative not so much of work schedules as of the fact that people were so relaxed about this obligation before they came here. Prayer was not so important in Lebanon because "everyone there was Muslim. Religion was in the air." In Dearborn, the emphasis has to shift to the individual's responsibility for his or her religious well-being. Religion is not seen as something in the air here at all. Effort must be made if one is going to protects one's soul. Prayer, while being an orthodox part of religion, becomes what

Sami Zubaida refers to as an "instrumental" aspect of religion.[3] That is, people use it in an almost magical way to protect themselves or attain a desired end.

While this instrumental approach to prayer is fairly pervasive, it is less so for those with a political orientation to Islam. In their case, prayer is a statement of membership in Islam. It is a marker of their solidarity.

Salat, as I said, takes effort. Not everyone I have met here knows how to perform *salat*. If a person did not learn it as a child, chances are he or she will not learn it as an adult. One woman who grew up here told me that she had not learned *salat* "completely." Another young woman and her sisters, who had gone to a Christian school in the Bekaa, wanted to learn to pray before Ramadan but were too embarrassed to go to the sheikh and admit their ignorance. A stylish young woman from Bint Jubeil said that she had never learned to do *salat* and that her scarf-wearing mother had never learned, either. Still, religion is extremely important to them. They feel they know enough about their religion to know what is right and wrong.

It is my estimate that about 5 to 10 percent of the adults in this community pray three or five times a day and that perhaps another 20 percent pray on a fairly regular basis, as time permits. Older people are more likely to pray than young ones. The Shariʿa-minded are by far the most conscientious about doing *salat*.

As for the remainder who claimed to pray, they make an effort to do so during special times of the year, particularly at Ramadan. As several of my interviews took place during Ramadan, people were likely to say that they prayed regularly. They said they intended to continue to pray afterward as well, but it appears that they need dreams to remind them. During Ramadan, Wafa, my friend with the "prayer problem," greeted me at the door one day wearing her prayer cover, but the cloth would see little use until the next fast.

On the other hand, there are people such as the religiously knowledgeable Hajj Deeb, who does not allow work to interfere with his prayers. A repairman at Ford, he has obtained permission from his supervisor to take time for prayer. Going off to a small, sequestered place with his rug, he prostrates himself and prays.

Nisrene, a young mother who grew up in a nonpolitical but devoutly religious home near Nabatiyeh, does not answer the door or the telephone when she is praying. Her year-old son mimics her actions and attempts the words *"Allahu Akbar."*

That it is a struggle to keep *salat* alive in America is evident. Judging from my interviews and the contacts I have had with the

American-born and those who came here as young people before the new wave of immigrants arrived, there was a trend for people to grow lax about their prayers. Not that there was a lack of religious feeling or a desire to be "good Muslims," but the whole notion of this sort of ritualized prayer seemed to be losing its meaning. Although this is a tentative finding, I believe that prayer had begun to take on a more Christian style. "I pray in my heart" or "I pray in my own way" are comments I heard.

One woman who grew up in America says that she did learn *salat* as a child. Assigned a paper to present in class, she decided she would discuss her religion and include a demonstration of *salat*. Her classmates and teacher, none of whom was Muslim, did not disguise their amusement and caused her intense humiliation. Although an incident occurred immediately afterward that she considered "miraculous" and which helped confirm her in her religion, she rarely does *salat*. Prayer for her is communing with God. She makes up her own prayers as she goes along.

The course has now changed for these earlier immigrants and their offspring. The arrival of the new wave of immigrants and the resurgence of Islam in the world have caused the Americanized Muslims to pay closer attention to their religious obligations, including *salat*.

Fasting

Sawm (fasting) is quite different from prayer, at least from private prayer. First, unlike *salat*, one does not have to learn how to fast—one simply avoids eating, drinking, smoking, and having sexual relations from the first light of dawn until dark. Second, it is a far more public statement of religious convictions and identity. So, it is far more likely for people to fast than to pray.

The scholarly young son of an Iraqi family from Najaf who has taken an interest in my research scoffed at the notion of the Lebanese carrying through with the fast. "They fast for two or three days," he said with a wave of his hand, "and that's it." Certainly, there is some of this. One set of neighbors fasted for several days until they decided they wanted a picnic and brought out their grill to roast shish kebab. Another young neighbor proudly announced to me that she was fasting, but when I saw her a few days later, she was sipping a cup of coffee and smoking a cigarette. It is easy to focus on situations such as this, but to do so clouds the fact that there are a great many Muslims who are not eating during the daylight hours of Ramadan in East Dearborn. The restaurants may not be empty during the day, but their Muslim clientele is greatly reduced. Even those who take an occasional break for a few days tend to return to fasting. There are usually more people fasting at the beginning and the end of Ramadan than in the middle.

To indicate deepest piety, fasting is not limited to Ramadan. Occasionally, I would meet a person—usually very Shariʿa-minded but not always—who was fasting at different times of the year. According to the Hadith (at least, the Hadith referred to locally), the Prophet advised that Thursday is the most efficacious day to fast.

Classroom teachers in the East Dearborn schools have great difficulty with Ramadan as even children as young as eight and nine years forgo food during the day. Some teachers have tried to persuade young children not to fast, knowing that it is not obligatory for them to do so. School performance suffers, and teachers complain that children fall asleep during class or act out. On the other hand, at least in the school my children attended, the administrators have shown great sensitivity to the situation with Ramadan, planning evening activities so that they do not conflict with *iftar*, the breaking of the fast.

Iftar is commonly held at the Majmaʿ and at the recently opened Majlis. At 9:00 P.M., mothers will be dishing out food to their youngsters, the first they have eaten all day. (Some eat before the sun rises. During Ramadan 1990, this meant getting up at 4:30 A.M.) After dinner, these children will mill around the rooms of the building as their parents listen to sermons or visit among themselves.

Ramadan shows no signs at all of dying out in this community. The person who does not fast subjects himself or herself to chastisement and lectures from those who are fasting. For many of the Shariʿa-minded, Ramadan takes on a special significance. It is a time of close contact with other Muslims who share one's orientation. Especially at the Majmaʿ and the Majlis, the "strict interpretation of the law" view of Islam is strongly reinforced at this time. It is also a time when one can attempt to promote a "proper atmosphere" for the Muslim community. For example, a neighbor with a rather lax attitude toward religion was asked to turn his tape player off during Ramadan by another neighbor. He claimed it would awaken his sleeping child, but everyone knew the real reason for the request: this man considers popular music to be *haram* and especially offensive during this sacred time of the year.

For the community at large whose approach can be said to be more traditional, it is also a time for establishing one's religious credentials. Apparently, the sheikhs in Dearborn never eat in their own homes during Ramadan. One friend's husband attempted to invite a sheikh for *iftar*, but there was not one night that he had not already scheduled for dining with other believers. One of the homes this sheikh had already been invited to was that of Husayn. He had recently purchased and completely remodeled a large and expensive house of which he was very proud. Husayn's wife told me about the event in great detail. The guests dined on an elaborate meal of whole roasted lamb, chicken and rice, spinach and meat pies, salad, and so on. Here again, we have a case of displaying worldly success while also being purified by the pious act of feeding the sheikh.

The *Hajj*

If you walk the streets of East Dearborn in the middle of July, you will occasionally see a house whose porch has been decorated with crepe paper and balloons, sporting a banner written in bold, brightly colored Arabic lettering welcoming home a pilgrim. I assisted with the decorations a few days before Hajj Deeb returned home from Mecca. When he did arrive, the guests poured into his home to greet the man who had walked on the same soil and on the same path as the Prophet more than 1300 years ago. When I took my turn to visit, I was presented with a large black scarf for my head and some kohl for my eyes, which he had purchased in Mecca, and I was given a cup of the precious ZemZem water to drink. Though he had by then told the story of his pilgrimage many times over, he still rhapsodized about this incomparable experience.

Hajj Deeb has an American passport, so it was a simple matter for him to travel to Saudi Arabia. Relations between the Wahabi Sunni Saudis and the Shiʿa have never been good, but the attacks on the shrines by Shiʿa in Mecca during the *hajj* in 1979 have made relations positively hostile. Since that time, the Saudis have attempted to prevent Shiʿa from the Middle East from performing the *hajj*. Only very recently have restrictions let up, but having an American passport facilitates the process of getting a visa. The Shiʿa who do go to Mecca generally keep a low profile while there. During the *hajj* of the summer of 1990, there were approximately fifty pilgrims from the Dearborn area. These days, about two million pilgrims go to Mecca during the pilgrimage season each year from all over the world.

Like prayer and fasting, the *hajj* is considered obligatory in Islam, but it is also infused with extraordinary meaning. Barbara Metcalf has written:

> Travel to Mecca is travel of a very particular kind. To go to
> Mecca is to go home, to return to one's *ruhani watn*. To go to

Mecca is to perform an act of unquestioned value. Not only is the goal clear, but the place, in contrast to the destinations of some kinds of travel, is thoroughly known by vast resources of the culture in story and devotional song—now reinforced by techniques of reproduction and communication that make the Holy Places ever present. Moreover, the journey moves on the invisible lines which believers create by every prayer, posture at sleep, and burial in the grave; on the day the *hajjis* perform the ritual sacrifice, fellow Muslims everywhere perform their sacrifice and all are linked worldwide in celebration of the feast. By undertaking the *hajj*, the pilgrim in principle affirms his individual responsibility for obedience to God and claims his place among the community of faithful people.[4]

The Shiʿa of Dearborn take seriously the obligation to make the *hajj*. It is an obligation that is anticipated with both joy and trepidation. Only those few who rejected religion completely expressed no interest in making the pilgrimage.

Oddly enough, though, the responses I received regarding the *hajj* tended to be among the ones that clearly delineated the Shariʿa-minded—particularly the politically oriented—from the traditionalists.

Perhaps Adel's answers to the questions about pilgrimage best sum up, though in a slightly exaggerated way, the feelings of the more traditional Shiʿa in this community. He is a young man who supports his wife and child as a cook in a restaurant and through income from rental properties. Always at odds with his in-laws and often as not with his tenants and employers, he is always one to test the limits of the law and the social norms. In the summer, he goes about in shorts, a practice that tends to belie his insistence that he is a very pious man. He is, after all, a *sayyid* with a brother studying in a *madrasa*. He says he looks forward to the day when he will be a *hajj* and he expects he will be different afterward. Then, he says, he will "stay home, be retired, go to the mosque, and talk about religion all the time."

Almost invariably, the women who do not wear the scarf stated that they will wear it after they make their pilgrimage. They anticipate that the pilgrimage will be a turning point in their lives. Zahra D. said that the thought of making a pilgrimage was frightening for her because she knew how much her life would have to change afterward. She did not feel at all ready to make that sort of commitment at her young age of thirty-two. She realizes that she could no longer be careless about praying, fasting, or dress. She, of course, would not be able to shake hands with men anymore, either.

Najwa, who professed to caring deeply about her religion but seemed remarkably uninformed about its tenets, also said she looked forward to being a *hajja*. She believes people will respect her after she has made her pilgrimage. Asked if she thought she would change after pilgrimage, she said only that she would be much older then. When I specifically asked her if she would start wearing the scarf, she replied negatively. Another young woman was in the room at the time, and she gasped in horror at Najwa's comment. She wanted me to know that Najwa was mistaken about this matter and that a woman must wear a scarf after she has gone on pilgrimage.

The traditional *hajja* is unmistakable. She wears a white gossamer scarf that completely covers her hair and is almost invariably old. She is fully cognizant of the fact that she is to be treated with the utmost respect.

To the more traditional sort of Muslim, there is the assumption that the *hajj* is to be performed in one's later years. Clearly, the statement being made is that in one's later years it is easier and less inconvenient to be "holy." It is only natural that one will be sinful (i.e., lax in one's religious duties) in one's earlier years. Furthermore, young men are likely to be concerned with (or obsessed by) sex and, now that they are in America, fast and flashy cars. Young Lebanese women, while their body parts may be more covered than those of their non-Lebanese counterparts, are notably flashy in their attire. Proud of their thick manes of hair, the majority of school-aged girls do not opt to cover it. Once these young men and women are married, their appearance and behavior tone down considerably. Yet they still don't see themselves as ready to take on the responsibilities of being *hajjis*. These earlier years are a time for some religious leeway.

But once one reaches his or her fifties and sixties, there is rarely any excuse (except for poor health) for not making the pilgrimage to Mecca. At that point, one has little to lose and much to gain by doing so. Jane Fonda is not a role model for fifty-year-old women in this community. A woman at that age should be stout and dowdy in her appearance. She should be no sexual threat. Indeed, anthropologists studying the Middle East have referred to postmenopausal women as being symbolically men. As for mature men, they gain no respect by being dashing and rakish. In these later years, then, one should make a pilgrimage, the purpose of which is "purification and atonement" for one's past life. Then, when one returns home from pilgrimage, one leads a life of prayer and fasting. He or she will avoid shaking hands with the opposite sex and will try to avoid all other sins. In other words, the *hajj* is viewed as a rite of passage.

This life-cycle or rite-of-passage view of Islam infuriates the Shariʿa-minded. One should already be living a religious life before one goes on pilgrimage. And to wait until one is "too old to sin" suggests a lack of religious commitment. Young Ismael expressed the harshest criticism of this attitude. He looks upon the *hajj* as being a "spiritual education" but not a point in his life at which he starts following God's laws. He already does that. He simply hopes that on his pilgrimage, he will come to have a deeper understanding of religion. He believes that most people go on pilgrimage to gain status. He complained of *hajjis* who get upset if they are not called by that title.

Yet, even among the more Shariʿa-minded, there is a tendency to have some expectation of self-improvement after pilgrimage. Youssef is only in his thirties and has already made the pilgrimage. Strict in his conformity to most religious law, he does feel he has changed since becoming a *hajj*. Now he no longer attends weddings held outside the mosque (i.e., weddings where there is music and dancing), nor will he listen to music other than the chanting of the Koran or "anthems." These attitudes, he said, did not come suddenly but were building up prior to the *hajj* (again suggesting the view that the *hajj* should not be considered a rite of passage).

It should be noted that the traditional sort never mentioned having to give up music or attendance at weddings. To do so would be a sign of "fanaticism." Hajja Sharifi may pray and fast, even outside Ramadan, but she delights in visiting her nieces at their homes for an evening of music and traditional dance. And she certainly finds nothing wrong with attending her kinsmen's weddings in the local halls.

There is little likelihood that the more orthodox views of Islam will affect the general community's attitudes toward the *hajj*. First, the notion that the *hajj* is for purification purposes is deeply embedded. A person who is a *hajji* truly is expected to behave differently from a non-*hajji*, and he or she is subjected to criticism if he or she does not live up to the community's standards. Second, I have detected no real pressure by the Shariʿa-minded to encourage early pilgrimages. The points of contention in this community concern general behavior and modesty of dress, not something as individual as one's attitudes about and timing of the *hajj*.

Furthermore, even if there were pressures being put on the community for early *hajj*, there is the added consideration that the pilgrimage is expensive, and here in America there are so many things in which to put one's money. Better to wait until one has amassed one's fortune and then go on *hajj*.

Halal or *Haram* Meat?

Mr. M. told me that when he came here in the late 1940s, the people were "in doubt" about meat. By this, he meant that there was no way to be sure whether the meat one ate was prepared according to religious rules or not. Consequently, the people ate the meat they could buy in the markets and only avoided eating pork, about which there is no doubt. Under no conditions is pork *halal*.

Today there should be no doubt about the meat one eats. On the main business street of East Dearborn alone, within a space of about eight blocks, there are three Lebanese Shi'i-owned meat markets with signs in front announcing "*Halal* Meat." Other such shops are found throughout the eastern and southeastern sections of the city.

According to Khu'i, for meat to be *halal*, five conditions must be met:

> A slaughtered animal is *halal* if it is slaughtered by a Muslim. It is not *halal* if it is slaughtered by a nonbeliever or even by a monotheist. It is not conditioned on faith. According to the most reliable opinion, he need not be a Shi'i if he is judged to be a Muslim and if he is not an enemy or of a group such as the Kharijites or certain extremist Shi'te sects that have been judged to be non-Muslim.
>
> The animal may be slaughtered by a Muslim woman or even the young child of a Muslim, so long as he or she knows the difference between right and wrong.
>
> It is only permissible to slaughter the animal with an iron implement so long as one is available. . . . If there is no iron available, then the use of a sharp implement of some other material is acceptable.
>
> It is obligatory to cut through four things: the esophagus, the windpipe, and the two arteries.
>
> Correct slaughter of an animal is based on the following conditions:
>
> First condition: the animal to be slaughtered and its place of slaughter must both face the *qibla*.
>
> Second condition: that the person who is to slaughter the animal says the name of God.
>
> Third condition: that the blood drain out in the correct way. If it comes out slowly or in drops, the meat is not *halal*.
>
> Fourth condition: that the throat be cut in the correct place, not on the nape of the neck. It is a precaution to place the knife on the throat and then cut the jugular veins. It is not sufficient to stab beneath the jugular veins and then cut upwards.[5]

When I asked people if they ate *halal* meat, they almost invariably said that they did. However, this does not mean that they do not eat meat that is not *halal*. Men are far more likely than women to eat meat that is not religiously sanctioned, principally because men spend much more time outside the home. If they are on the main street of East Dearborn, there is no difficulty obtaining *halal* meat in Shiʿi-owned and -operated restaurants. However, once outside the neighborhood, there is no guarantee of finding *halal* meat. Besides, the men—especially those with a traditional view of Islam—confess that they are sorely tempted by Burger King hamburgers. Women have fewer such temptations. If they eat out, it will be with relatives or close friends who are also likely to buy meat from the local markets.

However, the topic of *halal* meat did elicit some curious responses. Mahmoud, the engineering student who could scientifically prove the existence of *jinn,* said that there was only one market in town from which he would buy meat. He was certain that the other markets did not butcher their meat properly. One of the sheikhs reportedly expressed the same concern and avoided eating meat. Ali, the entertainer-entrepreneur, would not give me a yes-or-no answer to my question concerning his meat preference but only replied that there was no place that really sold *halal* meat.

I did not take these comments very seriously until my scholarly Iraqi friend, a woman who is the very vision of Islamic propriety, told me about her own visit to the meat market that I frequent. When she ordered meat, the butcher asked her (of all people) if she wanted "*lahme halal* or *haram.*" She left the shop indignantly.

While shopping in the meat section of a large grocery store in town, I saw a Lebanese man and his *hijab*-covered wife loading up their cart with steaks that were on special. Quite taken aback, I went to one of my chief informants who is an employee at this same store. He laughed at me and said, "What do think? This happens all the time." He then explained that money is the determining factor. If meat at the grocery store is cheaper than at the *halal* meat markets, the people, no matter how religious otherwise, will buy their meat "*haram.*"

Perhaps he is right, in some cases at least. Since questions have arisen about whether the meat at the Lebanese markets is truly *halal,* one could justify the purchase of meat at an American grocery. It seems, then, that some people are still "in doubt" just as Mr. M. was in the 1940s. On the other hand, Hajj Deeb and his family would not leave Dearborn for a vacation outside the area without loading up his cooler with enough locally purchased *halal* meat to last the entire family for a week. As most people will say, if the butcher shops are not selling *halal* as they say they are, then the sin lies with them and not with their customers. Only those with the most rigid interpretation of the law, then, would refuse to eat meat from a market that calls itself *"halal."*

For those who are truly in doubt about the local meat markets and want to be sure that they are eating properly butchered meat, there are farms in the area where one can purchase an animal and butcher it oneself. Of course, this is the most economical way to purchase meat as well, so wherein lies the true motive?

Obviously, the insistence on meat killed only by a Muslim who does not have enmity with the members of the House of the Prophet, that is, the Shiʿa, is a powerful tool in establishing a caste type of system in a community. This situation could only be realized in a community where the butchers claim to sell religiously sanctioned meat. To some extent, this caste system does exist. My experience leads me to believe that perhaps more than half of the adults in this community will only eat *halal* meat. I can say this with some confidence because I see that it is not just the meat itself that is somehow sacred but also what that meat becomes. *Kibbeh, kafta, kabbab*—these meats are truly "food." Notions of "pure meat" are melded with notions of "pure food." For the women particularly, I see a strong resistance to eating anything else. That food is important in Middle Eastern societies has been well documented. But now transported, it takes on almost quasi-religious connotations.

Thus far, I have not even discussed pork, the meat that is truly *haram*. One can forgo all other religious obligations and still avoid pork. The idea of eating pig meat is simply repugnant to a people who believe this animal is filthy. Mr. S., who said that he had eaten pork in the form of pepperoni on a pizza, did so to shock his wife. A man with an unusually positive view of America, he disapproves of his wife's narrow view of her religion and of the world and was making a statement. It was a radical statement. Linda, a professional woman who grew up in America, refuses to eat pork. She considers this to be a strong indicator of her religious convictions, but the idea of eating only *halal* meat seems rather alien to her.

The schools in East Dearborn do not serve pork in their lunch program. A letter goes home to the parents in English and Arabic reassuring the parents that they have nothing to fear on this front. But the meat is not *halal*, and I rather doubt that there will be any effort to introduce this into the school lunch program. The notion of religiously sanctioned meat is alien to this community, where there are no kosher delicatessens to have paved the way. Further, so long as the Lebanese do not feel their rights are actively being infringed upon or that they are being attacked by the outside community, they do not tend to make protests and demands. The line must be drawn at pork, but most Lebanese feel that some compromises have to be made, at least when dealing with American schools and employers.

Purity

As Fischer and Abedi point out in their introduction to Khomeini's *Resaleh,* or *Clarification of Questions,* fully a quarter of the three thousand problems deal with issues of purity, while the theme of purity relates to other problems as well. It is helpful to look at how Fischer and Abedi explain purity in Shi'ism. After warning the English reader that one must not confuse the purity code with modern notions of cleanliness, they say:

> Excrement for instance is always unclean or dirty, but the excrement of an animal whose flesh may be eaten is never impure. Purity has something to do with the state in which one can approach God: one must be pure for prayer. There is an interior aspect (the *batin*) which is all important, and there is an outer sign of the inner spirit. The rules of purification through various forms of ablution (the *vozu* before the formal prayer called *namaz* or *salat;* the full ritual bath or *ghosl* required after seminal emission, menstrual flow, afterbirth, touching a corpse) constitute these outer signs; in themselves they have no meaning and no efficacy if they are not accompanied with the inner spirit. . . . Nor is it merely a washing, but it is ritual, a washing done with the proper form and *niyyat.* Thus, prayers said by a peasant in a shirt stained with cow dung are perfectly valid; the shirt is dirty but not impure. Conversely, the wet hand of a non-Muslim may be clean, but is nonetheless always impure; so, too, a dog freshly washed is clean, but is nonetheless always impure and polluting.[6]

In no other area of religious life will a Shi'i living in America find so much difficulty as that of living up to the purity code. There are three mosques to pray in, and there are enough *halal* meat markets to provide for the entire community. One can still manage to fast if one tries, though certainly America is not geared to a fasting schedule. But if one wants to follow one's religion to the letter of the law, there will be serious difficulties in living up to the purity code. Problems will arise particularly when the Muslim must work and associate with non-Muslims. To refuse to shake an American's hand on the basis that he is impure is tantamount to slapping him in the face. I can safely say that the vast majority of Lebanese living in Dearborn realize the problem and ignore this injunction.

Fouad Ajami alludes to the fear of defilement, the Shi'a's fear of touching something, that is *najis* or impure. Musa Sadr addressed this problem head-on by ostentatiously purchasing and eating the ice cream served to him by a Christian ice cream vendor. As Ajami says, "The lesson was not lost on the crowd. Things hitherto impermissible were declared acceptable by a man of religion and a *sayyid*, a descendant of the Prophet."[7]

However, I have witnessed awkward moments of indecision. My husband and I had occasion to usher around a television correspondent who was interested in doing a feature story on Islam. We spent an afternoon with one of the local sheikhs and a visiting *qadi* (religious judge) from Lebanon. My husband, having to leave early, rose and stretched out his hand to the *qadi*, who glanced nervously at the sheikh. Almost imperceptibly, the sheikh gestured to the *qadi*, and the *qadi* reached out his hand to my husband.

Another of the local sheikhs apparently had little or no experience with non-Muslims when we first met him. When we were introduced, he placed his hand to his breast as a gesture of greeting and did not extend his hand to my husband. However, the interview proved to be quite cordial, and he seemed particularly pleased that we had spent some time in Iran. On departing, he initiated a handshake with my husband.

While one might be able to rationalize shaking hands with non-Muslims on the basis that it would cause bad feelings and turn Americans against Islam, there is no rationalizing one's feelings about dogs. As Khomeini and all Shi'i scholars have made so clear, dogs are *najis*. This is a teaching that the Lebanese definitely take to heart. The American propensity to have dogs roaming the house is a confirmation of how different the worlds of Muslim and non-Muslim are and how important it is that they remain separate.

A situation that seemed at first amusing but ended sadly involved our own dog. Young Wa'el befriended our then ten-year-old son, Nathaniel. A friendly child intrigued by the differences between our home life and his own, Wa'el spent a good deal of time with us. His parents showed no objection to this at all and were always warm and hospitable with us. But the main attraction for Wa'el was the dog, which became very devoted to him. (Incidentally, aware of the Lebanese distaste for dogs, ours was kept in the yard or in parts of the house where guests do not go.) At first, Wa'el bragged to his friends about his relationship with the dog, until word got to his parents that he was playing with it and actually touching it. His father's reaction was initially to chastise him; his mother's was to make him shower whenever he had been to visit us. I learned this indirectly from one of their relatives. Still, Wa'el came, and, despite my admonitions that he should not disobey his parents, he continued to play with the dog. The verbal scoldings turned into physical punishment, and finally Wa'el was forbidden to play at our home.

Roy Mottehedeh cites an amusing story of an Iranian who encounters a dog on his way to prayers. Having performed his ablutions, he did not want to have to perform them again. He simply uttered the words, "*En sha' Allah,* it's a goat," and went off to pray.[8] Dogs are not being mentally transformed into goats in this community. The anthropological theorist Mary Douglas proposed that laws regarding purity and permitted foods be seen as "signs which at every turn inspire meditation on the oneness, purity and completeness of God."[9] Yet, when considering the lives of Shi'a in Lebanon, who had to remain separate from their non-Shi'a countrymen, one cannot help but see these laws in more practical terms. They are important reminders that the Shi'a are "different." Following these laws is a means of rejecting incorporation into the dominant culture, whether it be that of the Sunnis in the Middle East or of secularized Christian culture in America.

Gold and Religious Conviction

Prosperity comes quickly in this community if you are fortunate enough to find the means to open a gold shop. The two gold shops on Warren Avenue, which import gold jewelry primarily from Saudi Arabia, Egypt, and Italy, are doing quite well. Women and even the smallest girls are dazzling in their 24-karat gold bracelets, necklaces, rings, and earrings. Despite the interest in investing in rental properties and businesses, wealth is still put into jewelry.

I was rather taken aback, then, when a woman at the Majma' told me that wearing gold jewelry is forbidden. "It will cause men to be attracted to a woman," she said. The sanction does not appear to be taking hold. Only two women I interviewed wore no jewelry whatsoever, although most women who wear the *hijab* wear relatively conservative amounts of jewelry. Layla, who wears the *hijab,* only recently learned about the ruling against gold from other women at the Majma'. She confirmed what they said with a sheikh visiting from Lebanon. She has removed all but a couple of bracelets and her rings.

The vast majority of women I spoke with had never heard of any injunction against wearing gold and swore that I was mistaken in my information. During a visit with Wafa and her sisters, I brought up the subject of gold. Wafa said, "These Muslims will all tell you different things." She claimed she herself had asked one of the sheikhs about wearing gold, and he had told her it was *halal* for women but not for men. Men, though, are allowed to wear silver. I asked why she thought gold was forbidden for men. Her sister said that it was because the gold passes through the skin into the bloodstream and has an ill effect on them, but Wafa cut her off, telling her that what she was saying was all wrong and that I should not listen to her. Others, though, offered the same explanation as Wafa's sister.

At an engagement I attended at the Jamiᶜ, Sheikh Chirri stated that it was permissible for a woman to wear gold but not for a man. The newly engaged man wore a ring of silver. Obviously this issue has yet to be definitively settled.

Among the men themselves, there is little agreement in this community about whether or not gold is allowed. Most men who eschew wearing gold jewelry do so because they simply don't think that such adornment is masculine, but there are those—both traditional and Shariᶜa-minded—who will not wear gold for religious reasons. However, the general perception in the community can be summed up in the statement of one man who had been raised in Dearborn and grew up attending the Jamiᶜ: "Only the Hizb Allah believe that gold is forbidden."

Makeup

A similar controversy exists about makeup, but more women appear willing to conform to sanctions about the former than the latter. Approximately a third of the women I interviewed said they only wear makeup for their husbands or if they are at an all-female party. This is interesting, because makeup, among those who use it, tends to be applied lavishly. To refuse to wear it is to make a very definite and visual statement about one's religious orientation.

Shaking Hands with the Opposite Sex

Aside from the injunction not to shake hands with *kuffar* (unbelievers), shaking hands with members of the opposite sex is also proscribed. On this issue, there is more agreement than there is about gold and makeup. People know it is wrong for a woman to shake a man's hand, and vice versa. After all, the Prophet did not shake hands with the women when he accepted their allegiance in Mecca. But I estimated that approximately a third of the men and half of the women follow this rule completely.

There were comments expressing the belief that shaking hands is a friendly gesture. Although people realized it was religiously forbidden, they could not understand why this was so and made the decision for themselves to shake hands. Iman, who is struggling to follow the rules of her religion, did admit that when she is introduced to an American man, she shakes hands so that she "will not cause bad feelings."

When a Shariʿa-minded man was introduced to me, he would generally place his right hand to his chest. I never initiated handshakes with men but was surprised on a few occasions when men whom I knew were strict followers of the law reached out their hands to me. After speaking with one of these men for a while, I asked why he had shaken my hand. Basically, it was because he thought I would expect this. He explained that he does not follow the laws exactly, that he does have "some sins," and that shaking hands with women was one of them.

Of course, after one is a *hajji,* one must surely follow the restriction about shaking hands with the opposite sex. Though for the recent immigrants this does not seem to be such a problem, for those who have lived here for many years, or who have grown up here, the question of whether or not a *hajji* will shake hands with a woman to whom he is being introduced is not easily answered. I was told, "We try our best to avoid it."

Catholicism, of course, does not have the equivalent of *halal* meat or proscriptions against gold jewelry or shaking hands with the opposite sex. Yet parallels do exist between Shiʿism and Catholicism. The Catholic church's prohibition against eating meat on Friday comes to mind. Eating fish became a "badge of individual integrity and identity."[10] This dietary rule expressed not only Catholics' desire for separateness but also their moral superiority over Protestants. The Lenten fast, while hardly as rigorous as that of Ramadan, was an occasion for publicly demonstrating this superiority.

Certainly, the highly ritualistic, devotional, and sacramentalized Catholicism that held sway through at least the first half of this century could be interpreted as an earnest attempt to ensure that the dividing line between Catholic and Protestant did not become fuzzy. Children in Catholic schools were reminded repeatedly that it was only through the Church that they could attain salvation. Should a child be so unfortunate as to have a Protestant parent or some other close relative, he or she was supposed to pray devoutly for that person's conversion.

Tensions regarding whether to emphasize or deemphasize the differences between themselves and their non-Shi'i neighbors are as great in Dearborn as they were in many immigrant Catholic communities. Should a Shi'a make accommodations with American society, or should he steadfastly observe the letter of the law in order to maintain his distinctiveness?

Ultimately for the Shi'a, as for the Catholics, the real question emerges: what really constitutes true religion anyway? The answer will help determine how Shi'ism survives in America.

Living with the Supernatural

Anthropologist Clifford Geertz wrote, "Our problem, and it grows worse by the day, is not to define religion but to find it."[11] In writing about Morocco and Indonesia, Geertz realized he was studying Islamic societies undergoing tremendous structural changes, ones in which "the machinery of faith" was wearing out.

The Lebanese, first in Lebanon and now in America, have undergone radical changes that necessarily impinge on the structural aspects of their religion but also test the strength and resiliency of their individually held faith. In this section, I am concerned with the individual and what he or she believes. This is not the realm of formal or communal religion, but, rather, it is the realm of the heart, soul, and mind. In a sense, I am trying to find an aspect of religion that one cannot find if one defines Islam only in its scriptural sense.

I am concerned with how much importance people attribute to the supernatural and how they see their earthly lives interact with it. Do they see otherworldly concerns shaping their lives, affecting what they do? How are the Koran's numerous warnings about hell (al-Nar, "the Fire") and its promises of paradise (Jannah) seen in this community? The Koran's treatment of the afterlife is very sensuous. One can almost see and hear and smell the delights of paradise and feel the agony of the fire of hell when reading the Koran. Do the Lebanese Shi'a accept this view of an afterlife, or do they opt for a more symbolic interpretation? Are there differences in opinions between the Shari'a-minded and the traditionalists? Is life in urban America affecting their views?

How do people view God, or Allah? Is he principally a punitive creator, or is he benign? Is death to be feared or merely accepted with resignation? Or is there truly a life of beauty and ease to be anticipated? Erika Friedl, in her study of poor Iranian village women, states that "for a great many women only death means a true end to hardship (or joy, as the case might be); in this sense death is seen not as a hopeful release from earthly shackles into the pleasures of heaven but as release into nonexistence, back-to-dust finality."[12] In the case of the Lebanese, who have faced years of death and destruction and, particularly with the Shi'a, a great deal of poverty, do they share this view of death with their Iranian coreligionists?

If people do have hope for a better life in the next world, how does one attain admittance into paradise? Is it through following religious law, or is there some other way to redemption?

The idea of deliverance from a world of disorder and tyranny is a common theme in world populations and certainly among peasants who have experienced a large share of the world's tyranny.[13] However, relief from tyranny does not have to be confined only to the afterlife. Millenarian movements concern themselves principally with establishing utopian societies here on earth. Such thinking is built into Shi'i eschatology. Twelver Shi'ism is almost defined by its anticipation of the return of the Twelfth Imam, referred to as the Qa'im or, more so in this community, as the Imam Mahdi. The son of the Eleventh Imam, it is believed that he went into occultation in A.D. 872 at the age of five years and has continued to live in occultation until this day. He will remain hidden until the Day of Judgment, at which time he will appear, conquer his enemies, and bring justice and peace to the world. According to the Shi'i philosopher 'Allama Tabataba'i, "the future will see a day when human society will be replete with justice and when all will live in peace and tranquillity, when human beings will be fully possessed of virtue and perfection. The establishment of such a condition will occur through human hands but with Divine succor. And the leader of such a society, who will be the savior of man, is called in the language of the *Hadith*, the Mahdi."[14]

The Mahdi is to be the leader in the Final Days, appearing before the Day of Resurrection when souls will be joined with their bodies. He and other members of the family of the Prophet, most notably the Imam Husayn, are to have a role in the judging of souls who will be sent to either paradise or hell. As the *raj'a*, or return, of the Mahdi is so central to Shi'ism, it is important to ascertain how the community under study views his return. Finally, there is also the question of supernatural beings, specifically the *jinn*, and their role in this earthly existence. Before entering into this realm, we will first discuss eschatological concerns.

The Existence of the Afterlife

I posed the question "If a person does not follow the laws of Islam, what will happen to him?" With only a few exceptions, my respondents automatically answered, "He will go to hell." In view of the fact that the Koran mentions and describes hell so often, this is not surprising.

However, it should be noted that most people in this community do not follow the laws of Shi'i Islam exactly. There is considerable laxity about prayer, fasting, and strict modesty for women. While honesty is a virtue people want associated with their names, business people are not always absolutely scrupulous about income taxes. It is common to hear men and women talk about obtaining "cash jobs," whereby they earn money that does not have to be reported to the IRS, which is beneficial both to them and to their employers. There are other ingenious tactics utilized for "beating the system" as well. While the Muslims in this community value honesty as one of the virtues of the Prophet and the imams, they also see their survival as important. It can be argued that this sort of chicanery is not as offensive as cheating a customer. Face-to-face relationships invariably have a more salient impact on people's behaviors. The inclination to manipulate and cheat the U.S. government is certainly not surprising in view of the long history of indifferent and even malevolent treatment of the Shi'a by the Lebanese government. (In fact, what is truly surprising is that more people did not share this negative attitude. There were obviously many who believed it to be their Islamic duty to follow all the laws of the land in which they reside.)

Do those who are lax in their adherence to the rules and in ethical matters see themselves as being destined for that most horrid of places, *el-Nar* or hell? The answer to that question is emphatically no.

The people in this community tend to see themselves as being in God's favor. Responses indicated that others would go to hell, but they did not envision this scenario for themselves. This idea was reinforced when I asked questions about the next life, and almost invariably people spontaneously described paradise but had to be asked specifically to describe hell. Why are these Shiʿa so optimistic about the next life?

This question can be answered at least partially by referring to the responses to my questions regarding moral values. Specifically, I asked, "What is the worst thing a person can do?" and "Who are the best people?" I wanted to know what people truly considered to be the worst offenses and what characteristics they admired the most. Was the person who prays and fasts, performs the *hajj*, and pays the *khums* the one most admired in this community? And, on the other hand, was the person who is negligent in these duties the worst?

Very few, it seems, see the world in these terms. Those whose lives are most strongly influenced by the Shariʿa told me that it was imperative to follow all the rules of religion, to live by the Five Pillars of Islam. Hajj Youssef said that the best people are "very, very strict about their religion and won't even allow a TV or a radio in their home." To Ismael, the best person was the one who knows the truth and follows it—especially the Shiʿa." Um Hamood thought the worst thing a person could do was not pray.

But these responses were in the minority. The vast majority of people with whom I spoke saw "goodness" in more universalistic terms and did not necessarily insist that a person needs to be a Muslim to be considered good. Even Iman, who conscientiously prays and fasts, said the best people were "warm, loving, caring, and clean people." And Suad, a wearer of the black ʿabaya and a regular at the very pro-Iranian Majlis, said that the best people are "those who are good to others, kind and generous. They are people who love others."

These comments do not sharply contrast with those of the more traditional Zuheir, who values kindness and caring in others. Zahra D. saw her "nonreligious" (but obviously beloved) husband as being the best sort of person, because "he is honest, tolerant, funny, helpful, optimistic, and determined."

Hurting another in any way was generally considered to be the worst thing a person can do. Whether killing someone or causing trouble through backbiting, the act of harming one's fellow man was definitely *haram*. Ali A. referred to backbiting as being like "killing a soul very slowly. This is what Arabic people today are doing to each other. Backbiting is the most *haram* thing a person can do." His feelings were reiterated by others. During a visit to Ghalia's home one day with her sisters, I found her in quite a frenzied state of mind. Someone was making trouble between her husband and her brother through what she swore were lies. She was expecting the worst.

Concern with gossip is natural in a community that uses this form of social control so readily. Gossip and slander, while helping to ensure that cultural and religious mores are upheld, also have the deleterious effect of playing havoc with people's lives.

One woman I knew has suffered considerably from her community's jealousy. Rumors abound that her family's business wealth is generated through drug sales. These rumors, she says, reached the police, who sent undercover agents to investigate. She claims that the police found no grounds for the accusations, but the rumors have not abated. "If this jealousy hurts my family, we will close our business," she told me.

The war in Lebanon also directly affected some of the responses. Khalid saw the most despicable of persons being one who "betrays his nation or his own cause." The best of people to him are "the honest politicians who are leading their people against all odds, like Imam ʿAli, the Prophet Muhammad, Nabih Berri, and Imam Musa Sadr." Ali S., who, like Khalid, supports Amal, shared Khalid's feelings. He hates people who commit treason and deceive their people. He said that Hizb Allah fall under this category.

Several men mentioned hypocrisy as the most hated of sins. As Hajj C. said, "I like people who practice what they preach." There were surprisingly few mentions of sexual misbehavior. Najwa, who, in her pedal-pushers and short-sleeved pullovers, is an interesting contrast to the rest of the married women in the neighborhood, said that immodest dress was the most *haram* thing for a woman. From Al Januub, she accused the women of the Bekaa for their immodesty. For men, she said, at least for married ones, going out with women is the worst thing. Only two other women mentioned adultery.

I do not believe that the dearth of comments relating to sexual behavior is a result of any lack of concern with this matter. Rather, I think the two particular questions I posed served as an inkblot test. I noticed frequently that people responded with statements that reflected what they had been experiencing lately. I knew in many cases that women particularly, but also men, were concerned with what others were saying about them, so they were prone to seeing gossip as particularly reprehensible. Comments reflect other hurts and slights as well. Mona, who has had to rely on considerable assistance from her friends, said that she finds those who help but don't want praise to be the most admirable. Ali A., who said he considers gossip to be the cause of "a soul's slow death," suffers from much division in his family which he attributes to others' interference and gossip.

In general, I believe that the majority of people in this community set greater stock by peaceful coexistence with family and neighbors than following precisely all the laws of Islam. However, they feel a person should strive to live a good life in the name of God, not just for some humanistic belief system. Several respondents mentioned that the best people are religious, although they frequently added that they did not necessarily have to be Muslim. Zahra conceded that some of the best people she has known have been Christians. But not to believe in God at all seems almost incomprehensible in this community. The worst accusation a person can have made against him or her is to be called an atheist.

The legalistic aspects of religion tend to be downplayed by the majority of Shiʿa in this community. While religion is deeply important to them, they are more likely to stress the spirit rather than the letter of the law, again reflecting the Lebanese Shiʿa's relative isolation from the scholarly centers of Shiʿism. This tendency also would be strengthened by the Christian influences in Lebanon.

When discussing prospects for the afterlife, a number of individuals mentioned that good deeds were more important than strictly adhering to religious rules. This was heard from both new immigrants and earlier ones. As the recently arrived Dr. B. stated, and others also reiterated, "Good works are paramount." The elderly Zahria, who was raised in the United States, said, "Each person is judged individually, not just by whether he follows the laws of religion or not." In these responses, I heard an invocation of some other source of morality than that of scriptural religion. Such ideas are anathema to the Shariʿa-minded, who believe that all wisdom and guidance come from the sacred texts and that good works are certainly not enough to save one's soul.

Another factor that can influence people's expectations for the next life is reliance on God's mercy and forgiveness. "God is forgiving" was a phrase I heard repeatedly. Zuheir feels it is wrong not to abide by the Koranic rules. Yet, he added, he knows that he is supposed to pray but does not because he is "too lazy." He fears God yet perceives him as being "loving, caring, and forgiving." I also heard repeatedly that God is just. He weighs the good and the bad. Several individuals referred to the Koranic image of a scale on which God or his angels actually compare the good and bad actions of a person during his entire lifetime. Most people seem confident that their good actions have counteracted any evil they may have done.

That God is forgiving is something both the Shariʿa-minded and the traditionally religious can agree on. Yet there are differences even on this matter. The Shariʿa-minded Iman made it clear that God's forgiveness won't come on one's deathbed. One must beseech God's forgiveness while one still has time to prove one's faith and sincerity. No such radical change in behavior seems to be required for the traditionalist. Forgiveness can come at any stage, even at death.

Finally, I believe that this community's optimism is closely linked to the circumstances under which the people have been practicing their Shiʿi beliefs. They are a people who have always had to share their environment with non-Shiʿa, be they other Muslims or Christians. These others were constant reminders to the Shiʿa of their spiritual edge over the rest of the world. They were the only ones to pledge their loyalty to the Imam Ali and the other imams. They were the descendants of those who suffered persecution for their beliefs. And they alone had the Imam Husayn as their savior.

Suffering in This Life

When people said that they believed there was a punishment in the next life, I asked if they believed that God punished in this life as well. This community seems to be about equally divided between those who believe that God punishes only in the afterlife and those who believe that God punishes sinners in this life as well.

Those who expressed a belief only in an otherworldly punishment often commented that people can enjoy a very prosperous life here yet have to face a terrible fate after death. In other words, worldly success was no indicator of God's favor, as it is believed to be in the Calvinist tradition. Though this community tends toward upward mobility, there is still a great deal of suspicion about those who have done very well materially. For those who have not managed to achieve the American dream, there is a great deal of envy of those who have. Accusations that a well-to-do shop owner or other entrepreneur has made his fortune through drugs or some other illegal activity are extremely prevalent. Apparently, those who have not been materially successful find some comfort in their belief that the rich will ultimately suffer. The envy found in this community probably reflects a common idea among people of peasant background: there is only so much good to go around; anyone who takes too much is depriving his neighbor of his share.

As for those who have suffered misfortune in this life, one should not assume that they are being punished by God for their sins. After all, God tests his loved ones. Zuheir commented that the best people are those who suffer most in this world. Several people commented that the question about suffering in this life was very complicated and had various possible answers.

There is earthly punishment for transgressors, however. Both the Shariʿa-minded and the traditionalists believe this. Traditionalists, though, tended to give "superstitious" explanations for the afflictions. Ghalia believes that a person's mind will become confused, and Saroya believes that even members of the offender's family can face illness or other misfortune if God is displeased with a person. Zahra D. is afraid that if things are going too well in her life, she will face a punishment. Therefore, she is trying to be more conscientious in her religious obligations.

The Shariʿa-minded take a more logical approach. They believe that Islam is the perfect prescription for living. If one does not follow this prescription, one's life cannot possibly be healthy and happy. One will fall into paths that lead to destruction. In other words, this suffering is not a direct result of God's punishment but rather a self-inflicted type of punishment, just as by not following the safety rules for using a dangerous machine, one may cut off one's fingers. As Samira put it, "They are making trouble for themselves by not following God's laws that are made for us to live our life by. Here in the U.S., there is always a need for government and police, but in an Islamic society, one knows how to follow Islam. No other rules are necessary. If a person follows the rules of Islam, they have no problems."

Two men I interviewed referred to a different sort of worldly punishment, that inflicted by the government. When asked if a person is punished in this life for disobeying Islamic law, Maher said, "Nothing happens to a person in this life because we don't have an Islamic government. In the next life, the offender will get what is coming to him. If a person is punished by a non-Islamic government for a crime, he still must pay the penalty for having offended God. If he is punished the Islamic way, his debt is paid. He is forgiven by God." Ali, a college student, replied, "If a person does not follow the laws of Islam, what will happen to him depends on whether there is an Islamic government or not. If there were, they would take care of the sinner, but when there is none, the person must be left to God." Both of these men, of course, believe that an Islamic government would serve as God's representation on earth and would be a vehicle for the salvation of souls. If people are punished here, they would be spared punishment in the next life. Outside Iran, they believe, no such government and, therefore, possibility for forgiveness exists.

Those Who Don't Believe

Mona, the woman who studied with Musa Sadr's sister in Lebanon, who came to the United States wearing *hijab,* and who refuses to wear blue jeans or a bathing suit because they are "against religion," gave a startling response to my questions about the afterlife. She said, "In the Holy Book, it says there is a heaven and a hell, but I am not sure about that. No one has ever come back from death to report about the next life, so I don't think there is a next life. However, the Koran tells us to stay away from trouble, so you should. I don't believe that God punishes anybody. If you are bad, you have no respect either from yourself or from others. A person should not be good just because of reward in the next life."

The only others to voice such doubts were those who had questions about the existence of God. Mona does not question God's existence. She was shocked and appalled when a Lebanese Shiʿa, a very disreputable man in the community, said that he wasn't afraid of God, so he certainly wasn't afraid of Mona and her brothers. Over and over again, she repeated his words, trying to comprehend them. And yet, in front of another Lebanese woman during the interview, she said she doubted the existence of the next life. I waited for a reaction from the other woman. It never came. Could it be that others have such doubts but can't bring themselves to voice them? Yet Mona said what I had observed earlier. One can follow the Koran, not because of a fear of punishment but because it presents a way of life that people view as the correct path to follow. It is also the path sanctioned by all of one's family and closest friends. It probably seems more realistic to fear them in their tangible presence than to fear God.

There were a few bona fide nonbelievers, or at least serious doubters, in my sample, but even these had some surprising thoughts to share about life after death. Ridwan, the social scientist, said that he is "skeptical" about the next life. He does not believe in punishment. He thinks of religion as serving communal, psychological needs. "Religion is part of a heritage, and you feel you are part of it," he said. He likes to pray on Friday at the mosque to experience this communal feeling. Yet, while he is "not convinced there is an afterlife," he added that he still fears God.

Husayn, who feels "religion has no place in our lives anymore" (yet who shares many of the same moral views as the believers), does not concern himself with whether or not there is a God. He stated that he does not believe in punishment for sins and that the end of the body is the end of life. But he does experience some fear that was evident in his recounting of a movie he had seen about a woman suffering greatly before her death. In the movie, a woman died but came back to life for a moment—just long enough to tell the woman who was preparing her body for burial that she was still suffering just as greatly in the next life as she had in this one. Husayn told me that he had a fear of something like this but then repeated that he did not believe in an afterlife.

The Imam Mahdi

The time of the Advent or "Return" of the Imam is known to God alone, but it will be heralded by numerous signs ... of which the most celebrated are the coming of the wicked and hideous Sufyani, whose army the earth will finally swallow up. The appearance of a figure in the sun; the multiplication of misleading divines and lawyers and of poets; the abounding of tyranny and oppression; the appearance of Antichrist (Daj-jal) riding on his Ass; the assembling of 313 chosen supporters of the Imam in Taliqan of Khurasan, etc. After a "reign of the Saints" lasting seventy years, the Imam will die, poisoned by a woman named Maliha, and the Imam Husayn will return to earth to read the Burial Service of him. This is the beginning of what is called the "Lesser Resurrection" (Qiyamat-i-Sughra), when the Prophet and all the Imams, as well as their chief antagonists, shall return to earth for a while, and fight their battles over again, but with a different result, since the unbe-lievers shall be uniformly defeated. In this first temporary Res-urrection only those who are purely believers or unbelievers (Mùmin-t-Khalis or Kafir-i-khalis) will come to life. Then they will again disappear from the face of the earth, and, after forty days' anarchy and confusion, the tribes of Gog and Magog (Yajuj u Majuj) will burst through the Wall (Sadd) which keeps them back, and will overrun the earth, and eat up all the grass and herbs, and drink up the rivers.

The "Greater Resurrection" (Qiyamat-ii-Kubra), when all the dead shall be raised to life in the same bodies they had while on earth, recreated by God's Power as a broken brick can be remade from its original materials, will be inaugurated by the blast of Israfil's trumpet, which shall draw into itself all the spirits of the quick and the dead, so that no living thing shall remain on earth save the "Fourteen Immaculate Ones" (Cha-hardah Ma'sum). Then, when their bodies have been recreated, Israfil will again blow his trumpet, and the spirits will emerge from it like a swarm of bees, and fly each one to its own body. All animals will also be raised to life to undergo the Reckoning and be judged for their acts of violence towards one another. Then the Balance (*Mizan*) will be set up for the weighing of the good and bad acts of each soul, and the scroll of each man's deeds, written down by the Recording Angels Saʿig and Shahid, will be placed in his hand.[15]

When I asked young Shariʿa-minded Ishmael when he thought the Imam Mahdi would return, he responded, "It is not allowed to make such predictions." But he could not help adding, "There are signs that it may be coming soon. The Islamic Republic in Iran and the social problems like sexual freedom and other corruptions are also a sign." Maher, also very strict in his interpretation of the law, said, "The Imam Mahdi will come when he gets permission from God, and anyone who tells you otherwise is a liar." But his equally Shariʿa-minded wife on another occasion told me that she was studying with a visiting sheikh from Lebanon who was not at all reticent about making some predictions. She reported that he told his class that the war in Lebanon, Arab against Arab, Jews coming back home, all these things, and many more must happen before the Imam Mahdi comes with Jesus to bring justice to the world. Changes of weather patterns are another indication of his coming. From her understanding of what the sheikh was teaching, she is convinced that the Imam's return is imminent. Indeed, one of the most sought-after religious books in the community is a popular account in Arabic of the prophecies of the Mahdi that shows how they are in the process of fulfillment.

While there are some like Maher and Ishmael who are resistant to sharing their opinions about the time of the return, the sheikhs are less so. When Sheikh Berri was asked this question, he quoted the scholar Ibn ʿArabi on the subject, citing prophecies that strongly suggest that the believers are justified in their hopes that the Mahdi will return in their lifetimes. Sheikh Chirri very directly teaches that the Mahdi will return soon. During one of his sermons, he said, "Can the Mahdi defeat all enemies of Islam? Muhammad is 'bigger' than the Mahdi. Why do we expect one man, the Mahdi, to change the whole world? The reason: when the Prophet Muhammad was in the world, there was not the technology to broadcast to the world."

To my question about the Imam Mahdi, the ardently pro-Iranian Samira gave a most novel response. She prefaced her answer with a disclaimer that she knows when he would return, but continued, "There are signs that he will come, such as when there is much oppression on earth. Also, Shiʿites won't be allowed to go on *hajj*.

There will be computers, and women will dress like men. *El Mahdi* has been known to come without people realizing it at the time. He performs miraculous cures, and people he has helped will recognize him when he comes. He could be on this street right now." Actually, I am surprised I did not hear more about encounters with the Mahdi. There is a fair amount of folklore about people who have met him, since, after all, he is not dead but simply in hiding.

Only those who question the divine origin of Islam truly doubt the return of the Mahdi. Skeptic Husayn thinks that the issue of the return is a purely political matter. He believes that "the Shi'a use the Mahdi to reinforce their conviction that the imams are the rightful successors [to the Prophet] so as to oppose the Sunnis." The Sunnis also have a belief in the advent of a Mahdi figure, but the Shi'i beliefs are directly linked with the belief in the imamate, they are far more specific, and the prophecies do include some very anti-Sunni aspects.

Six of my respondents told me explicitly that the Mahdi would return before the year 2000. These tended to be the most traditional and least educated, but, while the more educated in my sample resisted the temptation to use that exact date, it was apparent that they see the Mahdi's time as having come.

The American experience has not weakened people's belief in and longing for the Mahdi. Hajj C., a second-generation American, told me, "He doesn't have to come in my lifetime, but I would like to respond to his call." He said he was prepared to give up everything to follow the Mahdi. Hajj M., also a second-generation believer, said that it was Sheikh Chirri's insistence that the Imam Mahdi would appear soon that was instrumental in making him a more observant Muslim.

Life in America would not necessarily weaken this belief and, in fact, may strengthen it. After all, America is the birthplace of some of the most activist millenarian movements, in which people have dedicated their lives and fortunes to preparation for Christ's return. Some of my more Americanized informants are well aware of how eagerly American Christians await the return of Christ. The two returns, that of Christ and that of the Imam Mahdi, according to Shi'i belief, are supposed to occur more or less simultaneously. Therefore, the Christian beliefs reinforce those of the Muslims. Also, the Muslims can look forward to a time when they will have the upper hand, even in predominantly Christian America. Abdo, one of the most ostensibly assimilated of my respondents, said, "The Imam Mahdi will come prior to the return of Christ, who will meet him in Jerusalem. He will ask Christ to pray, and Christ will tell him that he will follow him." Certainly, the vindication of Islam in the eyes of the Christian world would be a major triumph for Islam and something to anticipate.

That the expectation of the Imam Mahdi's return is not simply considered a theoretical matter but something close to the hearts of the local Shiʿa was reflected in Minnie's comments. A traditionally religious woman raised in America with a high school education, she said, "All people will rise from the dead [when the Mahdi comes]. The punished people will carry coffins on their backs wherever they go. Allah will talk to each one alone about their sins. I think it will be soon because I hear about it too much from my family."

A translation of the late highly esteemed scholar Ayatollah Muhammad Baqir al-Sadr's words on the coming of the Imam Mahdi appears in the religious bookstore in Dearborn. In one of his essays, he writes:

> The Mahdi is not only an embodiment of the Islamic belief but he is also the symbol of an aspiration cherished by mankind irrespective of its divergent religious doctrines. . . . This belief is not merely a source of consolation but it is also a source of virtue and strength. It is a source of virtue because the belief in the Mahdi means the total elimination of injustice and oppression prevailing in the world. It is a source of inexhaustible strength because it provides hope which enables man to resist frustration, howsoever hopeless and dismal the circumstances may be.[16]

One of the signs from the traditions for the return of the Mahdi is that "death and fear will afflict the people of Baghdad and Iraq. A fire will appear in the sky and a redness will cover them."[17] The events that arose out of the Iraqi invasion of Kuwait may well serve to strengthen faith for some.

When the Virgin Mary appeared at Fatima and Lourdes, the children who encountered her were initially denounced by the Church as impostors. The clerical hierarchy knew full well that through the visions of these children, religious power was being transferred from the Church to the "spiritually pure" laity. The Church, unable to discredit the children, ultimately had no choice but to give credence to the apparitions and incorporate reverence and visitations to the sacred sites as part of Church belief. Still, an uneasy relationship maintains between the clerics and those who experience their deepest religious convictions through apparitions of the Virgin. The religion that the Virgin Mary represents—the nonconformist, antiestablishment religion of the individual—continues to be a threat to the status quo of the Church. In 1960, there was much speculation among American Catholic adults and children alike about what was contained in the letter believed to have been given to the oldest child at Lourdes by Mary and passed on to the Pope. Many believed that we were on the eve of enormous political and social changes associated with the return of Christ and, by implication, the disempowerment of the Pope and church hierarchy.

The Imam Mahdi, too, may well be seen as the antithesis of established religion and government. His ever-promised appearance holds a latent power as great as, if not greater than, that of the Virgin. The governments of Iran, since the Safavids, have had to pay lip service to their belief in him but have always dreaded the announcement that he has appeared. For example, when Ali Muhammad, the Bab, proclaimed in Iran that he was the Mahdi, he was imprisoned and executed in 1850 by Nasir al-Din Shah with the full support of the higher levels of ʿulama. A substantial number of the lower-ranking ʿulama, on the other hand, chose to follow the Bab, many of whom were tortured and killed as a result.

The ʿulama and the lay Shiʿa of Dearborn can well afford to anticipate the appearance of the Mahdi, as it is only through him that their greatest hopes of ascendancy could be realized. The Shiʿa of Dearborn are not revolutionaries out to establish an Islamic regime in America, but the Imam Mahdi, with Christ at his side, has the power to transform the entire world.

Jinn

As a girl in her late teens, Wafa's sister had turned down many suitors. She had a friend with a brother who wanted to marry her. She rejected him.

One day, while still in Lebanon, the family was involved in a huge housecleaning project in preparation for the arrival of an uncle. While Wafa was helping to air the mattresses, a ball-like object fell from one of them. She took it and began to bounce it off a wall. The "ball" came open, and inside she found paper with writing. She took it to her father, who recognized it as a curse. He, in turn, took it to her grandfather, who was a sheikh and had many books and knew about sorcery. The curse, he said, was on Wafa's sister. She would either never marry or have a disastrous marriage. He directed Wafa's father to dissolve the paper in water, but it would not dissolve. He consulted his books and said that Wafa's father and sister must get on a boat and go to the middle of the sea. Her father would have to immerse the girl seven times in the water and throw away the paper. He did so, and the curse was broken. Wafa's sister is now a happily married woman with children.

I had known Wafa for more than a year before she told me this story. She only told me because I had brought up the subject of the *jinn*. Earlier in the week, I had heard that a very Shari'a-minded woman had consulted a woman who speaks to the *jinn*. This is all I had heard; there were no details. So, when Wafa telephoned me, I asked her what she knew about the *jinn*. She knew plenty. There was the woman who was being seduced by the *jinn* until one night people found her naked in the cemetery. The *jinn* also came to the hospital room and took Wafa's grandmother to paradise; I am told that there are photographs of this, but I have not seen them. For Wafa, the *jinn* are a reality and a force to be reckoned with. To protect oneself from them, one must say *"Bismallahi Rahmani Rahim,"* and they will leave the potential victim alone.

After listening to Wafa's stories, I began to wonder if all Shi'i Lebanese carried within their psyches the same fears and apprehensions about these mysterious creatures.

The *jinn* are mentioned in the Koran and are considered servants of God, somewhat in the same manner as humans and angels are. They are a part of the established religion. *The Encyclopedia of Islam* states: "According to the Muslim conception [they are] bodies composed of vapor or flame, intelligent, imperceptible to our senses, capable of appearing under different forms and of carrying out heavy labors. They were created of smokeless flame (Kur'an, LV, 14) while mankind and the angels, the other two classes of intelligent beings, were created of clay and light. They are capable of salvation; Muhammad was sent to them as well as to mankind; some will enter Paradise while others will be cast into the fire of hell."[18]

While the *jinn* are part of Islamic creed, the question arises of whether it is acceptable to use incantations and spells to compel the *jinn* to accomplish something desirable. On many occasions, the Prophet was asked about the efficacy and truthfulness of charms, omens, fortune-telling, and the like. In each case, he either condemned these practices or advised against them. It is interesting that he condemned them but did not appear to suggest that these practices were absurd or impossible. In the Koran, Sura CXIII states:

Say: I take refuge with the Lord of the Daybreak
   from the evil of what He has created,
   from the evil of darkness when it gathers,
   from the evil of the women who blow on knots,
   evil of an envier when he envies.[19]

It has been left up to the theologians to determine what is allowable regarding people's involvement with the *jinn* and with magic.[20] In Wafa's family, there are sheikhs who have gone off to the Atabat to study. She has told me that some of them believe it is acceptable to learn all one can about the *jinn* in order to control them, while others, though firmly convinced of the existence of these spirits, feel that "one should take refuge with the Lord" and avoid such matters. The latter attitude conforms to that of Ibn Khaldun, the fourteenth-century Arab scholar who wrote in considerable detail about supernatural forces. He gave an example of a sorcerer who entered into a pact with the *jinn*, thereby making his spell more forceful. While he noted that "no intelligent person doubts the existence of sorcery," he warned that sorcery, the use of talismans, and dealings with astrology are harmful and should be avoided.[21]

The sharp dichotomy between religion and magic has proven time and again in anthropological studies to be a false one. While there are differences between the two, magic tends to be entwined with religion, whether it is the religion of primitive or complex societies. In Islam, magical forces of a variety of types have a particular legitimacy both because Islam was founded in a culture where magic played an essential role and because of the Koran's recognition of its potential force. The Koran rejects forces that challenge the power of God but never denies the existence of such forces. The *jinn* have a particular significance because they are specifically referred to in the Koran. Yet, for those who see religion in a highly scientific, rational way such as many Shariaʿ-minded tend to do, the *jinn* would seem to pose a problem.

It was my task to find out what people believed about the *jinn*. Did they indeed put full credence in their existence? Did educated people believe in them? Were people from one region more inclined to believe than those from another region? If people believed, did they have experiences with them, and were they likely to try to contact the *jinn*?

One comment I heard repeatedly was that it was the people from Bint Jubeil and Tibnin, two villages in South Lebanon, who were most "knowledgeable" about the *jinn*. However, when I asked people what their beliefs were regarding these spirits, I found no difference between people from these villages and those from other areas.

Mr. S., from Machghara in the Bekaa, still becomes quite visibly shaken when he talks about his visit to the shrine of Sitt Zeinab. He was kneeling next to his mother when he noticed a woman beside him dressed in white who suddenly vanished into thin air. He had no doubt that she was a *jinn*.

Um Ali, also from Machghara, told me that a female relative had kicked a cat that was in her way and suddenly became incapable of functioning. She had lost her mind, Um Ali said. The woman was taken to the hospital, but the doctor could find nothing physically wrong with her. Someone came and read the Koran over her, and she became well.

Another woman, again from Machghara, used to wash dishes in the bathroom and dump food in her toilet. One day, when she walked into the bathroom, she saw a vision of a huge sheikh standing in the tub. She consulted a sheikh, and he told her to stop flushing food in the toilet. She followed his advice and never saw the vision again.

Hajja Sharifi, from another village in the Bekaa, told me that in the olden days, "when people were very good, a goat came along and was hurt and needed help. A man came and gently took care of it. When he did, the goat spoke to him and thanked him. Now it is different. People aren't good, and now the *jinn* may hurt you. They usually look like monkeys, covered with hair, but they can take any form. If you are suspicious that you are dealing with the *jinn,* you always say '*Bishmallahi Rahmani Rahim.*' Then they will go away and leave you alone. If you are throwing hot water away outside, always say, '*Bismallah . . . ,*' because you might accidentally throw hot water on the *jinn,* which makes them furious, and they will drive you mad."

One evening, I was having coffee with my young neighbors. One of them was seventeen-year-old Mariam from Bint Jubeil, who was expecting a baby any day. Reading the coffee grounds from a demitasse cup, she began telling the fortune of the other woman, who was from Ayetini in the Bekaa. I personally have only known people from Bint Jubeil who read fortunes, and the two young women agreed that it is only Bint Jubeilis who know how to read fortunes, though I am not sure if this is true. I then asked Mariam about *jinn* and whether she had had experience with them. She had a story to tell, but she wanted me to be clear that fortune-telling was just for fun, whereas the *jinn* were for real. She proceeded to tell me that when she was fourteen years old, she returned to Lebanon to become engaged. She claimed that she was very frightened travel-ing by herself because she was afraid people would think she was a "bad girl." (I learned later that she was also extremely unhappy about the engagement, which was to a cousin she did not know. There was a boy in Dearborn whom she liked very much. Her father eventually threatened him when he continued to show an interest in Mariam.) When Mariam reached her village, she went to a sheikh who talks to the *jinn*. She paid him "a lot of money," and he gave her a piece of paper with writing, tightly bound in tape, to place under her shoulder when she went to bed at night. After that, she was calm. This young woman and her family have had much expe-rience with supernatural forces, two of her infant siblings having been killed through "supernatural means."

It may be instructive to look at Mariam's case to understand her and her family's involvement with the supernatural. This is a family steeped in Lebanese tradition. While Mariam's family took the great leap to come to the United States, there was no wish on their part to leave Lebanon behind. They simply needed a safer place to live and one that provided an opportunity to make a living. In this way, they are very typical of many families I knew. Mariam posed a threat to their traditional ways, however. A pretty, spirited teenage girl who was fascinated by all that America offers its youth, she dared to show an interest in a boy not hand-picked by her family. While a more religiously sophisticated family would try to control their daughter's behavior through norms prescribed by scriptural religion, this family taught their daughter that it was the *jinn* whom she needed to fear if she were to break society's rules. Using such reasoning, one would expect that belief in the *jinn* might increase among traditional Shi'a in America, at least in the short run.

An overwhelming majority of Lebanese Shi'a in Dearborn may have claimed that they place some credence in the existence of the *jinn*, but there is considerable disagreement about their role in the world otherwise. A minority specifically stated that they be-lieved in the *jinn* "because they are mentioned in the Koran." These people claimed to have no knowledge of these spirits otherwise and said that they were not important in their lives. These tended to be the Shari'a-minded who want to downplay any mystical or mysteri-ous aspect of religion. In fact, a couple of women who wear full *hijab* chided me for asking about the *jinn*. They both wanted to know why I would bother to ask such a question, as they believe that the *jinn* are not an important part of religion. One of the women who objected had gone to a sorceress to consult the *jinn*. She never admitted this to me, but a close relative of hers did.

Generally, the more highly educated also made it clear that *jinn* for them were a matter of faith. They believed in the Koran, so they must accept the *jinn*. But even this was not a consistent finding. I was quite taken aback when college-educated Dalal, who claimed no religious sentiment whatsoever, told me, in all seriousness and with conviction, a story of a man being raised up to the ceiling because of the *jinn*. "If the man said '*Bismallah* . . . ,' he would fall," she told me.

Not all Shiʿa who were either born in America or spent their formative years here were as definite about the role of the *jinn* as Mariam's family. One woman saw them as angels (although actually they are supposed to be distinct from angels). One man portrayed them as the subconscious struggle between good and evil. Another said that anyone who said he could contact the *jinn* was having hallucinations. These responses all suggest Western influence. Yet Hannah, who was born here but whose parents originated from a village in the south, told of a most remarkable experience.

Hannah is a widow who was left to raise three children. She told me that before her husband died, she saw a woman in the doorway of her home wearing black. The woman had only one eye in the middle of her face, and she knew that this woman comes only when there is an imminent death. Her husband died days later while her younger daughter was at camp. A teacher from the camp called Hannah and said that the daughter had been frightened by a dream of a woman dressed in black and was afraid something had happened to her father. Hannah believed these were visitations from the *jinn* and that they have played an important role in her life.

However, several people, both the traditional and the Shariʿa-minded, felt that the *jinn* used to live in the days of the Prophet but are no longer with us. One man who does not consider himself to be religious said that God chained the *jinn* so that they can no longer control people's lives. An elderly woman who only recently made the *hajj* told me she does not believe in the *jinn* but that when her father was a young man, he was walking one day in a forest in the Bekaa and came across a goat. He tried to kill it, but he couldn't; it just vanished. But she doesn't believe such things.

For those who believe that the *jinn* are still among us, these spirits are quite terrifying. "They are black and hairy and come upon us suddenly," exclaimed Najwa, from Bint Jubeil, shaking herself as though shaking off the spirits. The other woman in the room at the time kept repeating *"Bismallahi Rahmani Rahiim"* over and over again but was only half glad when this exciting topic came to an end.

While having coffee with a few young women one day, I mentioned that I would like to meet someone who has contact with the *jinn*. "No, don't do it, Linda," one of them warned. "Something terrible will happen to you." Then the stories flowed of children being kidnapped by *jinn* who live in cemeteries, of *jinn* removing a man's appendix at night, of goats that transform themselves into women before one's very eyes . . . *Bismallah!*

The Evil Eye

Ibn Khaldun writes: "Another psychic influence is that of the eye—that is, an influence exercised by the soul of the person who has the evil eye. A thing or situation appears pleasing to the eye of a person, and he likes it very much. This creates in him envy and the desire to take it away from its owner. Therefore, he prefers to destroy him."[22]

When Mariam's mother lost one of her babies, it was because of the evil eye of a jealous woman. There is nothing one can do about the person with the evil eye. He or she does not harm intentionally, as would a sorcerer. One can take precautions against such harm, however, and precautions appear to abound among this community, particularly in protecting newborns from the evil eye of another.

When a baby is born, friends and neighbors are expected to visit. The guests are served *einar*, a pudding made with nuts and cinnamon which is actually considered to have healthful benefits for the mother. Sometime during the visit, the guest invariably smuggles some money into the infant's clothing or blankets as a gift. In case any of these visitors should have the evil eye, the baby is equipped with a piece of protective jewelry bearing a robin's-egg blue bead. Such items, which can be found even in grocery stores, are affixed to the inner side of the baby's shirt. Sometimes a minuscule Koran will also be attached. It does not matter whether the person is traditional or Shari'a-minded in religious viewpoint; the amulet appears in any case. In Lebanon, the fear of the evil eye was deeply embedded in the culture and reinforced by both religious writing and a traditionally high infant mortality rate. Brian Spooner found that the fear of the evil eye is greater among peasants (such as the Lebanese) than among nomads. Peasants are very concerned with guarding their privacy and feel a need to put up a protective wall against outsiders, whom they consider threatening. Nomads, on the other hand, have no private life, and "the stranger-guest is an integral feature of the life of the community."[23]

The parents of a child are not the only ones who can take precautions. The admirer of the baby can also do so. He or she should always accompany any words of admiration with the exclamation *"Smullah!"* (colloquial for "In the name of God!"), thereby invoking God's protection for the child.

Amulets and invocations aside, I observed no obsession with protecting the child from supernatural forces. All the mothers I knew readily took their children to the doctor, and, if a child were ill, none of them spoke about the *jinn* or the evil eye having caused the illness. These babies and older children had colds and flu and ear infections just like their American counterparts. While blue beads and miniature Korans might continue to be used and their efficacy believed in, they seem, at least in many cases, to have taken on the role of religious symbols and not simply superstitious objects. In fact, they seem very much akin to statues of the Virgin Mary which can either contain supernatural powers or remind people of their deep devotion and reverence for the "Mother of God."

In Detroit ... one Polish woman attributed the death of a friend's child, obviously a victim of infantile paralysis, to a malady she described as "tangled hair." "Tangled hair" resulted from bewitchment countered by clipping the matted hairs off and placing them beneath the sufferer's pillow. Bewitchment, Poles believed, was carried out by the power of the 'evil eye' possessed by magicians, witches, persons considered malevolent, and sometimes even by animals. . . . A belief in magic gave immigrant Poles a resource for explaining—and thereby coming to psychological terms with—the stresses and losses they daily found in an often hostile alien world they could not control.[24]

Priests and nuns have not tried to obliterate folk religious beliefs but rather have generally sought to reinforce the use of substances and objects that have an institutional basis such as holy water, medals, holy cards, rosary beads, and the like.

While French Canadians in Quebec still go to shrines seeking cures for a variety of maladies, Polish-American Catholics no longer attribute children's deaths to bewitchment. Belief in supernatural intervention in human lives rarely vanishes entirely among people. In urban settings such as Detroit, beliefs associated with agrarian life tend either to fade or to take on a new meaning and be sustained in a fashion that does not seem so contrary to sophisticated urban culture. For example, the use of medals among Catholics does not necessarily mean that they are expecting miracles. Rather, they are a sign of Catholic identity and a desire to feel close to the saint whose image is engraved on the medal. Occasionally, relics or images that have been used in a more "orthodox" fashion might revert to their more magical uses. A case in point would be the apparitions and miracles associated with a statue of the Virgin Mary in a northern New Jersey town during 1993. Frequently, such extraordinary occurrences can be linked to problems existing in the community. One problem might be tensions between the clerical hierarchy and the laypeople. In the case of French Canadians who visit shrines in remote regions of Quebec, we find that there has been a shortage of high-quality modern health care. Perhaps if modern health-care facilities were available to the people, there would be a diminished belief in the curative powers associated with shrines. A variety of societal factors affect what types of beliefs will be sustained, how strong these beliefs will remain, and what meaning will be given to them.

As mentioned above, the Shiʿa are already showing some shift in the meaning they give traditional beliefs. The proliferation of scholarly sheikhs in the community and the ascendancy of the Shariʿa-minded in Dearborn will affect the emphasis placed on the supernatural. Those striving to live by the Shariʿa do not see, for example, the *jinn* as important in their daily struggle to lead an Islamic life. College education, which is being pursued by many, seems already to be dampening traditional views of supernatural forces. A very traditional woman with a college-educated daughter regaled me with vivid stories about encounters with the *jinn*. But when she finished, she added that she was quite certain that there were no *jinn* in America. "They just live in Lebanon," she told me.

Women and the Family

On a typical summer Sunday afternoon in East Dearborn, the streets, normally full of the sounds of children, are remarkably quiet. The houses are closed up, and the cars are gone from streets and driveways. This is the day for the family picnic.

There are fine parks with outdoor swimming pools in East Dearborn, but that is not where the Lebanese neighbors are to be found. They are far more likely to be on the "non-Arab" west side of town, at a park not any more pleasant than the ones on the east side but with a far larger swimming pool than any of the others in town.

There are remarkably few non-Arabs in this park on Sundays. Sunday has become the day for the Lebanese.

The smell of shish kebab and garlic-marinated chicken fills the air as women in all manner of dress, from full *hijab* to village dress to blue jeans, cluster at tables, visiting back and forth from one group to the next. "The group," though, is the family. Parents, children, cousins, aunts and uncles, grandparents—they are all there.

As Laurel Wigle found in her study of the south end of Dearborn, kinship, which in the Lebanese case is extended out through entire villages with endogamous marriages, has shown no obvious signs of weakening.[25] The cousin marriages in Dearborn are not necessarily through the patrilineage; a mother's sibling's child appears to suffice.[26] With so many complex interrelationships resulting from these marriage patterns, anyone who is not related is considered an outsider; the word often used is *stranger*. The result is that one has an extremely large circle of relatives with whom to socialize and on whom to rely.

Along with sex, alcohol, and drugs, family breakdown is another evil that this community wants to guard itself against. Ali H., a twenty-year-old college student who also works at a gas station to help pay family expenses, has expressed to me repeatedly that he finds the family situation among Americans to be appalling. "Nobody cares about anyone here," he said. He looks forward to marrying a relative from his village in the Bekaa. These endogamous marriages, of course, strengthen the bond between religion and family.

When Wigle conducted her study in the south end looking at, among other things, the relationship between marriage and religion, she did not distinguish among Yemenis, Palestinians, and Lebanese. She saw the Sunni/Shiʿa division as inconsequential because people told her that they did not differentiate between the two sects for purposes of marriage. I contend that they told her this so as to put on "a good face" for the outsider. Barbara Aswad also found that half of the Lebanese women she interviewed said they would permit a child to marry into another Islamic sect,[27] but in actuality there are very few Shiʿi/Sunni marriages in this community. Four of the cases I know of involve Shiʿi men with Sunni wives; in only one is the wife a Shiʿa married to a Sunni. In one case, the wife has conceded and now calls herself a Shiʿa. In another case, there is continual bantering between the couple, with the husband, who is an ardent admirer of the imams ʿAli and Husayn, teasing his wife that she belongs to "that filthy sect." In a third case where the woman is a Sunni, the family at large has difficulties contending with her, and

WITHOUT FORGETTING THE IMAM / 176

when they discuss her, they remind their listeners that she is a Sunni. In a fourth case, the Shi'i identity of the man and his family is not strong, and there appears to be no tension over the matter of religion. The situation of the Shi'i woman married to a Sunni man appears to be fairly harmonious.

There is no ban per se on the Shi'i/Sunni marriage, but when the preference is for cousin marriages, this is only going to reinforce the notion that religion, specifically Shi'ism, and family are inseparable.

Husbands, Wives, and Shi'ism

Shireen Mahdavi gives an excellent account of the development of Shi'ism and its direct effect on women, particularly as related to the development of the role of the *ulama* and the concept of *ijtihad*, the process by which the learned men come to understand the meaning of religious dogma. She cites three of the *ulama* or *mujtahids* who are involved with interpreting the position of women in Iran: Tabataba'i Nuri, and Motahheri.

Although these three *mujtahids* reside in Iran, the country about which Mahdavi is writing, this discussion is very relevant to the study of the Dearborn community. The writings of these three men can be found at the local mosques and bookstores, and Motahheri's writings have even been translated into English. The opinion of all three *mujtahids* is the same: the psychological and physical differences between men and women make it imperative that men should have control over the lives of women. Only men can initiate divorce, and only men can have multiple spouses. All three of these learned men are emphatic that a woman's body should be completely covered, leaving only the face and hands exposed. All three assume that "man's sexuality in the face of temptation is uncontrollable,"[28] which justifies their position in favor of *mut'a*.

According to the *ulama*, the Shi'i ideal is that of a wife who is totally obedient to her husband, who accepts his contracting other wives, whether permanent or temporary, and who has no legal recourse to divorce if she is unhappy with the marriage for any reason. In Khu'i's words: "A wife must not leave her house without the permission of her husband whenever her absence might prevent her husband from taking his pleasure in her—or anytime, as a precaution. If she leaves without his permission, she is recalcitrant. She is not prohibited from doing other things without the permission of her husband, so long as these do not prevent her husband from taking his pleasure in her."[29] And: "The husband is obliged to supply his permanent wife with maintenance, including food, clothing, shelter, bedclothes, curtains, instruments for cleaning, and everything else that is required in his state of life, so long as she lives with him."[30]

We will now look at how well the Lebanese live up to this ideal.

Scarves, Veils, and Other Bones of Contention

"Wearing *hijab* is the 'first thing' for women in Islam. It makes you feel spiritual." The muezzin was calling the faithful to prayer at the Majma'as Neifa, a middle-aged woman, said this. She added, "It makes you feel spiritual, the way the prayer call does." She has worn the scarf for ten years and decided to do so because she knew she had to "choose between paradise and hell." She lived in the United States at the time of her decision to don the *hijab*. I told her that I knew many Lebanese women who loved their religion but did not wear the *hijab*. She told me that sooner or later, they would decide on their own to wear it. She said that it is in the Koran that women must veil themselves and that in the days of the Prophet, all Muslim women wore the *hijab*. *Hijab*, she said, is for the protection of women so that men do not look covetously at them. She thinks that much of the rape in this society has to do with women going around with their bodies exposed. Men cannot bear the temptation.

Until the Iranian Revolution of 1979, the trend in the Levant was to abandon all types of veiling. The removal of the veil was considered a good indicator of women's emancipation, a sign of modernization.[31] However, even in areas where modernization had not deeply penetrated the society, the Lebanese had only a limited form of veiling. Emrys Peters describes peasant women in South Lebanon in the 1970s as being comparatively independent. Male/female division of labor was not strict, and women played a productive role in the economy. They also inherited property and received a bride wealth settlement upon marriage. They covered their faces only in the presence of men who were strangers. Peters's description of these women suggests that economic factors were of paramount importance in defining a woman's place in society, as well as her attire.[32]

But since the revolution, there has been a trend throughout the Middle East toward defining women's role in religious terms so that the matter of dress would be more influenced by dogma than by occupation. Also, there is a pervasive desire to disassociate "modernization" and "Westernization." It is significant that the most orthodox people I have met refer to themselves as "modern" Muslims. For these women, the veil is, as Anne Betteridge states when referring to Iranian women on the eve of the revolution, "an indication of spiritual independence and self-worth."[33]

There is a general consensus in this community that women should be modest and that this includes wearing a head covering. However, disagreement arises over what kind of covering and at what age a woman needs to begin to cover.

The kind of covering a woman wears says as much about her as not wearing a scarf at all. Someone who is conscientiously trying to follow a marja° will dress so that only her face and hands, below the wrist, are showing. Her ankles may show, but essentially nothing else. So women who are Shari°a-minded will dress like this. They are then considered to be wearing hijab. But there are the politically Shari°a-minded and the nonpolitical sorts, and there are subtle and not-so-subtle ways of making distinctions among themselves.

At least some members of the community believe that a woman is showing her affiliation with Hizb Allah by wearing her scarf, which is very large so that the end is fastened with a pin near the left ear. A friend's cousin wore her scarf that way to a doctor's office once, and the doctor asked her if she had joined Hizb Allah. The woman had not, and after this she quickly changed her style of wearing her scarf. In addition, though, women who are identified with Hizb Allah will also wear long, loose-fitting "coats" over their clothes, which are worn anytime they set foot outside the house. These are generally made of light fabric which easily blow in the wind. They can be particularly cumbersome when a woman tries to play tennis or badminton in them, which I have seen on occasion.

There are women who are Amal supporters who also fasten their scarves on the left side. However, these women do not wear the coatlike covering but rather simply very modest dress. It is more difficult to ascertain by appearance whether one is an Amal supporter or not. Attending what amounted to an Amal rally at the Jami° one evening, I found a wide variety of costumes. In fact, two or three women I had previously associated with Hizb Allah turned out to be Amal supporters. Their dress was ambiguous enough that I could not tell what kind of statement they were making.

I am not the only one who suffers from this confusion. Zahra D.'s sisters-in-law wear their scarves pinned on the side along with long, very modest dresses. Another Lebanese woman approached one of these sisters-in-law one day when Zahra D. was with her. The woman asked, "Do you wear your hijab for Hizb Allah or Amal?" Zahra angrily blurted out, "She wears it for God."

On the other hand, there are Amal supporters who do not normally wear the scarf. There is wide variation on religious matters in
this organization.

Another way of wearing one's scarf to announce one's adherence to the laws of Islam is to wear it balaclava-style, like the
medieval knights wore under their helmets and armor.

For those who want to make it very clear that Khomeini is
their leader, both religiously and politically, there is the *chador* (Iranian) or the *'abaya* (Iraqi). Within the short span of a year, there have
appeared in Dearborn an increasing number of these black shrouds,
which have been worn over the centuries in places such as Iran and
Afghanistan but not in Lebanon. Normally, with the *chador*, only
the eyes, nose, and mouth show, but occasionally one will find a
woman who chooses to reveal only her eyes. The wives of two of the
sheikhs wear the *chador*, one obviously more willingly than the
other. They are apparently serving as role models for a growing
number of women.

The traditional way of covering one's hair in Lebanon was simply to wear a scarf babushka-style, tied under the chin. These scarves
are not as large as their modern equivalents and may or may not
cover all the hair. If even the slightest bit of hair is exposed, this will
be sufficient evidence that a woman is not truly Shari'a-minded and
is probably apolitical. (There is a way of pleating one's scarf to ensure
that not a bit of hair ever shows.) A majority of middle-aged women
can be seen wearing babushka-type scarves at least part of the time.

The younger women who hold traditional religious attitudes
feel that there is plenty of time to wear the scarf in one's lifetime.
They prefer to wait until they are plump and gray and not so attractive before covering their hair. The irony, of course, is that the scarf
is supposed to prevent men from being sexually stimulated by a
woman's beauty, but these women don't want to wear the scarf
until they are less likely to be sexually stimulating.

There is a way for younger women to wear a scarf without
looking dowdy or political. They can tie it at the nape of the neck,
gypsy-style, still revealing a great deal of hair. Aware that they still
look very attractive, they can also claim to be fulfilling their religious duty. But, interestingly, not many women opt for this solution, presumably because it is associated with a "peasant" look.
They prefer either to go bare-headed until their beauty forsakes
them or to wear *hijab*.

What does the scarf mean then?

For the young women who wear the full *hijab*, many of whom
are indeed very attractive underneath the layers of cloth, the *hijab*

does succeed largely in hiding their charms. (Even among these, I have found a few women who still can manage to look glamorous while completely following the rules.)

Only about 20 to 25 percent of school-aged girls, at the elementary and high school level, cover their hair, usually in a complete fashion. These girls, and their families, are projecting the message that they are sexually off limits. (It should be noted, however, that some young girls wear their scarves as they walk to school but remove them when they enter the classroom. They complain that the Arab boys pull off their scarves—much like non-Arab girls in America have traditionally had their braids pulled—in school. But the question arises, of course, of whether this is just an excuse for ridding oneself of the unfashionable and annoying garment.)

A great many women are wearing the scarf who cannot possibly view themselves as sexual temptations. Hajja Sharifi, the mother of several adult children, is an example. Gray, wrinkled, and extremely stout, she will allow no man to see her when she is not wearing her white gossamer scarf. Once, she and I were visiting with her nieces in one of their homes. When the niece's husband started to enter the apartment, Hajja Sharifi called to him to wait, while she properly adorned herself. Yet none of the other women did so, in spite of the fact that they were the ones who were young and pretty.

My conclusion is that the scarf in this community has very little to do with men and their sexual urges. A woman wears a scarf as a statement. A woman who wears the full *hijab* is announcing her total commitment either to following the Shari'a or to following a political movement. For an elderly *hajja,* such as Sharifi, it is an announcement that she has undergone an important rite of passage and should be treated with great deference.

Anthropologists studying the Middle East have found that a woman who has borne children and is more advanced in years has far more power than a young woman.[34] Wrinkles and matronliness have a definite advantage among Middle Eastern women. In this community, at least, the scarf only serves to enhance a woman's position as it shows that she has religion behind her.

Modesty in America

Mona from Bint Jubeil wore the *hijab* when she came to America but found it inconvenient here. (She also claims she found it dangerous during the hostage crisis because of anti-Middle Eastern sentiment.) Saroya, from the same village, did not wear the scarf upon arrival here, nor for some years later, but she finally decided to. A serious illness had made her see her mortality.

Wafa had never worn a scarf either in Beirut or in Tibnin where her family originated. When she came to America, the Iranian Revolution was under way, and she decided to put on the scarf. That lasted about two weeks. She has not worn it outside a mosque since. The scarf does not fit with her business and her relatively extravagant lifestyle.

Iman's mother, back in southern Lebanon, wore the scarf. When Iman decided to start to wear one while living in Dearborn, she chose to follow the *mujtahids'* injunction about covering all but the oval of her face. America's free-wheeling style chastened her.

Nisrene from Nabatiyeh has worn the scarf, *hijab*-style, since her teens (a bit late for this village, so she incurred some criticism). Since living in Dearborn, she has not changed her style of dressing.

The above examples reflect how divergent are opinions about the scarf. They also suggest that there are no real answers to the question of whether life in America is going to encourage or discourage the use of the scarf. Economic and occupational circumstances, education (of both a secular and a religious nature), political views, and individual personality are going to influence a woman's decision whether or not to veil.

Of course, the issue of veiling pertains to minor daughters as well as to adult women. The ambivalence families feel about this issue is striking. Some Shari‘a-minded families seem to have come to terms with the problem fairly easily. The daughter's identity may be so strongly Islamic that she herself wishes to wear the *hijab*. But most families have not resolved the issue as amicably as that. After all, they realize, their children do attend American schools, and veiling is not an American custom. They see that their children are going to be more affected by American values, and they realize they must make some adjustments. But the question of how much to compromise is a constant preoccupation. There does appear to be unanimous agreement among this population that America's greatest failing is in the area of moral values relating to sex, drugs, and alcohol. Dressing modestly, whether with or without the scarf, is still going to be considered of paramount importance if one is to protect oneself against the onslaught of American sexual freedom.

The case with Sarah's family exemplifies this concern. One day I took the sixteen-year-old Sarah shopping. We picked out an oversized top and a skirt that reached just to the middle of her knee. She had tried on several pairs of slacks, but I could see that she definitely wanted the skirt, so we bought it. Still, she had reservations. Her mother does not wear the scarf and in some ways shows unusual openness to American life and has never required Sarah to wear the scarf, so I did not expect that the length of this skirt, which was not so very short, would matter. When we arrived home, she had to model her clothes. The top was fine, but there was much tittering from her mother and brothers about the skirt. Sarah's father would have to give the final verdict when he came home from work. I saw the top on Sarah several times, but the skirt only once, several months after the shopping trip. Nothing more was ever said about it. While Sarah never openly rebels, she does have her quiet struggles for greater freedom.

Men's Views on the Scarf

Thus far, I have focused only on women's attitudes toward the scarf. Yet the injunction that women should wear scarves originated with men. Furthermore, according to religious law, women are supposed to be obedient to their husbands. In a patrilineal society such as is found in Lebanon, it is also expected that all females are under the jurisdiction of their male kinsmen, particularly their fathers and brothers and, when married, their husbands. It should follow that it is actually the men of the household who are deciding whether or not their womenfolk need to wear the scarf.

My findings do not corroborate this assumption at all. The debonair Dr. B. told me that a woman should cover her hair and every part of her body that is pretty so that she will not be considered a sex object. Dr. B.'s wife wears no scarf at all, nor do the women in his office, nor do his numerous female cousins whom I know. His sister wears the ʿabaya, but that is because she is married to a sheikh.

Mustafa's wife was very surprised to hear that her rather nonreligious husband had a favorable view toward the scarf and believed that eventually his wife would decide to wear it. But it is her decision, he said.

Deeb's bare-headed wife was also surprised on hearing her husband's views. He feels that women who are out in the work world should cover themselves completely. He stated that women's immodesty causes a great deal of trouble. "Men cannot work properly," he said. "And there are a lot of unwanted pregnancies because women don't dress properly." His wife laughed at him when he said this.

When Saroya decided to wear the scarf, her husband was furious and threatened to divorce her. He was concerned that she would appear to be influenced by politics. She compromised by tying the scarf at the nape of her neck, still covering almost all of her hair. That way, everyone would know she was wearing it only for religious reasons.

Diab wants his wife to wear the scarf and told me a man can divorce his wife if she disobeys him in this matter. "Wearing the *hijab* is the first thing in religion," he said with great feeling. He told me this several months after his wife stopped wearing the scarf. She has not returned to wearing it yet. She became pregnant soon after he expressed this opinion, and he has not initiated a divorce.

The cases presented here clearly show that typically in this community, the decision to wear the scarf is the woman's decision. Some women stated that they did not think their husbands had any influence on their decision about wearing the scarf. Nor did the women think that the men had any right to influence them. Um Zuheir put it best when she said wryly, "My husband doesn't worry about my scarf."

The majority of men agreed that the decision to wear the scarf lay with the woman. When both husband and wife are Shariʿa-minded, there is no question of whether or not a woman should cover herself, but exactly the way she does so appears to be hers to decide. Even elementary and high-school-aged girls appeared to be given a fair amount of leeway. My observation was substantiated by a Lebanese school counselor. It would be interesting to pursue this line of research.[35]

Men's World / Women's House

While the Lebanese who have come to the Dearborn area have been adjusting to the idea that there are educational opportunities for their daughters as well as for their sons, they are still ambivalent about the idea of a woman working outside the home after she is married. Barbara Aswad, in comparing Yemeni and Lebanese women in Dearborn, found that the latter do think it is permissible for their daughters to hold some types of jobs, and they are far more open to even married women working than are Yemeni women.[36] Some of the more respectable occupations for women include working in family stores, teaching, pharmacology, and medical or dental technology.

Even with a more liberal attitude toward women's education and occupation, there remains the desire to marry off daughters at a young age (for the sake of virginity), and therefore women's careers have not become a major issue here. I suspect, though, that it may become a major issue soon. During an art class for fourth and fifth graders at my sons' school, the children were asked to make cut-out drawings of themselves dressed in their "future career clothes." I am told that an overwhelming number of young Lebanese girls pictured themselves as doctors and nurses.

Amina is a university student studying English literature. She is a serious student who would like to have a career, though she also expects to marry. She realizes that the traditional Lebanese woman's role would be difficult for her to follow. When she was in her mid-teens, young men and their parents came to her father's home, where she still lives, and made marriage proposals, something that is common in this community. She turned down these proposals. Sarah, who endured her family's disapproval of her short skirt, also has rejected suitors in order to pursue college studies. Her mother expressed both pride and misgivings about her daughter's decision. The fact that the mother had come to terms with it was surprising in view of the fact that her elder daughter had married at the age of seventeen. Both Amina and Sarah come from the same village in the Bekaa and have parents with very little education. Yet these parents have accepted—to some degree, at least—their daughters' ambitions. These cases notwithstanding, there is still great ambivalence in this community over the issue of higher education versus early marriage for girls.

Layla is seventeen and expecting her first child. At the age of fourteen, she returned to her village of Bint Jubeil to become engaged to her cousin who was also living in the United States. She completed only two years of high school but expresses no regret. Her neighbor, Zeynab from the Bekaa, was also engaged while in high school. She did graduate, but now that she has been married for a few years, she expresses regret that she did not have more schooling. Her husband resists the idea of her taking any college courses or working outside the home at all. Her job is to stay home and take care of their child and the house.

I attended a huge wedding of a teenage girl, not yet out of high school. Radiant with excitement on her wedding day, she expressed no hesitation about her marriage. As I sat at the table at the party, a friend from Bint Jubeil, who was married at the age of thirteen herself, pointed out other women who had been teenage brides. There were many. Since it is illegal to be married in the state of Michigan before the age of sixteen, those who do not wish to wait simply go to another state that permits marriage at an earlier age.

While it is interesting to know that girls continue to marry at a young age, it is more interesting for this study to discuss what they are doing after they marry.

By and large, they are cleaning their houses. They are mopping walls and floors, washing windows, disinfecting their bathrooms, and scrubbing their kitchens. Frequently, they have two kitchens, one upstairs for show and one in the basement where they actually cook, although this one is also cleaned avidly. In fact, the main floor of most houses is just for receiving guests. The refinished basement is where the family tends to spend its time. There is never any mess or clutter. The women have total intolerance for the slightest disarray, let alone dirt.

Of course, the question arises of whether this passion for cleanliness has anything to do with religion. I believe it does. Or, to be more precise, I believe the Lebanese Shiʿa believe it does. A second-generation Lebanese, giving a sermon at the Jamiʿ one day, commented that "Islam is the cleanest religion." Islam very much in this case means Shiʿism and its purity code. Mazzaoui's comment that Arab Shiʿism takes an exoteric form as opposed to the esoteric Iranian Shiʿism is pertinent here. I believe the Lebanese are interpreting the purity code in such a way that it leads them to an almost compulsive attitude toward cleanliness, which would be consistent with their practical, nonmystical approach to religion.

Women do not spend hours a day cleaning their houses because their husbands come home from work to inspect them. Anyone watching a Lebanese woman doing housecleaning knows that she does it from her own heart. No one has to tell her. However, her husband does share her values on cleanliness. When a house is purchased by a Lebanese man, he immediately repaints it and often sets about gutting it, removing the drywall, carpets, tile, bathroom fixtures, and so on. Everything should be new and clean. People who have just purchased a used home invariably tell me that it was "filthy" when they bought it. How much this is a reaction to living in a house owned previously by unbelievers I cannot say, but the zealousness with which the house is stripped does suggest that fear of impurity is at least partially the cause.

One could argue that this obsession with cleanliness is Lebanese rather than specifically Shiʿi Lebanese or that it is common to all Shiʿa, regardless of nationality. As for the latter theory, to my knowledge no one has ever commented on the Iranian Shiʿa's overcommitment to cleanliness, and in my time spent with Iranians I never observed anything comparable to the Lebanese attitude. (This is not to say that Iranians are dirty, simply that there is more variation in household cleanliness standards than is found among the Lebanese Shiʿa.) As for it being a generalized Lebanese trait, Judith Williams offers some indirect evidence that it is not. In her study of

Haouch el Harimi, a Sunni village in the Bekaa, she presents a striking contrast to the Shi‘i community in her description of toilet training: "The child's training toward cleanliness proceeds rather casually. Most of the time the child's bottom is left free and women seem unperturbed if he soils in their lap or about the house."[37] She cites other research in Sunni villages to suggest that this approach to toilet training is widespread.

I observed no such casualness in Dearborn. Soiling a carpet or a mother's skirt would never be met with serenity. The woman who is "lazy" about toilet training faces criticism from family and friends. By the time a child is eighteen months old, diapers should be a thing of the past. American theories that a child should not be toilet trained until he or she is ready are greeted with contempt. This is just another indicator of American slovenliness. This attitude toward toilet training is in keeping with every other aspect of the Lebanese Shi‘a's life. Comments they make on a daily basis indicate that cleanliness and religion are linked in their minds.

Mut‘a

When I discussed the role of the *marji‘ taqlid* in the community, I introduced the topic of *mut‘a*, translated as "temporary" or, more correctly, "pleasure" marriage. I cited the "official" definitions of this type of marriage and some of its requirements and restrictions. Throughout the centuries, the topic of temporary marriage has been debated, largely because the Sunnis reject it. The second caliph, Omar, who is almost universally hated by the Shi‘a as the great usurper of the Imam ‘Ali's position, abolished the practice, although it appears that it was permissible in the time of the Prophet. The imams, those descendants of the Prophet's daughter, Fatima, and her husband, ‘Ali, who became the religious leaders of the Shi‘i community until the occultation of the Twelfth Imam in the ninth century, have elucidated on this subject. The belief that *mut‘a* is acceptable, and actually something religiously encouraged, is part of Shi‘i dogma. Shahla Haeri offers an account of the practice of *mut‘a* in the shrine cities of Iraq and Iran and explains the rationale behind the practice: "*Mut‘a* marriage is an institution in which the relationships between the sexes, marriage, sexuality, morality, religious rules, secular laws, and cultural practices converge. At the same time it is the kind of custom that puts religion and popular culture at odds. Whereas religiously there is no restriction for virgin women to contract a temporary marriage, popular culture demands that a woman be a virgin for her first permanent marriage."[38] It is this tension between religion and popular culture that is of greatest interest to me.

I have not elected to focus on *mut'a* because it is a practice that is rampant in this community. Rather, I have done so because people's reactions to this institution reveal so much about their attitudes toward religion and toward women.

Soon after I arrived in Dearborn, I occasionally heard rumors that *mut'a* was being encouraged by the sheikhs. To be more specific, young men in public places were discussing the matter in terms that suggested that the sheikhs were saying that a young man could have an affair with an American woman as long as he formed a contract with the woman making her a *mut'i*.

More than a year elapsed before I was actually to encounter people who claimed to have formed a *mut'a* marriage. The first was a middle-aged woman who had just fled her husband, leaving behind her older children. She claimed to be homeless, and through neighbors I became involved in her problems. When the issue of legal assistance came up, she said that she was actually divorced from the man she had just fled. However, some time after the divorce, she had returned to him as a *mut'i* and had lived with him ever since. Various members of this family, which has become notorious in the community, have had problems with the law and have actually been imprisoned, mostly for drug dealing. My impression is that this woman simply returned to her former husband and now refers to their relationship as *mut'a* to preserve some sense of dignity before her God-fearing neighbors. It is highly doubtful that any contract was ever involved.

The second case was that of a young man, Mahmoud S., who, as he told me quite bluntly, simply desired a sexual relationship that was religiously sanctioned. He said it was futile in his circumstances to hope that a Lebanese girl would marry him because he was a student and had no job yet. He began to approach American women to ask them if they would agree to a *mut'a* marriage. He reported that all of them laughed at him except one. This woman, a divorcee, married him temporarily. She eventually converted, at least nominally, to Islam, and they have since married in the presence of a sheikh with the purpose of forming a permanent union. I have been told that it is not uncommon for temporary unions to end up as permanent marriages.

In 1989, Sheikh Berri wrote a small book entitled *Temporary Marriage in Islam*, which was published locally. The fact that he would take the time and effort to write such a tract indicated that there must be a fair amount of concern regarding this issue, at least in some circles.

As time passed, I began to realize that aside from attitudes toward religion, the issue of temporary marriage would also help to illuminate this community's attitudes toward women and marriage. While initially I feared that people would not be forthcoming, I found to the contrary that there were many who were willing to expound on the subject and to share their personal views (that is, after they recovered from the initial shock that I knew about the practice).

Sheikh Berri's Text on *Mut'a*

Sheikh Berri formulates his treatise in a conventional style used in Shi'ism. (Unfortunately, the translation of Berri's text does not do justice to his facility with language. He is known for his excellent Arabic, and, though he has become quite facile with English in a short period of time, he apparently did not feel qualified to write in English.) This small book is based on questions he has received regarding the topic. The answers are framed in response to the concerns of one young man who says that "in his heart [he feels] it [temporary marriage] is an immoral act." The young man goes on to say that he would not accept *mut'a* for his sisters and doesn't believe that the other *mu'minin* brothers (good Muslims) would do so, either.

Berri prefaces his comments with a scenario about a beautiful girl (one has a definite sense that she is American) who has seduced a believer and given him AIDS. In this way, he couches his argument in favor of *mut'a*, substantiated by the sayings of the early imams, in terms of it being a solution to the pressures of a highly sexualized environment.

Not surprisingly, the caliph Omar is condemned for having made *mut'a* illegal. Berri cites, as his first defense, proof from the Koran that it was permissible in the times of the Prophet. On the other hand, he still seeks logical justification for the practice in these modern times: "Isn't corruption to let the young men and women fall in the traps of adultery, weird sex, and homosexuality? Or is it maybe to seek God's protection, words and his laws of marriage and the organization of sexual relationship the corruption. Therefore temporary marriage is one of chastity and love, and a form of decency and conservativism and is not an indecency. Nor is it like the 'friendship' of boys and girls which was known before Islam, and is revived by the Western culture."[39]

He goes on to address the issue of a man allowing his sister to form a temporary marriage: "Is the standard that the brother accepts or rejects? Isn't it first the satisfaction of Almighty God's will and then the sister herself? Or maybe the religion of God should submit to the desires of the brother and his jealousy. Anyway some brothers do accept. Also, why would a brother in many cases allow himself to do things he prevents his sister from doing? Doesn't he do that to protect 'himself' from social shame? And that 'shame' is not it a fake and an improper one? And did it not originate from 'tradition' not the right sensing? If not, why then would he do things that he does not allow her to do?"[40]

While one should not forbid *mut'a* for virgins on general principles, Sheikh Berri does not condemn the father who will not permit his virgin daughter to form a *mut'a* marriage, as long as permission is denied on the grounds that he is safeguarding her well-being.

He continues, "Temporary marriage is seen as a way of avoiding sinfulness, especially during young maturity." It is also a means of protecting oneself from sexually transmitted disease, because a man is supposed to choose a "virtuous woman" as his *mut'i*. Berri dispels the idea that this type of union is purely for sex, saying instead that love can exist in a temporary union, as it can in a permanent one.

He also states that "temporary marriage is not encouraged when the continuous [marriage] is available."[41] Addressing the issue of how many temporary wives are allowed at one time, he cites sources saying that four is the limit (as it is in so-called continuous marriage) and other sources saying there is no limit.

A great deal is being said about this community in the above quotes from Berri's book.

In the first place, the young man inquiring about the practice has strong misgivings about it. Sheikh Berri does not have to inquire about his hesitations. The idea of *mut'a*, especially for a virgin, runs contrary to the value Lebanese culture places on virginity. Sheikh Berri claims that the Koran permits the practice, while Lebanese culture insists that it is forbidden. But Berri is a Lebanese himself and the father of daughters. He finds a loophole. The father can reject *mut'a* for his daughter on the grounds that it is personally not good for her. In doing this, he rejects the notion that culture is more powerful and important than religion while at the same time he protects the cultural norm of virginity for unmarried women. Furthermore, he reinforces the Islamic (and cultural) prerogatives given to the male head of the household.

It is indeed very striking that he should advocate a sister having the same rights as her brother in matters of sexuality (although he also indicates that the father has authority to forbid the union). It can be argued, of course, that he is simply giving the *mujtahids'* opinions on the matter. But Sheikh Berri has carefully selected what he has presented about *mut'a*. What he has given us is not a hodge-podge of quotes from the imams and the *mujtahids*. (Indeed, Khomeini and other ayatollahs are far more ardent in their encouragement of the practice than is Berri.) Rather, he is responding to issues of Lebanese culture and the problems he is having to deal with in the United States. By saying that a girl can elect to form a *mut'a*, he is giving a way out to the headstrong girl, who, defying her parents' authority, has a sexual relationship with a man outside marriage. Meanwhile, he is still protecting the rights of the father.

When I interviewed Maher, a man affiliated with the Majma' who has a close ear to the ground in the community, he said that while it is not recommended that a young girl form a *mut'a* marriage, he could see that in the case of a rebellious daughter who wanted to have a sexual relationship, *mut'a* could be a solution. By stating that the possibility exists for a girl to form a temporary union, Berri is thereby discouraging families from taking drastic measures against her. By drastic measures, I am referring to the possibility of killing her, something that was not unusual in Lebanon, especially in the Bekaa. In fact, in 1987 in Dearborn, a Shi'i man killed his teenage daughter on the grounds that she was having an affair with a man and destroying the honor of the family.

In this text, Berri is addressing young unmarried men who are not yet in a position to marry. He is attempting to discourage casual sex and is encouraging sex within religiously sanctioned parameters. When he addresses the issue of married men forming *mut'a* marriages, he cites traditions that discourage the practice for married men, though he could easily have found ones that do the opposite. He chooses to quote from the Imam Al-Rida, who is reported to have said, "but do not persist on pleasure marriage where it would keep you occupied from your continuous wives. Then they would reject the faith, complain, and then accuse us and curse us."[42]

Sheikh Berri has given us the legalistic view (albeit a relatively conservative one in comparison to that of other *'ulama*) of the practice of *mut'a*. The question now arises of how this view fits with that of the community.

Community Attitudes toward *Mut'a*

For elderly Hajja Sharifi, the worst thing a person can do is to commit stupid acts—things that are *haram* (forbidden)—stealing, drinking, becoming *mut'is*. Like Sharifi, young Ghalia is also from the Bekaa, and she also hates *mut'a*. "It should never be allowed," she said. Nisrene, from the religiously strict village of Nabatiyeh, doesn't like it, either: "If you want to get married, do it the ordinary way." From Bint Jubeil in southern Lebanon, Najwa, still in her teens but married with a baby, said that *mut'a* is *haram:* "only Hizb Allah have *mut'a*." In her home village in the Bekaa, Amina has heard that *mut'a* is now practiced and is causing a great deal of trouble in families. "It's all because of Hizb Allah," she said. "We never had *mut'a* there before." Elderly Um Zuheir, who recently made her pilgrimage to Mecca and who originates from Ba'albek and a Beirut suburb, says that *mut'a* is "against religion."

Samira dissents from this view. The "born again" young woman who spent her school years in America heartily approves of the practice. Wearing her gigantic scarf and flowing "coat," she lectured me on the virtues of *mut'a*, which she supports "100 percent." She went on, "It is a rule sent by God to man. We cannot forbid it because of this." I asked her for her personal opinion on the matter, but she said she could not give me one, that she must tell me only what is written in the books. "*Mut'a* is to protect society. It is for married men, but not married women, because man and woman are different. Man has a much stronger sex drive. A woman isn't always interested in sex like a man is. When a woman is pregnant or menstruating, she has to refuse her husband because it is *makruh* [undesirable but not prohibited] to have sex during these times, especially during menstruation. You can have a deformed child if you get pregnant during your period. So a man can get a *mut'a*. She cannot stop her husband from doing this. She should not ask him about it even."

There are others in this community who share Samira's religious and political views, but I have yet to hear such a forceful defense of *mut'a* from any other woman. The Shari'a-minded tend to pay lip service to the practice. And they all agreed that it was not for a virgin and that they did not see it as being for married men, either. Lila, also part of the earlier immigration and, like Samira, having opted for a strict interpretation of religion, tended to justify *mut'a* on the grounds that it was part of religious dogma. She realizes that her husband is entitled to have a *mut'a*, and they have discussed the subject. He apparently has no intention of getting one, which Lila admitted was good because she "would probably kill him" if he did. She also said that she saw it being abused by young single men, and she was not hesitant to chastise them for this.

It was almost unanimous that *mut'a* was not for virgins, but the dissenting view on this came from an interesting source. The one woman I interviewed who rejects religion for leftist ideology said that she saw *mut'a* as a good way to legitimize sex for unmarried women, though, she added, such a thing wouldn't be socially acceptable.

Selwa, a Shari'a-minded woman but one who is not political, claimed that she does not agree with *mut'a*. This raised the hackles of an Iraqi woman who asked, "How can you not agree with something your religion preaches? You might not like to practice it, but to say you don't agree with it is wrong." This is the "religiously correct" response for Lebanese women to use with the issue of *mut'a*, but apparently they have not learned it yet. Most of them reject the practice quite emphatically.

How do these responses fit with those of the men? Ali S., a young, married, college-educated man from the south, said, "Perhaps *mut'a* was a reasonable practice in the early days of Islam, but it has lost its purpose as far as I am concerned. It is no different from dating. Just because the name of God is said doesn't make it good."

Khalid, also from the south and with a college education but more religiously learned than Ali, replied initially, "It is legal prostitution." He then retracted this statement and admitted he was confused about the issue. "It is supposed to be a religious thing, and I guess I am leaning toward accepting it, but I don't quite see how a man can have more than one wife." He found it more acceptable for a single man than for a married man. But only a divorced or widowed woman could be a *mut'a*.

Ali H., a college student from the Bekaa, said that he disliked *mut'a*, which was something that only Hizb Allah did. Ashraf, a college graduate who grew up in the Beirut suburbs, could not find justification for *mut'a* but was being pressured by a relative sympathetic to Hizb Allah to form a *mut'a* marriage.

Muhammad T., who grew up in the United States and worked in a factory all his adult life, sees *mut'a* as a good idea, especially in view of the current conditions in America. "Every man can have a *mut'a*," he said, but quickly added that he has never had one. (His wife was in the other room at the time watching TV and seemed not to be listening. However, when he made this last comment, she looked toward me with a smile that said, "He knows what's good for him.")

But there are men who both approve of the practice and follow it. Muhammad F., a college student, is one of them. "It is a good solution for us because we are young students, and it is our only choice." This way, he said, they could have sex and not go against Islam. I asked Muhammad if it was possible to form *mut'a* marriages here with Lebanese girls. He said that a man could form a

temporary marriage with a free woman—someone divorced, widowed, or a virgin over eighteen, if, that is, she was living in the
United States. If she was in Lebanon, she was under her father's or
brother's guardianship, but not so here. He added that he rejected
the Lebanese cultural attitudes against virgins being *mut'is*.
Muhammad, young, serious-minded, and pro-Iranian, serves as a
model of the sort of person who will form a *mut'a* marriage in this
community. But he is not the only type.

Hassan, unmarried and a nightclub swinger on Saturday
nights, but in the Jami' on Sunday mornings, was, in some respects,
more liberal in his interpretation of *mut'a* than anyone else to whom
I spoke. Any man, whether married or not, according to Hassan, can
have a temporary marriage, though he should know the woman
first and not just walk up to her and make a proposition. The
woman should be divorced or widowed.

Hassan parts company with almost everyone else I interviewed. According to my findings, those who believe a married
man can form a *mut'a* relationship don't usually form them themselves. *Mut'a* remains for them a theoretical proposition, so to
speak. A few older men, and I noted that they were ones who had
spent long periods of time away from their wives at certain points in
their married lives, said that *mut'a* was a way for them to meet their
sexual needs while remaining within the law of Islam. Generally,
though, those who do form *mut'a* relationships are the unmarried
young men who do not see themselves as able to take on the responsibilities of marriage but are eager not to sin. However, as college
student Issa added, *mut'a* is not to be taken lightly. If the woman
becomes pregnant, it is up to the man to support the child.

Ali B.'s case was the most surprising. Around forty years of
age and the image of the Lebanese nightclub entertainer, he was
married with children to a Muslim woman. Having spent most of
his life in America before the new wave of immigrants arrived, he
had adjusted to American society more than most of the people in
the community I have known. I was startled to learn that he himself
had a *mut'a* wife. I ascertained from him that this woman was also
Muslim and Arab but not Lebanese. Furthermore, this union was
formed in the presence of a sheikh, and people were invited to the
occasion. However, the marriage was not legal under American
law. He told me that a man is entitled to as many as four wives if he
can treat them all equally. He assured me that he could treat his two
wives, one of whom he referred to as a *mut'a* wife, equally. Actually, I believe he has confused the two types of marriage, permanent
and temporary. On the other hand, by calling his second marriage

mut'a, he has found a way around the American law against polygamy.

While the views expressed here are admittedly diverse, there are some definite overriding themes. It is apparent that *mut'a* was not a burning issue in Lebanon before the Iranian Revolution. A number of the people I spoke to had only become aware of it recently and since they had been residing in the United States. It is certainly not viewed as a Lebanese tradition. The fact that Sharifi knew of the practice, as did the older woman who said she had returned to her divorced husband as a *mut'i,* suggests, though, that the idea is not completely foreign to the Lebanese. In fact, it was probably only practiced by sheikhs and women who somehow found themselves on the periphery of society, much as Haeri discovered in Iran. In Lebanon, though, far away from the shrine cities, it was presumably done on a much smaller scale.

The consensus of the community is that, at best, *mut'a* is a hard pill to swallow. Women I spoke to, both formally and informally, overwhelmingly tended to express their dislike for the practice, and I often heard the comment that it was against religion. Some Shari'a-minded women have brothers who have formed *mut'a* unions, and they are quick to justify their brothers' behavior, but they also mention the limitations imposed on the union. They want *mut'a* to be seen as a serious matter and something very different from American "boyfriend-girlfriend" relationships.

While more men tended to accept the practice as justifiable, there was still no overwhelming praise of it. Mr. S., a mechanic from the Bekaa, said that it was acceptable for a man to form a *mut'a* marriage if he were going to be away from his wife for a long period of time. However, he added that it was far preferable for him to be loyal to his wife.

Only those who had totally accepted Khomeini's view of religion would accept the idea of a virgin as a temporary wife, and not even all of them. Maher is a case in point. While he knew such a thing was religiously permissible, his Lebanese values kept him from truly accepting this idea.

That this is a monogamous community has come across very strongly in my research. While men expect loyalty from their wives, wives can and do make the same demands. Considering that this is a community whose religion teaches that the men can have up to four permanent wives and an unlimited number of temporary ones, the men certainly aren't taking advantage of their options. While it could be argued that American law would prohibit taking multiple wives, there are ways around this law (such as Ali B. used) if men are inclined to seek them. The Shi'i Lebanese, whether here or in Lebanon, have not viewed polygyny as the norm. It does occur in Lebanon, but it is definitely the exception rather than the rule.

Afaf, a pretty, bright, and spirited woman from the Bekaa, claimed that she would not like to live in Iran or Pakistan; she had heard that women were treated badly there. In those countries, "men can have more than one wife!" she said with disgust. Wafa told me that she would leave her husband immediately if he ever cheated on her "even once!"

It should also be noted that divorce is still greatly frowned upon among the Lebanese living in the Dearborn area. One of the great fears in this community is that divorce will become more prevalent as a result of influence from American society. I have discussed this matter with Sheikh Berri, who admits to spending a great deal of his time counseling troubled couples. He does see divorce on the rise and expresses concern for this problem. However, he has also done some research on divorce rates in America and finds that there is no comparison between those rates and the ones he finds among his flock. Sheikh Burro also expressed grave concerns that the Muslims in this community would begin to follow American patterns in matters of divorce, reminding me of the saying that divorce is "the worst of the things that are [religiously] permitted." Clearly, divorce will be discouraged actively by the clergy.

Berri's little book on the subject of *mut'a* has not become a best-seller in this community. Except for women such as Samira and her close acquaintances, the few women I have known who are curious about what is contained in the book are too embarrassed to go to the bookstore to purchase it. They fear that the shop owner will think they want to apply the practice themselves.

Whether or not people read the book or even know of its existence, there is obviously a growing awareness of the practice as well as a growing concern that young men will "misinterpret" the use of *mut'a*, that they will seduce Lebanese girls into forming temporary unions. Um Hamood, well educated in the teachings of Islam and very Shari'a-minded, scolded a young man who formed a *mut'a* marriage. She asked him if he would allow his sister to form such a union. She said "this shut him up." She conceded that it was acceptable to form a *mut'a* if one could not marry but added, "We really hate this practice." Though I have been led to believe that most of these *mut'a* marriages are with Americans, it is obvious from comments of Um Hamood and others that some Lebanese girls are involving themselves in these unions. Should the girls in this community see *mut'a* as a legitimate way to fulfill their sexual needs, this community could face extraordinary turmoil in the near future, which, I believe, would ultimately force the extinction of the practice in Dearborn.

Mosques and Women

One Sunday morning at the Jamiʿ, a dozen or so women, members of the women's auxiliary, were in the kitchen busily preparing a meal to be served after the conclusion of the sermons. At the same time, the woman in charge was arranging the food order for a children's picnic. While there may no longer be dancing and music at the mosques, the purely social occasions do remain an important part of mosque life. As with any church in America, the social functions would not exist without the women.

When I asked people about the differences between Islamic life here and back home, half of the women who had lived part of their lives in Lebanon told me that women were in the mosque much more frequently here than they had been in Lebanon. In fact, some women told me they had never set foot inside a mosque before they came to Dearborn. A group of women from the Bekaa recalled how they had occasionally congregated outside the mosque during holidays but rarely went inside. It had been a men's domain. In the 1970s, Prothro and Diab reported that "in the Levant generally women are not to be found at the daily prayers at the mosque, do not attend the Friday services, and are not even present in the mosque at funerals of close relatives."[43] In the Dearborn area, the situation is far different. Except for *salat*, women are as likely as men to attend affairs at all three mosques. Interestingly, men never volunteered that this was one of the differences. In cases where I specifically mentioned my observations about women in the mosques, they grudgingly admitted that these were correct.

Another difference noted was the issue of sexual segregation inside the mosques. In towns and villages where women did attend mosques on occasion, the two sexes were expected to be isolated from each other. A woman who has been attending the Jamiʿ since it first opened its doors said, "Over here, the women and men are together for ʿAshura. Back home, they were separate."

At the Majmaʿ, the men and women are still separate for ʿAshura, although for strictly social occasions that appeal to the general community, men and women do sit together.

There are other differences between the Majmaʿ and the Jamiʿ as well. A women's auxiliary does not exist at the Majmaʿ as it does at the Jamiʿ. This is not surprising because second- and third-gener-

ation American Shiʿa with exposure to American voluntary organizations are less likely to be found at the Majmaʿ than at the Jamiʿ.
Yet the absence of this organization does not appear to keep "the
sisters" from playing an important role. Rather than being in the
kitchen, they can be found in the meeting rooms. Women come and
go almost as freely as men to socialize and to study under the
sheikh or one of the more learned "brothers." A few are involved in
children's classes.

Not everyone at the Majmaʿ likes to concede that women are
spending more time there. The very Shariʿa-minded wanted to
make it clear that a woman's place was in the home, not in the
mosque. Yet one woman in *hijab*, an open advocate of Harakat
Amal, expressed great indignation upon seeing for the first time a
sign in a college cafeteria reading, "Please Bus Your Tray. Your
Mother Does Not Work Here." She resented the fact that women
were being portrayed as domestic servants and not as active members of society.

Whether or not they want to admit it, women are spending
considerable amounts of time at the Majmaʿ—and these are the
Shariʿa-minded. One man who admitted that women were at the
Majmaʿ more than they had been in the mosque in Lebanon said it
was because the women were bored at home. Living in Dearborn,
he argued, they did not have the same opportunities to visit in one
another's homes as they did back in the village. I must say I have
not noticed a lack of visiting in this community. But, whatever the
reason, women are present in the mosques, and this is bound to
have an effect on the religious life of the community.

"Religion is a woman's job." These words, uttered by an Ital-
ian-American Catholic woman, reflected the sentiments found in a
community where family, home life, and religion were closely
linked. In this ethnic community, it was the women who filled the
churches on Sunday morning, not the men.

While church attendance was more evenly balanced between
the genders in other ethnic communities, nineteenth-century immigrant Catholic women were seen as preservers of morals and
virtues. Between 1830 and 1920, "the importance of domesticity was
continually stressed throughout the culture, and woman was placed
upon a pedestal, enshrined as the moral guardian of the family."[44]
Later, women continued to be active, especially in the devotional
religion that took hold in the churches.

Yet they did not run the churches. Men, as the ones responsible for the public sphere of life, were vestry members and participants in regional and state conventions. Men were the parish trustees, and only men could vote for such trustees.

A visit to a Catholic church today shows how much the scene has changed. A man might stand beyond the communion rail and consecrate the Eucharist, but his role is very much diminished. Without the women of the parish, it is unlikely that the local churches would have remained such potent forces in the lives of Catholic Americans. Of course, Vatican II is partially responsible for these developments. More importantly, though, it seems that American Catholics were simply influenced by the same social forces that affected the Protestant churches in this country.

In her study of the role of women in religion in New England, Nancy Cott wrote that as early as the mid-seventeenth century, "while the church hierarchy remained distinctly male the majority of women in their congregations increased and ministers felt compelled to explain it."[45] By the nineteenth century, Protestantism had been feminized, and ministers took for granted that their congregations were largely comprised of women.

Women may have started out in Christian churches as simply a quiet majority, but they eventually became politically powerful. Again, quoting from Cott, "Women's prayer groups, charitable institutions, missionary and education societies, Sabbath School organizations, and moral reform and maternal associations all multiplied phenomenally after 1800, and all of these had religious motives."[46] Voluntary associations were as common among these early American women as they were among men, but the focus for women was always religious.

It is generally assumed that sexual segregation, at least for women, will have a deleterious effect on gaining formal power. But Cott says that sex-segregated prayer meetings served as "prototypes of religious organizations exclusively for women."[47] Cott offers various explanations for women's involvement in religion, but perhaps the most persuasive is that it allowed them the one arena of life where they could exercise their "full range of moral, intellectual, and physical powers."[48]

Cott's findings are indeed very relevant to this discussion. While currently the men in the mosques hold all the formal power, the fact that women are increasingly finding a place for themselves at the mosques is bound to upset the status quo. Not meek and retiring by nature—even the casual observer notices this—the Lebanese women in this community will, I believe, begin to assert themselves more and more in the running of the mosques, even though at the present time they seem to accept the power structure as it is. I do not see this change resulting from a Western-style "women's liberation" movement; rather, I see it evolving in the same manner as it did for Catholic and Protestant women and for the same reasons. Changes most likely will occur within the framework of Islam, only with an expanded interpretation of the role of women. Outside ideology probably will not play a role directly. The Lebanese women already wield considerable influence in their homes. The vast majority of Lebanese women jointly control the family finances and share decision making with their husbands.[49] Lebanese women do not need to look to American women as role models.

However, American approaches to organization will have, and already are having, an effect. For example, a few women, those of the earlier wave of immigration who have been educated in America, obviously do wield some power because of their intimate knowledge of American society and their administrative competence. From observing their behavior, it is obvious that they have an "insider's" role in the mosques.

In the summer of 1990, there was a dinner (catered by one of the local Lebanese restaurants) in honor of "the ladies," as they are always called, because they had raised ten thousand dollars for the Jami'. Several speakers, who were all male leaders of the mosque, praised the women for their efforts on behalf of the Islamic Center. Finally, the head of the women's auxiliary, a second-generation American, came to the podium and was presented with a plaque. In her acceptance speech, she said, "We [the women] have finally gained recognition, and it took ten thousand dollars to do it." She said this goodnaturedly, and it drew laughter, but she is the same person who said to me on another occasion, "Islam gave women their rights, and the Arabs took these rights away."

Also of interest on this occasion was the fact that a city board member, a woman of Lebanese extraction, presented an award to the women's auxiliary. This was the second time I had witnessed a woman of Lebanese background address a gathering at a mosque in Dearborn (with the exception of the woman being presented the award). The first time was at the Majma', where the woman was a lawyer with the law firm representing the Majma' in its attempt to build a school. In both cases, these were professional and public women who had to be treated with special deference. No doubt, as time goes on, there will be more such occasions. People with political clout and community influence are valued, whether they are men or women. The leaders of the mosques are well aware of women's importance to the Islamic community and are not likely to want to alienate them. Denying a prominent woman, whether Muslim or not, access to the podium on the basis of her sex would certainly be to no one's benefit. (However, it is yet to be seen whether the Majlis would allow such an occurrence.)

While an individual woman's moment at the podium expounding on essentially nonreligious topics is not significant in and of itself, it does at least send the message to the congregation that traditions cannot always be strictly adhered to in America. Furthermore, the young girls witnessing these assertive and confident women speaking publicly before men and other women will certainly be influenced. Some of these young girls already have had the experience of performing recitations, either singly or in groups, at the Jami' and the Majma' as part of their Arabic school programs. I believe that such seemingly small instances of visibility in the mosques will lead to larger roles for women and girls in the running of the religious community.

Another factor that will likely affect women's place in the religious community is the influence of the non-Arab Muslim women who frequent the mosques. These women are mostly Americans who have married Lebanese men. They are extremely fervent about their religion and are among the most heavily covered of the women in the community. While they are very conservative in their religious views, they also bring with them some very American behaviors and attitudes. For example, when I first met these women at the Majma', they were running a rummage sale for Lebanese orphans. Except for their dress, they could have passed for the ladies' auxiliary in any American church. When the earthquake struck Iran, it was these American women who organized garage sales and bake sales to raise money. Such activities draw in the Lebanese women to some extent, and ultimately these isolated activities could lead to the organization of full-fledged voluntary associations.

While voluntary associations did begin to appear in the Beirut suburbs before the outbreak of civil war, they seem to have been totally under male control.[50] A different situation could occur in Dearborn since women now have a central place for congregating— the mosques. Furthermore, there are pressing issues that concern women, particularly those involving the morals of their children. This could be a rallying point for women to organize themselves.

CHAPTER 4

Gathering Strength: The Emergence of American Shi'ism

When the natural world, the former context of the peasant ideas, faded behind the transatlantic horizon, the newcomers found themselves stripped to those religious institutions they could bring along with them. Well, the trolls and fairies will stay behind, but church and priest at very least will come.[1]

SOMETIME AFTER I completed my fieldwork in Dearborn, I visited a mosque in another part of the country during Ramadan. Although Shi'a were certainly not unwelcome at this mosque, Sunnis were the only ones in attendance. Those present on that occasion originated from Pakistan, Egypt, Nigeria, Saudi Arabia, and Syria. The women were downstairs, the men upstairs. There was no contact whatsoever between the two groups. As I sat with the other women, I reflected on how different an experience this was from the ones to which I had grown so accustomed. While cordiality and hospitality were not lacking, something was missing—and it was not just the men. I realized afterward that what I had found missing was the sense of utter coherence and deeply felt understanding that comes only when all present share in that indefinable essence called culture.

The Islamic group I studied in Dearborn is both distinctively Lebanese and distinctively Shi'i. They are unique. They may share a common set of Islamic values and practices with Muslims all over the world, but their Shi'ism differentiates them in a deep and significant way from Sunnis and all other groups of Muslims. Their Lebanese characteristics, in turn, differentiate them from all other Shiʿa as well. Therefore, to see them as characteristic of all Muslims in America is as helpful as viewing early Irish and Italian Catholics in the United States as interchangeable components of a single religious community. True, in both cases some traits are shared, but it is in the differences that we find the richness and texture that constitute a human community.

It is its "declaration of distinctiveness" that makes this Lebanese Shiʿi community seem so vital and strong. These are a people who have made a decision to be true to their beliefs; not to give in to pressures for uniformity either with the larger American culture or with their Sunni brethren. They certainly have not succumbed to puritanical Saudi Wahhabi pressures, something that is becoming commonplace in Islamic mosques in the United States.[2]

Some might argue that their distinctiveness fosters divisiveness. It is my contention that it actually fosters a sense of well-being—a sort of collective mental health—in the community at large. The mosques, the clerics, the rituals are a bridge tying homeland (usually the village) to life in the new land. These things make the transition far less jarring than it might be. They serve the purpose of buffering the individual from the onslaught of new and "foreign" ways and provide a framework of values within which to confront difficult choices and experiences. For this community, and perhaps for all sincere Shiʿa, religion can still provide the means of challenging the status quo.

That being said, I do not mean to imply that everyone in this community shares a uniform standard of religious belief and praxis. To the contrary, there are significant differences in the way people in this community approach religion. These differences relate to the way people emphasize the importance of Islamic law, the Shariʿa. To describe these people, I have not used the usual terms such as *Islamist, fundamentalist, neo-fundamentalist,* because they have all had connotations associated with them that would be misleading if applied to this community. I have chosen to use the term *Shariʿa-minded,* coined by historian Marshall Hodgson before the recent period of Islamic resurgence in the world—a resurgence commonly associated with negative events in the eyes of the West. While I did identify a subgroup that I have referred to as being political, most of the Shariʿa-minded are not involved in politics. On the other side of the equation are the *traditionalists,* a term I use loosely to describe a wide variation of approaches that lack the rigorous legalistic approach of the Shariʿa-minded.

The diversity in this community has not torn it apart. The various approaches to religion tend to coexist without being terribly disruptive to overall functioning. Some might have more religious prestige than others, but this can be counterbalanced by other forces, such as money or even political clout in Dearborn government. People who fall into one category tend to recognize, though often grudgingly, the benefits that others offer. Also, family continues to be the centripetal force in the community. Diversity of religious views may exist within a single family, but it is not allowed to destroy the family fabric.

What I have described is a brief moment in this community's history. Needless to say, the situation that prevails today cannot continue indefinitely. New generations raised in America will inevitably bring about changes.

The American Experience

America has been a great modifier of religion. Religion certainly does not die on American soil, but it is always transformed. While religious pluralism has characterized American society, the pluralism is, to some degree, superficial. Common threads run throughout the religions that have been transplanted in America. Capitalism, the dissolution of the extended family, the immigrants' break with traditional village ties, geographic and social mobility, and contact with innumerable other religions and nationalities have produced a style of religion unique in the world.

The nineteenth century was a time of pronounced new developments in American religion. Religion was no longer embedded in every other aspect of life but became compartmentalized. The unity of large communities through the church broke down, as new churches and sects proliferated across the American landscape. Frequently addressing unlettered audiences, preachers taught a religion of the heart rather than the head, with highly emotional sermons stressing forgiveness and love rather than commands for obedience. These developments eventually affected, at least to some degree, all religious communities in America, and their effects are felt to this day.

In their book *Habits of the Heart*, Bellah et al. offer an analysis of contemporary American life, including Americans' attitudes and approaches to religion. Religion for Americans, these researchers have found, is something "individual, prior to any organizational involvement."[3] American religion tends not to be based on an overriding religious authority but is something very private, personal, and individualistic. The privatization of religion and the idea that each individual chooses his or her own religious beliefs has also meant that religious diversity, at least to a certain extent, has been possible.

> The American pattern of privatizing religion while at the same time allowing it some public functions has proven highly compatible with the religious pluralism that has characterized America from the colonial period and grown more and more pronounced. If the primary contribution of religion to society is through the character and conduct of citizens, any religion, large or small, familiar or strange, can be of equal value to any other. The fact that most American religions have been biblical and that most, though of course not all, Americans can agree on the term "God" has certainly been helpful in diminishing religious antagonism. But diversity of practice has been seen as legitimate because religion is perceived as a matter of individual choice, with the implicit qualification that the practices themselves accord with public decorum and the adherents abide by the moral standards of the community.[4]

Of course, anyone at all familiar with American society knows that religion is not solely a matter of the individual's relationship with God. Organizational commitment is also a feature of American life. But this commitment is generally not broad-based. When people speak about involvement in "the church," they are speaking about the local church. This is the case even among Catholics who have traditionally identified themselves strongly with the Church as represented by the Pope, cardinals, and bishops. Among American Catholics, however, it is the local priest instead who has the greatest influence.

In America, religion has developed a therapeutic value for people. It is a place of refuge in a difficult world. Bellah and his colleagues found that Catholics share with Protestants a desire for warm, personal churches and "personal and accessible priests."[5] In other words, religion, like the family, is supposed to be a means of emotional support in a society that "places enormous pressures on people to marginalize and isolate them and force them away from community."[6] Not emphasized in these churches, whether they be Protestant or Catholic, is divine law, the type of law that induces people to make sacrifices and to deprive themselves of worldly pleasure. In other words, while religion might comfort and sustain, it does not command and restrain.

Placing Shiʿism in American Society

When Khalid made the comment that religion was a refuge from a sinful world, he was not talking about the emotional support he received from his mosque congregation and from his sheikh. Nor was he referring to some vague, private relationship with God that Americans speak about. Khalid was talking about the importance of following the laws of his religion. For Khalid, and for the Shiʿi community at large, these God-given laws are a means both of preserving order and goodness in the world and of counteracting evil. God, in these people's eyes, might be loving, but he also makes demands.

These demands are not to make one feel good about oneself. One fasts because God commands it. Of course, the society acts as God's surrogate by enforcing this obligation on others. At this point, the community is strong enough in its sense of identity—an identity completely infused with Shiʿism—to exert pressure on its members to fast, to abstain from drink, and so on. Again, this is not to say that everyone abides by the laws. But those who do not are marginalized; they are aware of their sins and know better than to flaunt them.

Judging from the trends we find in the larger society, how long can we expect this situation to prevail? A number of factors will continue to support this religious approach. First, as long as new immigrants continue to flow into Dearborn, the community can more or less maintain its distinctive ethnic and religious identity. It is these recent immigrants who have promoted the enactment of Shiʿi rituals, particularly those associated with the Imam Husayn, and have enhanced the use of Shiʿi symbols through sermons, books, mosque decorations, and so on.[7]

While the intensity of the Shiʿi experience was lacking in the lives of earlier immigrants and their children, today's children, on the other hand, hear the names of the imams repeatedly invoked, see increasing numbers of shrouded women, witness men beating their chests in a display of remorse and anger over the tragedy of the death of the Imam Husayn and over the tragedies in their own lives. Immigrants have been key to this experience, and, in the short run at least, they will continue to have a tremendous impact on the religious lives of the community. Thanks to these immigrants and the sheikhs who have been brought to this country to teach them, America is not going to be the place where the imams are forgotten.

Other factors strengthen ties to the old country. Unlike the early Catholic immigrants who could only rely on the exchange of letters if they remained permanently in this country, the Lebanese have the telephone, homemade recordings and videos, and ultimately the airplane to reconnect families.

Even more important to keeping the faith is keeping marriage endogamous. Research conducted in Canada has shown that children are far more likely to identify themselves as Muslim if both parents are Muslim than if only one parent is.[8] As we have seen, the Lebanese Shiʿa are strong advocates of marrying not only other Shiʿa but often people with village and kinship ties.

In addition, the role of the *marjiʿ taqlid* has been strengthened, and this institution affects the lives of Shiʿa living in America. While there are Shiʿa who reject the institution, there are growing numbers who do accept it. Also, the new sheikhs coming from the Middle East speak as proponents of the *marjiʿ* and through their pulpits encourage people to be *muqallid* to one or another of the possible candidates for the role, thus stressing the need to conform to a strict model of Shiʿism and not one adulterated by secular influences.

The countervailing forces are, of course, powerful. While the children might be exposed to strong influences within their homes and mosques, what they experience in the schools and playgrounds and on television and in movies relentlessly tugs at them to take a different course from their parents.

Even the establishment of full-time elementary and high schools would not completely inhibit the acculturation of the children into American society. In the words of a Yiddish educator from the early part of this century. "We thought we could raise our children according to our spirit, and through our schools insulate them from the community in which they grew up. Today we know that we cannot control the intellectual development of our children, and that both the home and community have a much greater impact on their education than we do."[9]

The statement quoted above by Bellah et al. reminds us that religious tolerance (at least at the superficial level of "we all believe in the same God, so what difference does it make what we call ourselves?") can have a devastating effect on the preservation of religious dogma and traditions. The perception that all religions are equal means that all religions are interchangeable. Religious "conversions" or simply moving from one denomination to another have been particularly commonplace since the 1960s as people sought a church or religion within which they felt "comfortable." Choosing one's religion, after all, is an inalienable right. In America, membership in a religion is voluntary, despite how contrary this notion has been to Muslims and Catholics alike.

Yet all has not been homogenization in American society. The picture is far more complex than that. Ethnicity and religious diversity continue to flourish, though in more muted forms than they did when people were "fresh off the boat." The community will change. America will have an impact, but Shi'ism will not disappear. Of course, to talk about religion in America today is not the same as talking about it in the 1950s when Will Herberg coined the phrase "the American way of life" or in the mid-1960s when Bellah used the term "civil religion." We live in an ever-changing society, one that is affected by and affects religion.

A Possible Picture of the Future

Certain trends toward what has been an "American religious model" are already appearing in Dearborn, one of which is a tendency for the mosques to develop a congregational style. The Jami' is the epitome of congregationalism. It has a board of directors largely constituted of successful businessmen responsible for hiring a sheikh who is expected, in the words of Irving Howe, "to minister to the 'spiritual needs' of his congregants but . . . best be cautious in making spiritual demands on them."[10] The Majma' has a different type of organization. It is dominated by the sheikh who founded the mosque and remains its spiritual guide. Also, the influence of the institution of the marji'iya is felt at the Majma' and, thus, functions more like a traditional Catholic church in this respect. When the day comes, however, that Sheikh Berri's (or, in the case of the Majlis, Sheikh Burro's) position needs to be filled, chances are fairly high that the governing bodies of those mosques will also assume greater power and limit the authority of their sheikhs. It also seems likely that as the mosques become increasingly established, people will select a mosque in which they feel most at home and will become its "members."

The sheikhs themselves assume more and more of the role of pastoral counselor that so many priests and ministers play in this society today. Gone are the days of quiet, contemplative reading and discussion of erudite matters. Sheikhs in this country spend a considerable amount of their time helping with all manner of problems, be they personal, social, or religious. They also do not see it as being to their benefit to isolate themselves from the rest of the religious leaders in the community. The roundtable group established in the area that includes several priests and ministers includes members of the 'ulama as well.

But what about the lay men and women of Dearborn? What predictions can be made for them? Will they continue to pray, fast, eat *halal* meat, wear *hijab*? The answer is probably fairly obvious: yes and no. I believe the community will become more bifurcated in its approach to religion. Those who do not adhere strictly to the Shari'a now probably will produce children and grandchildren who will view these laws as relics of the past.

Ramadan, among this group, probably will be treated in a token way with occasional fasting, most likely at the beginning and end of Ramadan. Head coverings probably will be relegated to the mosque, and selection of mosques will be based on the ability of the sheikh to accept a wide range of religious attitudes. (Selection of the sheikhs will be problematic for these people for a while. Sooner or later, the *'ulama* will have to have at least part of their education in the United States.) These are the people for whom private religion will assume the greatest meaning. And, these are the people who probably will find it easiest to spread out to the other Detroit suburbs.

But the picture really is not so simple as that. Frequently in the third or fourth generations, a kind of revivalism occurs among those whose families have become lax in their religious duties. Sometimes world events precipitate this phenomenon, as in the case of American Jews after the 1967 war. Sometimes other social forces were at work, as in the case of the Catholic Charismatic Movement of the 1970s. The people involved in these revivalistic movements try to reconstruct their lives on religious models and take a new pride in their heritage.

But there will be others who have never deviated. For those who will remain deeply committed to the Shari'a, Dearborn can provide a haven. Arabic might be relegated to the mosques eventually, but the *hijab* and *halal* meat can remain aspects of everyday life in this town. Events in the Middle East, along with the perception of hostility toward all things Arab and Muslim, will only serve to intensify the degree of isolation of many of these people. Of course, there will be a high attrition rate among this group, too, but endogamous marriage and a strong institutional base that supports a religious way of life will serve to perpetuate the Shari'a-minded approach to religion.

Animosity toward Muslims in America

For those who are concerned that American antipathy toward Muslims, be they Sunni or Shi'a, will continue or even intensify, it is helpful to look back on the history of Catholicism in America. I am writing this section of the book in southern Indiana, where the Ku Klux Klan was very strong in the 1920s. While African Americans were targets of their antipathy, anti-Catholic sentiment was at least as virulent and was shared by a majority of white Protestants in the state.[11] Nor was this hatred for Catholics relegated to isolated parts of the country. In fact, it was very widespread. The situation turned extremely volatile at times, such as after President William McKinley had been assassinated by a Polish anarchist in Buffalo, New York. When the Polish Catholic Congress met in that city three weeks after the assassination, the mood of the meeting was described as "militant and apprehensive."[12]

Anti-Catholic sentiment has not disappeared from America, but it is at a low enough level that it certainly does not hinder Catholics from participating in all spheres of activity. There is no reason to think that Muslims in general, and Shi'a in particular, will experience anything much different.

Afterword

When I lived in Dearborn from 1987 to 1991, the main world events that had shaped this community were the Lebanese civil war and the Iranian Revolution. The civil war had been the impetus for large migration and had strengthened the group's religious identity; the revolution had provided the ideological blueprint for religious revivalism among the Lebanese Shiʿa.

On a visit to Dearborn in June 1995 to attend the ʿAshura commemorations, I realized that there had been a paradigm shift caused by another major conflagration: the Gulf War of 1991. Dearborn was feeling the aftermath of this war as Shiʿi refugees from southern Iraq were joining their Lebanese coreligionists, benefiting from the inroads the latter had made in this Midwestern American city.

The Lebanese still own the stores and numerous restaurants, which now have new signs and smart, well-maintained storefronts. Indeed, the Lebanese business district now extends nearly a mile farther along Warren Avenue. The Dearborn Lebanese are no longer marginal shopkeepers but have become a community of established merchants with capital and stable businesses. The Iraqis are not the entrepreneurs the Lebanese are. If the Iraqis did not bring with them the extraordinary business acumen of the Lebanese, they did bring something else: an official "orthodox" view of Shiʿism. The Iraqis had grown up in the shadow of the tombs of the imams.

ʿAshura is almost by definition a dramatic time. In Dearborn, it is more so now than ever. The sense of mourning is enhanced by the greatly increased number of black ʿabayas both on the streets and in the mosques. This is the usual attire of women from the Atabat, and life in Dearborn is not about to change this very soon.

ʿAshura commemorations were held in all of the mosques in Dearborn during this past Muharram. There are more mosques now. Sheikh Attat, who had been brought from the Bekaa region of Lebanon by the Jamiʿ, left that mosque to form his own on Warren Avenue on the Detroit-Dearborn line. It is referred to as the Masjid.

After Sheikh Attat left, another sheikh was brought to lead the Jamiʿ, an Iranian by the name of Ilahi. History repeated itself in this case, too. Sheikh Ilahi, I am told, did not want to be a functionary. He wanted to truly lead the Jami', not be led by its board. And so, following a period of heated debate, he, too, left the Jami'. He has taken over a VFW hall on the corner of Warren and Schaefer and has converted it to the Dar al-Hikma, the House of Knowledge.

Sheikhs Attat and Ilahi took with them somewhat different groups, though there is, of course, overlap. Attat's Masjid appeals to traditional Lebanese, principally, it appears, from the Bekaa region. This mosque is most definitely an Arabic language mosque. Ilahi, on the other hand, is an Iranian and does not speak colloquial Arabic. He does know English, which, no doubt, weighed heavily in his favor when he was considered for the Jami'. His mosque is referred to as being for "Arab Americans"—younger generations who no longer are comfortable with spoken classical Arabic—although during 'Ashura one would not have guessed this. It should not be assumed that because it attracts Arab Americans, it is lax in its attitude toward the Shari'a. My impression was that this mosque sends the message that strict conformity with the law is the only acceptable approach.

The Jami' is still the largest and most diverse of the mosques. To the traditional Lebanese and the "Arab Americans" (a term used more commonly in the community these days) are added some of the very strict Shari'a-minded, many of whom are from Iraq. Sheikh Chirri passed away during the past year. Sheikh Attat having left the Jami', Sheikh Chirri was replaced by Sheikh Habhab, whose previous tenure at the Jami' ended precipitously in the earliest stage of my research.

Sheikh Hashim Hishami, the *khatib* who frequently led 'Ashura commemorations while I lived in Dearborn, has opened a small center himself which appeals to some of the Iraqi refugees, though obviously not to all of them.

This 'Ashura, Hishami's role as *khatib* was filled by men from out of town. One of them, Sayyid Hasan al-Qazwini, originally from Karbala and now residing in California, chanted the Majalis Husayniya in both the Jami' and in the Dar al-Hikma, thus necessitating coordination between the two facilities. While at the Majma', I met another *khatib*, this one brought to Dearborn for the occasion from Canada.

Aside from more mosques and more mourners, I also found a more intense and dramatic atmosphere during this 'Ashura commemoration. After the Majalis was completed in some of the mosques, young men gathered in circles to beat their chests. Again, this ceremony is led by Iraqis. Still, the fervor is kept behind the mosques doors. It does not spill over to the streets.

I believe the influx of Iraqis to Dearborn is having and will continue to have a significant influence on this community for a number of reasons.

First, the Iraqis have a sense of being the "keepers" of Shi'ism. Their lives have revolved around religion in a way that could not have been the case among the Lebanese, who did not have *madrasas* and shrines in their towns. Their number also includes many religiously trained men (and women) who strongly believe that there is only one interpretation of Shi'ism. In their eyes, deviation from this interpretation implies a lack of true religious commitment.

Second, it might be assumed, judging from past history of the Muslim community in the area, that the Iraqis will form their own cohort and become separated from the Lebanese. However, I do not think this will occur in the foreseeable future. I do not predict a split for a simple reason: money. The Lebanese, with their relatively large numbers and their strong mercantile abilities, can provide the financial resources to maintain and even build mosques and support clerics. It would not be in the best interests of the Iraqis, particularly the clergy, to alienate the Lebanese. The benefits the two groups bring to each other, the religious knowledge and prestige of the Iraqis and the relative wealth of the Lebanese, may serve to strengthen ties between the two groups. And while more Lebanese might be drawn to stricter conformity with religious laws, the Iraqis might, in turn, demand a little less conformity from the Lebanese. After all, the Lebanese need to fit into American society in order to carry out business ventures.

Third, the Iraqis bring with them a strong commitment to the institution of the *marja'*. The dynamics of how this institution will influence American Shi'a and how it will, in turn, be influenced by them is the subject of my current research.

Notes

Introduction

1. Sameer Abraham, Nabeel Abraham, and Barbara Aswad. "The Southend: An Arab Muslim Working-class Community," in Samir Y. Abraham and Nabeel Abraham, eds., *Arabs in the New World: Studies on Arab-American Communities* (Detroit: Wayne State University Center for Urban Studies, 1983), pp. 163–84.

2. Suad Joseph. "Women and the Neighborhood Street in Borj Hamoud," in Lois Beck and Nikki Keddie, eds., *Women in the Muslim World* (Cambridge: Harvard University Press, 1978), p. 544.

3. Laurel D. Wigle, "An Arab Muslim Community in Michigan," in Barbara C. Aswad, ed., *Arabic Speaking Communities in American Cities* (New York: Center for Migration Studies, 1974), p. 155.

4. For a discussion of the strategies employed by immigrants to the United States, see Alejandro Portes and Ruben G. Rumbaut, *Immigrant America* (Berkeley: University of California Press, 1990).

5. For historical information about early Muslim immigration, see, for example Mohammad Mahmoud Siryani, "Residential Distribution, Spatial Mobility and Acculturation in an Arab-Muslim Community" Ph.D. diss., Michigan State University, 1977; Michael Suleiman, "Early Arab-Americans: The Search for Identity," in Eric J. Hooglund, ed., *Crossing the Waters* (Washington, D.C.: Smithsonian Institution, 1987, pp. 37–54; and Gregory Orfalea, *Before the Flames: A Quest for the History of Arab Americans* (Austin: University of Texas Press, 1988).

6. Barbara C. Aswad, "The Lebanese Muslim Community in Dearborn, Michigan," paper, Centre for Lebanese Studies Conference on Lebanese Emigration, St. Hughes College, Oxford, 1989.

7. Suleiman, "Early Arab-Americans."

8. For a readable account of U.S. immigration policies, see David M. Reimers, *Still the Golden Door: The Third World Comes to America* (New York: Columbia University Press, 1985).

9. Nabeel Abraham, "National and Local Politics: A Study of Political Conflict in the Yemeni Immigrant Community of Detroit, Michigan," Ph. D. diss., University of Michigan, 1978, p. 111.

10. Siryani, "Residential Distribution."

11. Anthony Katarsky, "Family Ties and the Growth of an Arabic Community in Northeast Dearborn, Michigan," master's thesis, Wayne State University, 1980.

12. See Barbara Aswad, "Yemeni and Lebanese Muslim Immigrant Women in Southeast Dearborn, Michigan," in Earle H. Waugh et al., eds., *Muslim Families in North America* (Edmonton, Alberta: University of Alberta Press, 1991), pp. 256–81.

13. Samir Khalaf, "The Background and Causes of Lebanese Syrian Immigration to the U.S. before World War I," in Eric J. Hooglund, ed., *Crossing the Waters* (Washington, D.C.: Smithsonian Institution, 1987), p. 24.

14. Suad Joseph, "Family as Security and Bondage: A Political Strategy of the Lebanese Working Class," in Saad Eddin Ibrahim, ed., *Arab Society: Social Science Perspectives* (Cairo: American University of Cairo Press, 1985), pp. 241–56.

15. See Barbara C. Aswad, "The Southeast Dearborn Arab Community Struggles for Survival Against Urban 'Renewal,' " in Barbara C. Aswad, ed., *Arabic Speaking Communities in American Cities* (Staten Island, N.Y.: Center for Migration Studies, 1974), pp. 53–84.

16. "All Not Well Between Arabs, Non-Arabs," *Dearborn Press and Guide,* Jan. 19, 1984.

17. "The East End 'Melting Pot,' " *Dearborn Press and Guide,* Aug. 10, 1978.

18. In her 1989 article, "The Lebanese Muslim Community in Dearborn, Michigan," Aswad reported a decrease in intercommunity teenage fighting. While there does seem to have been a lull for a while, a series of incidents beginning in 1989 heightened tensions, particularly among high school students.

19. Irving Howe, *World of Our Fathers: The Journey of the East European Jews to America and the Life They Found and Made* (New York: Galahad Books, 1976), p. 51.

20. Smith, "Religious Denominations as Ethnic Communities: A Regional Case Study," in George E. Pozzetta, ed., *The Immigrant Religious Experience* (New York: Garland Publishing 1991), p. 357.

Chapter 1

1. For a discussion of the meanings and significance of Hijra, see Dale F. Eickelman and James Piscatori, eds., *Muslim Travelers: Pilgrimage, Migration, and the Religious Imagination* (Berkeley: University of California Press, 1990).

2. S. Husain M. Jafri argues this point persuasively in *Origin and Early Development of Shiʿa Islam* (London: Longman Group, 1979).

3. Moojan Momen, *An Introduction to Shiʿi Islam* (Offord: George Ronald, 1985), p. 12.

4. Ibid., p. 147.

5. Momen, in *An Introduction to Shiʿi Islam,* speculates that these people may have been converts from Ismaʿili Islam which had become very much hated in the Muslim world. Attempting to disassociate themselves

from the atrocities of the Isma'ilis, large numbers probably eagerly embraced the more respectable Twelver Shi'ism.

6. J. R. I. Cole, suggests that instituting this hierarchy could have been a means of controlling rebellious lower-level 'ulama, many of whom had become members of the messianic Babi movement of the nineteenth century. "Imami Jurisprudence and the Role of the 'Ulama: Mortaza Ansari on Emulating the Supreme Exemplar," in Nikki R. Keddie, ed., *Religion and Politics in Iran* (New Haven: Yale University Press, 1983), pp. 33–46.

7. See Abbas Amanat, *Resurrection and Renewal: The Making of the Babi Movement in Iran, 1844–1850* (Ithaca: Cornell University Press, 1989); and Hamid Dabashi, *Theology of Discontent: The Ideological Foundation of the Islamic Revolution in Iran* (New York: New York University Press, 1993), for a discussion of the institution of the *marji'iyat taglid tamm.*

8. Mikhayil Mishaqa, *Murder, Mayhem, Pillage and Plunder: The History of the Lebanon in the 18th and 19th Centures,* trans. by Wheeler M. Thackston, Jr. (Albany: State University of New York Press, 1988).

9. Ibid., pp. 20–21.

10. Cited in Augustus Richard Norton, *Amal and the Shi'a: Struggle for the Soul of Lebanon* (Austin: University of Texas Press, 1987), p. 14.

11. For an interesting discussion of *taqiya* and its opposite position, *ta'bi'a* (mobilization), see Fuad I. Khuri, *Imams and Emirs: State, Religion and Sects in Islam* (London: Saqi Books, 1990), esp. pp. 123–30.

12. See Charles Issawi, "The Historical Background of Lebanese Emigration 1800–1914," paper, Centre for Lebanese Studies Conference on Lebanese Emigration, St. Hughes College, Oxford, 1989; Norton, *Amal and the Shi'a;* and Joseph Olmert, "The Shi'a and the Lebanese State," in Martin Kramer, ed. *Shi'ism, Resistance and Revolution* (Boulder: Westview, 1987), pp. 189–201, for discussions about the economic conditions prevailing in Shi'i areas of Lebanon.

13. Norton, *Amal and the Shi'a,* p. 14.

14. Albert Hourani, "Ideologies of the Mountain and the City," in Roger Owen, ed., *Essays on the Crisis in Lebanon* (London: Ithaca Press, 1976), p. 35.

15. Fouad Ajami, *The Vanished Imam: Musa Al Sadr and the Shi'a of Lebanon* (Ithaca: Cornell University Press, 1986).

16. Eric R. Wolf, *Peasant Wars of the Twentieth Century* (New York: Harper and Row, 1968).

17. Ajami, *The Vanished Imam,* p. 71.

18. Khalaf, Samir, and Guilain Denoeux, "Urban Networks and Political Conflict in Lebanon," in Nadim Shehadi and Dona Haffar Mills, eds., *Lebanon: A History of Conflict and Consensus* (London: Centre for Lebanese Studies, 1988), pp. 181–200.

19. Suad Joseph, "Family as Security and Bondage: A Political Strategy of the Lebanese Working Class," in Saad Eddir Ibrahim, ed., *Arab Society: Social Science Perspectives* (Cairo: American University of Cairo Press, 1985), pp. 241–56.

20. Ajami, *The Vanished Imam,* p. 74.

21. Norton, *Amal and the Shi'a.*

Chapter 2

1. Michael Gilsenan, *Recognizing Islam* (New York: Pantheon Books, 1982), p. 72.

2. Whether religious sects tend to fuse or to split is, of course, of interest to researchers. While Nancy Conklin and Nora Faires, in their study "Colored and Catholic: The Lebanese in Birmingham, Alabama" in Eric Hooglund, ed., *Crossing the Waters* [Washington, D.C.: Smithsonian Institution,1987], p. 69–84), found a close and cooperative relationship between early immigrant Lebanese Maronites and Melkites, studies of more recently transplanted Lebanese communities cite a different situation. In Australia, for example, the Shiʿa and Sunnis are differentiating themselves in establishing mosques (Michael Humphrey, "Community, Mosque and Ethnic Politics," *Australian and New Zealand Journal of Sociology* XXIII, 2 [July 1987]: 233–45), and there is division among all Muslim groups, including the Lebanese, in Montreal (W. Murray Hogben, "Marriage and Divorce among Muslims in Canada," in Earle H. Waugh et al., eds., *Muslim Families in North America* [Edmonton Alberta: University of Alberta Press, 1991], pp. 154–84).

3. Alixa Naff, *Becoming American: The Early Arab Immigrant Experience* (Carbondale, Ill.: Southern Illinois University Press, 1985) It should be noted, however, that Gutbi Mahdi Ahmad states that Ross, North Dakota, holds the distinction of being the first American city to have had a mosque ("Muslim Organizations in the United States," in Yvonne Haddad, eds., *The Muslims of America* [New York: Oxford University Press, 1991], pp. 11–24).

4. Abdo Elkholy, *The Arab Muslims in the United States* (New Haven: College and University Press, 1966), pp. 76–77.

5. Sheikh Al Azhar is the head of the Azhar University in Cairo, the foremost Sunni theological institution. He is, therefore, the most prominent Sunni cleric in the world.

6. Muhammad Jawad Chirri, *The Shiites under Attack* (Detroit: Islamic Center of America, 1986), p. 107.

7. Ibid., p. 108.

8. Gregory Orfalea, *Before the Flames: A Quest for the History of Arab Americans* (Austin: University of Texas Press, 1988).

9. Jay Dolan, *The American Catholic Experience: A History from Colonial Times to the Present* (Garden City, N.Y.: Doubleday, 1985), p. 165.

10. Peter W. Williams, *Popular Religion in America* (Urbana: University of Illinois Press, 1989), p. 77.

11. Dolan, *The American Catholic Experience*, p. 181.

12. Ibid., p. 310.

13. For a discussion of interfaith cooperation in the United States, see Will Herberg, *Protestant, Catholic, Jew* (Garden City, N.Y.: Doubleday, 1955); and Williams, *Popular Religion in America*. The idea of an American "civil religion" was promoted by Robert Bellah in the 1960s. See his "Civil Religion in America," in William G. McLoughlin and Robert N. Bellah, eds., *Religion in America* (Boston: Beacon, 1968), pp. 3–23.

14. John Bowen, *Muslims through Discourse* (Princeton: Princeton University Press, 1993) and Olivier Roy, *The Failure of Political Islam* (Cambridge: Cambridge University Press, 1994).

15. See Gilles Kepel, *Muslim Extremism in Egypt: The Prophet and the Pharaoh* (Berkeley: University of California Press, 1985).

16. Marshall Hodgson, *The Venture of Islam: The Classical Age of Islam,* Vol. 1 (Chicago: University of Chicago Press, 1974).

17. Leslie Woodcock Tentler, "Who Is the Church? Conflict in a Polish Immigrant Parish in Late Nineteenth-Century Detroit," in George E. Pozetta, ed., *The Immigrant Religious Experience* (New York: Garland Publishing, 1991), pp. 419–54.

18. Robert Wuthnow, *Producing the Sacred: An Essay on Public Religion* (Urbana: University of Illinois Press, 1994).

19. J. R. I. Cole, "Imami Jurisprudence and the role of the ʿUlama: Mortaza Ansari on Emulating the Supreme Exemplar," in Nikki R. Keddie, ed., *Religion and Politics in Iran* (New Haven: Yale University Press, 1983), pp. 33–36.

20. Abbas Amanat, "In Between the Madrasa and the Marketplace: The Designation of Clerical Leadership in Modern Shiʿism," in Said Amir Arjomand, ed., *Authority and Political Culture in Shiʿism* (Albany: State University of New York Press, 1988), pp. 98–132.

21. The institution of the *marja* is found only among those who follow the Usuli as opposed to the Akhbari school of law. Those who follow the Usuli school are far more numerous. For a discussion of the differences between the Usulis and the Akhbaris, see Chibli Mallat, *Renewal of Islamic Law: Muhammad Baqer as-Sadr, Najaf and the Shiʿi International* (Cambridge: Cambridge University Press, 1993).

22. Moojan Momen, *An Introduction to Shiʿi Islam* (Oxford: George Ronald, 1985).

23. See Mottehedeh, *The Mantle of the Prophet* (New York: Simon and Schuster, 1985).

24. Augustus Richard Norton, *Amal and the Shiʿa: Struggle for the Soul of Lebanon* (Austin: University of Texas Press, 1987), p. 72.

25. Shahla Haeri, *Law of Desire: Temporary Marriage in Shiʿi Iran* (Syracuse: Syracuse University Press, 1989), p. 2.

26. Abuʿl-Qasim Khuʿi, *Minhaj al-Salihin,* Vol. 2, (Beirut: Daral-Zahra, n.2.), p. 265.

27. Chibli Mallat, *Shiʿi Thought from the South of Lebanon* (Oxford: Centre for Lebanese Studies, 1988).

28. Momen, *An Introduction to Shiʿi Islam.*

29. Mallat, *Shiʿi Thought from the South of Lebanon,* p. 10.

30. Fouad Ajami, *The Vanished Imam: Musa Al Sadr and the Shiʿa of Lebanon* (Ithaca: Cornell University Press, 1986), pp. 127–28.

31. Norton, *Amal and the Shiʿa.*

32. For a discussion of the institution of the *marjaʿ* earlier in this century, see Hamid Dabashi, *Theology of Discontent: The Ideological Foundation of the Islamic Revolution in Iran* (New York: New York University Press, 1993),

Momen, *An Introduction to Shi'i Islam;* and Yitzhak Nakash, *The Shi'is of Iraq* (Princeton: Princeton University Press, 1994).

33. Tentler, "Who is the Church?" pp. 425–26.

34. Michael Fischer, *Iran: From Religious Dispute to Revolution* (Cambridge: Harvard University Press, 1980), p. 13.

35. For various perspectives on this topic, see, for example, the following edited volumes: J. R. I. Cole and Nikki R. Keddie, *Shi'ism and Social Protest* (New Haven: Yale University Press, 1986), Nikki R. Keddie, *Religion and Politics in Iran* (New Haven: Yale University Press, 1983) Peter Chelkowski, *Ta'ziyeh: Ritual and Drama in Iran* (New York: New York University Press, 1979).

36. Mircea Eliade, *The Sacred and the Profane: The Nature of Religion* (San Diego: Harcourt, Brace, Jovanovich, 1959), pp. 111–12.

37. Mayel Baktash, "Ta'ziyeh and Its Philosophy," in Peter Chelkowski, ed., *Ta'ziyeh: Ritual and Drama in Iran* (New York: New York University Press, 1979), p. 103.

38. Mary Hegland, "Two Images of Husain: Accommodation and Revolution in an Iranian Village," in Nikki Keddie, ed., *Religion and Politics in Iran: Shi'ism from Quietism to Revolution* (New Haven: Yale University Press, 1983), pp. 218–35.

39. Gilsenan, *Recognizing Islam,* p. 69.

40. Fuad Khuri, *From Village to Suburb: Order and Change in Greater Beirut* (Chicago: University of Chicago Press, 1975).

41. Schubel states that Sunnis from South Asia join the South Asian Shi'a in Toronto for their commemoration of 'Ashura. He attributes the use of the Urdu language as the major attraction of the services. Vornon Schubel, "Muharram Majlis," in Earle H Waugh et al., eds. *Muslim Families in America* (Edmonton, Alberta: The University of Alberta Press, 1991).

42. Dolan, *The American Catholic Experience.* For a colorful description of the Italian festa in East Harlem in the earlier decades of this century, see Robert Anthony Orsi, *The Madonna of 115th Street: Faith and Community in Italian Harlem 1880–1950* (New Haven: Yale University Press, 1985).

43. Williams, *Popular Religion in America,* esp. pp. 76–80.

44. Oleg Grabar, "The Architecture of the Middle Eastern City," in Ira M. Lapidas, ed., *Middle Eastern Cities* (Berkeley: University of California Press, 1969), pp. 26–46.

45. Ibid., p. 38.

46. Open-necked shirts became the attire for religious but nonclerical men in the Islamic Republic of Iran. Refusal to wear a necktie has remained an obvious symbol of the rejection of Western values.

47. Transition in leadership at the Jami' occurred during the course of this study. The position of assistant director had been filled by a few men. At this writing, Sheikh Sa'il Attat, who served as assistant director, acts as director of the Jami'. Though he has not learned English and is still very much concerned with the political life of Lebanon, his personable style and obvious flexibility seem to have won over both the new and old immigrants who frequent the Jami'.

48. Sheikh Chirri died in 1994.

49. This is not where people perform *salat*. The decorum required in each area is quite different.

50. When the people of this community speak of Islam, they are generally speaking about Shiʻi Islam. I therefore use the two terms interchangeably in the same way as they do.

51. This is apparently a problem that other Muslim communities have had to grapple with in the United States. For example, see Ahmad H. Sakr and Sami A. Arafeh, *Guidelines of Employment by Muslim Communities* (Lombard, Ill.: Foundation for Islamic Knowledge, n.d.).

52. Gilsenan, *Recognizing Islam*, p. 120.

53. Young men also act as ushers to control crowds during sermons, as they do, for example, for black Muslim groups in the United States. Gilles Kepel describes a similar situation of crowd control for the controversial Sheikh Kishk in Egypt in *The Prophet and the Pharaoh*. (Berkeley: University of California Press, 1985).

54. Fouad Ajami, "The Battle of Algiers," *The New Republic,* July 9, 1990, pp. 12–13.

55. Kepel, *Muslim Extremism in Egypt;* Roy, *The Failure of Political Islam;* and Henry Munson, Jr., *Islam and Revolution in the Middle East* (New Haven: Yale University Press, 1988).

56. Kepel, *The Prophet and the Pharaoh.*

57. Ajami, *The Vanished Imam.*

58. Khuʻi, *Minhaj al-Salihin,* Vol. 1, p. 316.

59. Michael Fischer and Mehdi Abedi, foreword to Khomeini's *A Clarification of Questions* (Boulder: Westview Press, 1984) p. xiv.

60. For further discussion of this topic, see Walbridge, "Arabic in the Dearborn Mosques," in Rouchdy, *The Arabic Language in America,* pp. 184–204.

61. Dolan, quoting historian Sam Bass Warner, in *The American Catholic Experience*, p. 204.

62. Dolan, *The American Catholic Experience,* pp. 207–8.

63. Mottehedeh, *The Mantle of the Prophet,* p. 30.

64. Fischer, *Iran: From Religious Dispute to Revolution.*

65. Victor W. Turner, "Religious Specialists," in Arthur C. Lehmann and James E. Myers, eds., *Magic, Witchcraft, and Religion: An Anthopological Study of the Supernatural,* 2nd ed. (Mountain View, Calif.: Mayfield, 1989), pp. 85–92.

66. Maurice Bloch, "Introduction," in Maurice Bloch, ed., *Political Language and Oratory in Traditional Society* (London: Academic Press, 1975), pp. 109–29.

67. Steven C. Caton, *Peaks of Yemen I Summon* (Berkeley: University of California Press, 1990).

68. Pascal Boyer, *Tradition as Truth and Communication* (Cambridge: Cambridge University Press, 1990), p. 83.

69. Patrick Gaffney, *The Prophet's Pulpit: Islamic Preaching in Contemporary Egypt* (Berkeley: University of California Press, 1994).

70. Richard Antoun, *Muslim Preacher in the Modern World* (Princeton: Princeton University Press, 1989).

71. Mottehedeh, *The Mantle of the Prophet*, p. 183.

72. Bloch, "Introduction," p. 24.

73. See Sakr and Arafeh, *Guidelines of Employment by Muslim Communities.*

74. John J. Bukowczyk, "Mary the Messiah: Polish Immigrant Heresy and the Malleable Ideology of the Roman Catholic Church, 1880–1930," in George E. Pozzetta, ed., *The Immigrant Religious Experience* (New York: Garlan 1991), pp. 55–81.

Chapter 3

1. Alfred Guillaume, *Islam* (Middlesex: Penguin, 1954), p. 155.

2. Michel Mazzaoui, "Shiʿism in the Arab World," in Seyyed Hossein Nasr et al., eds., *Expectation of the Millennium* (New York: State University of New York Press, 1989), pp. 253–55.

3. Sami Zubaida, *Islam, the People and the State* (London: Routledge, 1989).

4. Barbara D. Metcalf, "The Pilgrimage Remembered: South Asian Accounts of the Hajj," in Dale F. Eickelman and James Piscatori, eds., *Muslim Travellers: Pilgrimage, Migration, and the Religious Imagination* (Berkeley: University of California Press, 1990), p. 100.

5. Abuʿl-Qasim Khuʿi, *Minhaj al-Salihin* (Beirut: Dar al-Zahra, n.2.), Vol. 2, pp. 325–29. I have abridged the passage considerably, omitting discussions of special cases, errors that do or do not keep the meat from being *halal,* and other ancillary matters.

6. Michael Fischer and Mehdi Abedi, foreword to Khomeini's *A Clarification of Questions* (Boulder: Westview Press, 1984), p. xxi.

7. Fouad Ajami, *The Vanished Imam: Musa Al Sadr and the Shiʿa of Lebanon* (Ithaca: Cornell University Press, 1986), p. 133.

8. Roy Mottehedeh, *The Mantle of the Prophet* (New York: Simon and Schuster, 1985), p. 181.

9. Mary Douglas, *Purity and Danger: An Analysis of Concepts of Pollution and Taboo* (London: Routledge and Kegan Paul, 1966), p. 57.

10. Peter W. Williams, *Popular Religion in America* (Urbana: University of Illinois Press, 1989), p. 81.

11. Clifford Geertz, *Islam Observed* (Chicago: University of Chicago Press, 1968), p. 1.

12. Erika Friedl, *Women of Deh Koh* (Washington, D.C.: Smithsonian Institution, 1989), p. 10.

13. Eric R. Wolf, *Peasant Wars of the Twentieth Century* (New York: Harper and Row, 1968).

14. Allama Tabatabaʿi, *Shiʿite Islam* (Albany: State University of New York Press, 1975), p. 9.

15. Edward G. Browne, *A Literary History of Persia,* Vol. IV (Cambridge: Cambridge University Press, 1969).

16. Ayatollah Muhammad Baqir al-Sadr and Ayatollah Murtaza Mutahhery, *The Awaited Savior* (Accra: Islamic Seminary, 1982), pp. 25–26.

17. Cited in Moojan Momen, *An Introduction to Shi'i Islam* (Oxford: George Ronald, 1985), p. 169.

18. P. N. Boratav, "Djinn," in *The Encyclopaedia of Islam* 2nd ed. (Leiden: E. J. Brill, 1960), pp. 546–47.

19. This verse refers to the ancient practice of making magic by tying knots in cords and then blowing and spitting upon them in order to bewitch people. See J. G. Frazer, *The Golden Bough, Part II: Taboo and the Perils of the Soul* (London: Macmillan, 1927), p. 302.

20. Toufic Fahd, "Magic: Magic in Islam," in Mircea Eliade, ed., *The Encyclopedia of Religion* (New York: Macmillan, 1987), pp. 104.

21. Ibn Khaldun, *The Muqaddimah: An Introduction to History*, Vol. 3 (Princeton: Princeton University Press, 1967), p. 159.

22. Ibid., p. 170.

23. Brian Spooner, "The Evil Eye in the Middle East," in Mary Douglas, ed., *Witchcraft Confessions and Accusations* (London: Tavistock, 1970), p. 314.

24. John J. Bukowczyk, "The Transforming Power of the Machine: Popular Religion, Ideology, and Secularization among Polish Immigrant Workers in the United States, 1880–1940," in George E. Pozzetta, ed., *The Immigrant Religious Experience* (New York: Garland, 1991), pp. 84–100.

25. Laurel D. Wigle, "An Arab Muslim Community in Michigan," in Barbara C. Aswad, ed., *Arabic Speaking Communities in American Cities* (New York: Center for Migration Studies, 1974), pp. 155–68.

26. In a study of a village in South Lebanon, Peters found first parallel cousin marriages in 15 percent of one group and 18 percent of another group. Emrys Peters, "Aspects of Rank and Status among Muslims in a Lebanese Village," in Julian Pitt-Rivers, ed., *Mediterranean Countrymen: Essays in the Social Anthropology of the Mediterranean* (Paris: Mouton, 1963), pp. 159–202.

27. Barbara C. Aswad, "Yemeni and Lebanese Muslim Immigrant Women in Southeast Dearborn, Michigan," in Earle H. Waugh et al., eds., *Muslim Families in North America* (Edmonton, Alberta: University of Alberta Press, 1991), pp. 256–81.

28. Shireen Mahdavi, "The Position of Women in Shi'a Iran: Views of the 'Ulama," in Elizabeth Warnoch Fernea, ed., *Women and the Family in the Middle East* (Austin: University of Texas Press, 1985), p. 261.

29. Khu'i, *Minhaj al-Salihin*, Vol. 2, p. 279.

30. Ibid., p. 281.

31. Edwin Terry Prothro and Lutfy Najib Diab, *Changing Family Patterns in the Arab East* (Beirut: American University of Beirut, 1974).

32. Emrys Peters, "The Status of Women in Four Middle East Communities," in Lois Beck and Nikki Keddie, eds., *Women in the Muslim World* (Cambridge: Harvard University Press, 1978) pp. 311–30.

33. Anne Betteridge, "To Veil or Not to Veil: A Matter of Protest or Policy," in Guity Nashat, ed., *Women and Revolution in Iran* (Boulder: West-

view, 1983), pp. 109–29. Also see Arlene Elowe Macleod, *Accommodating Protest: Working Women, the New Veiling, and Change in Cairo* (New York: Columbia University Press, 1991).

34. For example, Susan Schaefer Davis, *Patience and Power: Women's Lives in a Moroccan Village* (Cambridge, Mass.: Schenkman, n.d.).

35. See Charlene Joyce Eisenlohr, "The Dilemma of Adolescent Arab Girls in an American High School," Ph.D. dissertation, University of Michigan, 1988. The author found that Arab teenage girls did not always share their parents' opinions on a number of variables, including the use of the scarf and dating.

36. Aswad, "Yemeni and Lebanese Muslim Immigrant Women."

37. Judith Williams, *The Youth of Haouch el Harimi: A Lebanese Village* (Cambridge: Harvard University Press, 1968), p. 31.

38. Shahla Haeri, *Law of Desire: Temporary Marriage in Shiʿi Iran* (Syracuse: Syracuse University Press, 1989), p. 3.

39. Abduʿl Latif Berri, *Temporary Marriage in Islam* (Dearborn, Mich.: Az-Zahra International, 1989), pp. 17–18.

40. Ibid., p. 19.

41. Ibid., p. 33.

42. Ibid., p. 34.

43. Prothro and Diab, *Changing Family Patterns*, p. 120.

44. Jay Dolan, *The American Catholic Experience: A History from Colonial Times to the Present* (Garden City, N.Y.: Doubleday, 1985), p. 252.

45. Nancy F. Cott, *The Bonds of Womanhood: "Women's Sphere" in New England, 1780–1835* (New Haven: Yale University Press, 1977), p. 126.

46. Ibid., p. 132.

47. Ibid., p. 134.

48. Ibid., p. 138.

49. Aswad, "Yemeni and Lebanese Muslim Immigrant Women."

50. Fuad Khuri, *From Village to Suburb: Order and Charge in Greater Beirut* (Chicago: University of Chicago Press, 1975).

Chapter 4

1. Oscar Hindlin, *The Uprooted* (New York: Grosset and Dunlap, 1951), p. 117.

2. Saudi Arabia, which promotes a truly "fundamentalist" approach to Islam, has financially supported Islamic institutions in the West. Saudi money, for example, built the large mosques in Washington, D.C., and in New York City. As a result, they have had an influence on the way mosques are developing in America.

3. Robert N. Bellah, Richard Madsen, William M. Sullivan, Ann Swidler, and Steven M. Tipton, *Habits of the Heart* (New York: Harper and Row, 1985), p. 226.

4. Ibid., p. 225.

5. Ibid., p. 232.

6. Ibid., p. 240.

7. Many new Shi'i immigrants today are from southern Iraq, refugees in the aftermath of the Gulf War.

8. W. Murray Hogben, "Marriage and Divorce among Muslims in Canada," in Earle H. Waugh et al., eds., *Muslim Families in North America* (Edmonton, Alberta: University of Alberta Press, 1991), pp. 154–84.

9. Irving Howe, *World of Our Fathers: The Journey of the East European Jews to America and the Life They Found and Made* (New York: Galahad Books, 1976), p. 207.

10. Ibid., p. 194.

11. Leonard Joseph Moore, *Citizen Klansmen: The Ku Klux Klan in Indiana* (Chapel Hill: University of North Carolina Press, 1991).

12. Daniel S. Buczek, "Polish-Americans and the Roman Catholic Church," in George E. Pozzetta, ed., *The Immigrant Religious Experience* (New York: Garland, 1991), p. 33.

Glossary

ʿ*abaya.* The all-encompassing black garment worn in some Arab countries.

Ahl al-Bayt. The family of the Prophet, particularly the imams and their near relations.

al-Nar. Hell.

ʿ**Ali ibn abi Taleb.** The cousin and son-in-law of the Prophet and the first imam of the Shiʿa.

ʿ**Ashura.** The tenth day of the Muslim holy month of Muharram, the time when Imam Husayn was killed in Karbala, Iraq.

Ayatollah. "Sign of God"; a high-ranking *mujtahid.*

bismiʿllah. "In the name of God." This invocation is used at the beginning of all books, speeches, and sermons, before undertaking any activity such as eating a meal. It is also used to ward off evil spirits.

chador. All-encompassing black garment worn by women in Iran.

fatwa. A religious legal opinion given by a *mujtahid.*

fusha. The classical or standard form of Arabic, as opposed to the colloquial form.

hadith. The sayings of the Prophet Muhammad.

hajj. Pilgrimage to Mecca.

hajji (fem. hajja). Title given to someone who has made the pilgrimage to Mecca.

halal. That which is permitted by Islamic law.

Harakat Amal. "Movement of Hope." The militia formed by Imam Musa Sadr among the Lebanese Shiʿa.

haram. Something that is forbidden by Islamic law.

Hashimite. The clan to which the Prophet Muhammad belonged.

Hidden Imam. The Twelfth Imam, who went into occultation and whose return is awaited by the Shiʿa.

hijab. Modest dress worn by modern Muslim women that completely covers the hair and all parts of the body except the face, hands, and feet. Usually the outfit includes a large scarf and a long, shapeless dress or coat.

Hijra. Originally referring to the journey of the Prophet Muhammad from Mecca to Medina, this term is used when referring to a migration that has been given a religious significance.

Hizb Allah. "Party of God." Militia in Lebanon that is more radical than its rival, Harakat Amal. It has advocated the establishment of a theocratic government such as that of the Islamic Republic of Iran.

Husayn ibn 'Ali. The grandson of the Prophet Muhammad and the third imam of the Shi'a.

husayniya. The gathering place in a Shi'i mosque, separate from where one performs *salat* (can be a building separate from the mosque).

'id. Holy day.

'Id al-Adha. Feast of sacrifice that takes place during the *hajj.*

'Id al-Fitr. Feast marking the end of Ramadan.

iftar. Breaking of the fast; the meal one eats each evening at sunset during Ramadan.

ijtihad. Process of arriving at judgments on points of religious law using reason and the principles of jurisprudence.

'irfan. Mystical knowledge usually concerning the esoteric meaning of the Koran.

Isma'ili. A Shi'i sect resulting from disagreement over who should be the seventh imam. The founders of the Fatimid caliphate in Egypt in the tenth through twelfth centuries.

Jannah. Paradise

jinn. Spirits spoken of in the Koran that can be either good or evil.

Ka'ba. Sacred enclosure at Mecca.

kafir (plural *kuffar*). Infidel (nonbeliever).

Karbala. Site where the Imam Husayn was martyred and buried, it became a shrine city in southern Iraq with a theological center.

khatib. The person who recounts the story of the death of the Imam Husayn.

khums. Shi'i religious tax that goes to the *sayyids* and to one's *marji'.*

khutba. The sermon given on Fridays at the mosque.

madrasa. A theological school.

Majalis Husayniya. The recounting of the suffering and death of the Imam Husayn.

marji'. Shortened form of *marji'iyat taqlid tamm.*

marji'iyat. The institution of the highest-ranking Shi'i leadership.

marji'iyat taqlid tamm. "The point of emulation" for devout Shi'a; a *mujtahid* who has attained the highest status among all Shi'i clergy to whom Shi'a turn for direction in their religious, social, and, at times, political lives.

Maronites. A Lebanese Christian sect that is affiliated with the Roman Catholic church. The Maronites have been the dominant group in Lebanon since the founding of the modern state of Lebanon.

marjid. Mosque.

mihrab. Prader niche that marks direction of prayer.

Muharram. Month during which the Imam Husayn was martyred. It is considered holy to Shiʿa.

mujaddid. The religious reformer who should appear every century.

mujtahid. A high-ranking Shiʿi cleric qualified to practice *ijtihad.*

muminin. Believers.

muqallid. Follower of a *marjaʿ.*

mutʿa. "Temporary" or "pleasure" marriage, allowable by Shiʿi but not Sunni law.

mutʿi. A woman who has contracted a temporary marriage with a man.

Najaf. The city in Iraq where the Imam ʿAli was killed, the site of the major theological center for Shiʿa.

najis. Ritually impure.

qadi. Religious judge.

qibla. The direction faced in prayer (for Muslims, this is Mecca).

Qom. A shrine city in Iran with an important theological center for Shiʿa.

rajʿa. Eschatological return, usually of someone of religious significance.

Ramadan. Muslim lunar month of fasting.

salat. Obligatory prayer.

sawm. Fasting.

sayyid. A descendent of the Prophet Muhammad through the line of the Prophet's daughter Fatima and her husband, ʿAli ibn Abi Taleb.

Shariʿa. Islamic law.

sheikh. A tribal leader or elder; the term is used in this text as the title of a religious cleric.

shibab. Muslim youths.

tafsir. Science of interpreting the Koran.

taqiya. Concealment of one's religious affiliation.

taʿziyeh. The term used by Iranians for the passion play commemorating the death of the Imam Husayn.

ʿulama. "The learned," or Islamic clergy.

wilayat al-faqih. "Guardianship of the jurisconsult," the doctrine that a cleric should be the head of the government.

waʿz. Exhortation; a kind of preaching.

za'im (plural *zu'ama'*). Lebanese leader or strongman.

Zaydi. A sect of Shi'ism common in Yemen.

ZemZem water. Water from the well that was said to have sprung from the ground when Hagar and her son Ishmael were in the desert dying from thirst.

Selected Bibliography

Abraham, Nabeel Y. "National and Local Politics: A Study of Political Conflict in the Yemeni Immigrant Community of Detroit, Michigan." Ph.D. dissertation, University of Michigan, 1978.

Abraham, Sameer, Nabeel Abraham, and Barbara Aswad. "The Southend: An Arab Muslim Working-class Community." In Sameer Y. Abraham and Nabeel Abraham, eds., *Arabs in the New World: Studies on Arab-American Communities*. Detroit: Wayne State University Center for Urban Studies, 1983. Pp. 163–84.

Ahmad, Gutbi Mahdi. "Muslim Organizations in the United States." In Yvonne Yazbeck Haddad, ed., *The Muslims of America*. New York: Oxford University Press, 1991. Pp.11–24.

Ajami, Fouad. "The Battle of Algiers." *The New Republic,* July 9, 1990, pp. 12–13.

———. *The Vanished Imam: Musa Al Sadr and the Shiʿa of Lebanon*. Ithaca: Cornell University Press, 1986.

Al-Sadr, Ayatollah Muhammad Baqir, and Ayatollah Murtaza Mutahhery. *The Awaited Savior*. Translated by A. Ansari. Accra: Islamic Seminary, 1982.

Amanat, Abbas. "In Between the Madrasa" and the Marketplace: The Designation of Clerical Leadership in Modern Shiʿism." In Said Amir Arjomand, ed., *Authority and Political Culture in Shiʿism*. Albany: State University of New York Press, 1988. Pp. 98–132.

———. *Resurrection and Renewal: The Making of the Babi Movement in Iran, 1844–1850*. Ithaca: Cornell University Press, 1989.

Antoun, Richard. "Key Variables Affecting Muslim Local-Level Religious Leadership in Iran and Jordan." In Fuad I. Khuri, ed., *Leadership and Development in Arab Society*. Beirut: Center for Arab and Middle East Studies, 1981. Pp. 92–101.

———. *Muslim Preacher in the Modern World*. Princeton: Princeton University Press, 1989.

Arjomand, Said Amir. *The Shadow of God and the Hidden Imam*. Chicago: University of Chicago Press, 1984.

Aswad, Barbara C. "The Lebanese Muslim Community in Dearborn, Michigan." Paper presented at the Centre for Lebanese Studies Conference on Lebanese Emigration, St. Hughes College, Oxford, 1989.

———. "The Southeast Dearborn Arab Community Struggles for Survival Against Urban 'Renewal.' " In Barbara C. Aswad, ed., *Arabic Speaking*

Communities in American Cities. Staten Island, N.Y.: Center for Migration Studies, 1974. Pp. 53–84.

———. "Yemeni and Lebanese Muslim Immigrant Women in Southeast Dearborn, Michigan." In Earle H. Waugh, Sharon McIrvin Abu-Laban, and Regula Burckhardt Qureshi, eds., *Muslim Families in North America.* Edmonton, Alberta: University of Alberta Press, 1991. Pp. 256–81.

Baktash, Mayel. "*Ta'ziyeh* and Its Philosophy." In Peter Chelkowski, ed., *Ta'ziyeh: Ritual and Drama in Iran.* New York: New York University Press, 1979. Pp. 95–120.

Bellah, Robert N., "Civil Religion in America." In William G. McLoughlin and Robert N. Bellah, eds, *Religion in America.* Boston: Beacon, 1968. Pp. 3–23.

Bellah, Robert N., Richard Madsen, William M. Sullivan, Ann Swidler, and Steven M. Tipton. *Habits of the Heart.* New York: Harper and Row, 1985.

Berri, Abdu'l Latif. *Temporary Marriage in Islam.* Dearborn, Mich.: Az-Zahra International, 1989.

Betteridge, Anne. "To Veil or Not to Veil: A Matter of Protest or Policy." In Guity Nashat, ed. *Women and Revolution in Iran.* Boulder: Westview, 1983, Pp. 109–29.

Bloch, Maurice. "Introduction." In Maurice Bloch, ed, *Political Language and Oratory in Traditional Society.* London: Academic Press, 1975. Pp. 109–29.

Boratav, P. N. "Djinn." In *The Encyclopaedia of Islam,* 2nd ed. Leiden: E. J. Brill, 1960. Pp. 546–50.

Bowen, John R. *Muslims through Discourse: Religion and Ritual in Gayo Society.* Princeton: Princeton University Press, 1993.

Boyer, Pascal. *Tradition as Truth and Communication.* Cambridge: Cambridge University Press, 1990.

Browne, Edward G. *A Literary History of Persia,* Vol. IV. Cambridge: Cambridge University Press, 1969.

Buczek, Daniel S. "Polish-Americans and the Roman Catholic Church." In George E. Pozzetta, ed., *The Immigrant Religious Experience.* New York: Garland Publishing, 1991. Pp. 31–53.

Bukowczyk, John J. "Mary the Messiah: Polish Immigrant Heresy and the Malleable Ideology of the Roman Catholic Church, 1880–1930." In George E. Pozzetta, ed., *The Immigrant Religious Experience.* New York: Garland, 1991. Pp. 55–81.

———. "The Transforming Power of the Machine: Popular Religion, Ideology and Secularization among Polish Immigrant Workers in the United States, 1880–1940." In George E. Pozzetta, ed., *The Immigrant Religious Experience.* New York: Garland, 1991. Pp. 84–10.

Caton, Steven C. *Peaks of Yemen I Summon.* Berkeley: University of California Press, 1990.

Chelkowski, Peter, ed. *Ta'ziych: Ritual and Drama in Iran.* New York: New York University Press, 1979.

Chirri, Muhammad Jawad. *Inquiries about Islam*. Beirut, 1965.

———. *The Shiites under Attack*. Detroit: Islamic Center of America, 1986.

Cole, J. R. I. "Imami Jurisprudence and the Role of the ʿUlama: Mortaza Ansari on Emulating the Supreme Exemplar." In Nikki R. Keddie, ed., *Religion and Politics in Iran*. New Haven: Yale University Press, 1983. Pp. 33–46.

Cole, J. R. I., and Nikki R. Keddie, eds. *Shiʿism and Social Protest*. New Haven: Yale University Press, 1986.

Conklin, Nancy, and Nora Faires. "Colored and Catholic: The Lebanese in Birmingham, Alabama." In Eric Hooglund, ed., *Crossing the Waters*. Washington, D.C.: Smithsonian Institution, 1987. Pp. 69–84.

Cott, Nancy F. *The Bonds of Womanhood: "Women's Sphere" in New England, 1780–1835*. New Haven: Yale University Press, 1977.

Dabashi, Hamid. *Theology of Discontent: The Ideological Foundation of the Islamic Revolution in Iran*. New York: New York University Press, 1993.

Davis, Susan Schaefer. *Patience and Power: Women's Lives in a Moroccan Village*. Cambridge, Mass.: Schenkman, n.d.

Dolan, Jay. *The American Catholic Experience: A History from Colonial Times to the Present*. Garden City, N.Y.: Doubleday, 1985.

Douglas, Mary. *Purity and Danger: An Analysis of Concepts of Pollution and Taboo*. London: Routledge and Kegan Paul, 1966.

Eickelman, Dale F., and James Piscatori, eds. *Muslim Travelers: Pilgrimage, Migration, and the Religious Imagination*. Berkeley: University of California Press, 1990.

Eisenlohr, Charlene Joyce. "The Dilemma of Adolescent Arab Girls in an American High School." Ph.D. Dissertation, University of Michigan, 1988.

———. *The Sacred and the Profane: The Nature of Religion*. San Diego: Harcourt, Brace, Jovanovich, 1959.

Elkholy, Abdo. *The Arab Muslims in the United States*. New Haven: College and University Press, 1966.

Fahd, Toufic. "Magic: Magic in Islam." In Mircea Eliade, ed., *The Encyclopedia of Religion*. New York: Macmillan, 1987, Pp. 104–9.

Fischer, Michael. *Iran: From Religious Dispute to Revolution*. Cambridge: Harvard University Press, 1980.

Frazer, J. G. *The Golden Bough, Part II: Taboo and the Perils of the Soul*. London: Macmillan, 1927.

Friedl, Erika. *Women of Deh Koh*. Washington, D.C.: Smithsonian Institution, 1989.

Gaffney, Patrick. *The Prophet's Pulpit: Islamic Preaching in Contemporary Egypt*. Berkeley: University of California Press, 1994.

Geertz, Clifford. *Islam Observed*. Chicago: University of Chicago Press, 1968.

Gilsenan, Michael. *Recognizing Islam*. New York: Pantheon Books, 1982.

Grabar, Oleg. "The Architecture of the Middle Eastern City." In Ira M. Lapidas, ed., *Middle Eastern Cities*. Berkeley: University of California Press, 1969. Pp. 26–46.

Guillaume, Alfred. *Islam*. Middlesex: Penguin, 1954.

Haeri, Shahla. *Law of Desire: Temporary Marriage in Shiʿi Iran*. Syracuse: Syracuse University Press, 1989.

Hegland, Mary. "Two Images of Husain: Accommodation and Revolution in an Iranian Village." In Nikki Keddie, ed., *Religion and Politics in Iran: Shiʿism from Quietism to Revolution*. New Haven: Yale University Press, 1983. Pp. 218–35.

Herberg, Will. *Protestant, Catholic, Jew*. Garden City, N.Y.: Doubleday, 1955.

Hindlin, Oscar. *The Uprooted*. New York: Grosset and Dunlap, 1951.

Hodgson, Marshall. *The Venture of Islam: The Classical Age of Islam*, Vol. 1. Chicago: University of Chicago Press, 1974.

Hogben, W. Murray, "Marriage and Divorce among Muslims in Canada." In Earle H. Waugh, Sharon McIrvin Abu-Laban, and Regula Burckhardt Qureshi, eds., *Muslim Families in North America*. Edmonton, Alberta: University of Alberta Press, 1991. Pp. 154–84.

Hourani, Albert. "Ideologies of the Mountain and the City." In Roger Owen, ed., *Essays on the Crisis in Lebanon*. London: Ithaca Press, 1976. Pp. 33–41.

Howe, Irving. *World of Our Fathers: The Journey of the East European Jews to America and the Life They Found and Made*. New York: Galahad Books, 1976.

Humphrey, Michael. "Community, Mosque and Ethnic Politics." *Australian and New Zealand Journal of Sociology* XXIII, 2 (July 1987): 233–45.

Ibn Khaldun. *The Muqaddimah: An Introduction to History*, Vol. 3. Translated by Franz Rosenthal. Princeton: Princeton University Press, 1967.

Issawi, Charles. "The Historical Background of Lebanese Emigration 1800–1914." Paper presented at the Centre for Lebanese Studies Conference on Lebanese Emigration, St. Hughes, College, Oxford, 1989.

Jafri, S. Husain M. *Origin and Early Development Shiʿa Islam*. London: Longman Group, 1979.

Joseph, Suad. "Family as Security and Bondage: A Political Strategy of the Lebanese Working Class." In Saad Eddin Ibrahim, ed., *Arab Society: Social Science Perspectives*. Cairo: American University of Cairo Press, 1985. Pp. 241–56.

———. "Women and the Neighborhood Street in Borj Hamoud, Lebanon." In Lois Beck and Nikki Keddie, eds., *Women in the Muslim World*. Cambridge: Harvard University Press, 1978. Pp. 541–57.

Katarsky, Anthony. "Family Ties and the Growth of an Arabic Community in Northeast Dearborn, Michigan." Master's thesis, Wayne State University, 1980.

Keddie, Nikki. *Religion and Politics in Iran*. New Haven: Yale University Press, 1983.

Keddie, Nikki R., ed. *Scholars, Saints, and Sufis: Muslim Religious Institutions since 1500*, 2nd ed. Berkeley: University of California Press, 1978.

Kepel, Gilles. *Muslim Extranism in Egypt: The Prophet and the Pharoah*, trans. by J. Rothschild. Berkeley: University of California Press, 1985.

Khalaf, Samir. "The Background and Causes of Lebanese Syrian Immigration to the U.S. before World War I." In Eric J. Hooglund, ed., *Crossing the Waters*. Washington, D.C.: Smithsonian Institution, 1987. Pp. 17–36.

Khalaf, Samir, and Guilain Denoeux. "Urban Networks and Political Conflict in Lebanon." In Nadim Shehadi and Dana Haffar Mills, eds., *Lebanon: A History of Conflict and Consensus*. London: Centre for Lebanese Studies, 1988. Pp. 181–200.

Khuʿi, Abuʾl-Qasim. *Manahij al-Salihin*. Beirut: Daral-Zahra, n.d.

Khuri, Fuad. *From Village to Suburb: Order and Change in Greater Beirut*. Chicago: University of Chicago Press, 1975.

———. *Imams and Emirs: State, Religion and Sects in Islam*. London: Saqi Books, 1990.

Macleod, Arlene Elowe. *Accommodating Protest: Working Women, the New Veiling, and Change in Cairo*. New York: Columbia University Press, 1991.

Mahdavi, Shireen. "The Position of Women in Shiʿa Iran: Views of the ʿUlama." In Elizabeth Warnoch Fernea, ed., *Women and the Family in the Middle East*. Austin: University of Texas Press, 1985. Pp. 255–72.

Mallat, Chibli. *Renewal of Islamic Law: Muhammad Baqer as-Sadr, Najaf and the Shiʿi International*. Cambridge: Cambridge University Press, 1993.

———. *Shiʿi Thought from the South of Lebanon*. Oxford: Centre for Lebanese Studies, 1988.

Mazzaoui, Michel. "Shiʿism in the Arab World." In Seyyed Hossein Nasr, Hamid Dabashi, and Seyyed Vali Reza Nasr, eds., *Expectation of the Millennium*. New York: State University of New York Press, 1989. Pp. 253–55.

Metcalf, Barbara D. "The Pilgrimage Remembered: South Asian Accounts of the Hajj." In Dale F. Eickelman and James Piscatori, eds., *Muslim Travellers: Pilgrimage, Migration, and the Religious Imagination*. Berkeley: University of California Press, 1990. Pp. 85–107.

Mishaqa, Mikhayil. *Murder, Mayhem, Pillage and Plunder: The History of the Lebanon in the 18th and 19th Centuries*. Translated by Wheeler M. Thackston, Jr. Albany: State University of New York Press, 1988.

Momen, Moojan. *An Introduction to Shiʿi Islam*. Oxford: George Ronald, 1985.

Moore, Leonard Joseph. *Citizen Klansmen: The Ku Klux Klan in Indiana*. Chapel Hill: University of North Carolina Press, 1991.

Mottahedeh, Roy. *The Mantle of the Prophet*. New York: Simon and Schuster, 1985.

Munson, Henry, Jr. *Islam and Revolution in the Middle East*. New Haven: Yale University Press, 1988.

Naff, Alixa. *Becoming American: The Early Arab Immigrant Experience*. Carbondale, Ill.: Southern Illinois University Press, 1985.

Nakash, Yitzhak. *The Shiʿis of Iraq*. Princeton: Princeton University Press, 1994.

Norton, Augustus Richard. *Amal and the Shiʿa: Struggle for the Soul of Lebanon.* Austin: University of Texas Press, 1987.

Olmert, Joseph. "The Shiʿa and the Lebanese State." In Martin Kramer, ed., *Shiʿism, Resistence and Revolution.* Boulder: Westview, 1987. Pp. 189–201.

Orfalea, Gregory. *Before the Flames: A Quest for the History of Arab Americans.* Austin: University of Texas Press, 1988.

Orsi, Robert Anthony. *The Madonna of 115th Street: Faith and Community in Italian Harlem, 1880–1950.* New Haven: Yale University Press, 1985.

Peters, Emrys. "Aspects of Rank and Status among Muslims in a Lebanese Village." In Julian Pitt-Rivers, ed., *Mediterranean Countrymen: Essays in the Social Anthropology of the Mediterranean.* Paris: Mouton, 1963. Pp. 159–202.

———. "The Status of Women in Four Middle East Communities." In Lois Beck and Nikki Keddie, eds., *Women in the Muslim World.* Cambridge: Harvard University Press, 1978. Pp. 311–50.

Portes, Alejandro and Ruben G. Rumbaut. *Immigrant America.* Berkeley: University of California Press, 1990.

Prothro, Edwin Terry, and Lutfy Najib Diab. *Changing Family Patterns in the Arab East.* Beirut: American University of Beirut, 1974.

Reimers, David M. *Still the Golden Door: The Third World Comes to America.* New York: Columbia University Press, 1985.

Roy, Olivier. *The Failure of Political Islam,* trans. by Carol Volk, Cambridge: Harvard University Press, 1994.

Sakr, Ahmad H, and Sami A. Arafeh. *Guidelines of Employment by Muslim Communities.* Lombard, Ill.: Foundation for Islamic Knowledge, n.d.

Schubel, Vernon, "The Muharram Majlis: The Role of Ritual in the Preservation of Shiʿa Identity." In Earle H. Waugh, et al, eds., *Muslim Families in North America.* Edmonton Alberta: University of Alberta Press, 1991.

Siryani, Mohammad Mahmoud. "Residential Distribution, Spatial Mobility and Acculturation in an Arab-Muslim Community." Ph.D. dissertation, Michigan State University, 1977.

Smith, Timothy L. "Religious Denominations as Ethnic Communities: A Regional Case Study." In George E. Pozzetta, ed., *The Immigrant Religious Experience.* New York: Garland Publishing, 1991. Pp. 353–72.

Spooner, Brian. "The Evil Eye in the Middle East." In Mary Douglas, ed., *Witchcraft Confessions and Accusations.* London: Tavistock, 1970.

Suleiman, Michael. "Early Arab-Americans: The Search for Identity." In Eric J. Hooglund, ed., *Crossing the Waters.* Washington, D.C.: Smithsonian Institution, 1987. Pp. 37–54.

Tabatabaʿi, Allama. *Shiʿite Islam.* Albany: State University of New York Press, 1975.

Tentler, Leslie Woodcock. "Who Is the Church? Conflict in a Polish Immigrant Parish in Late Nineteenth-Century Detroit." In George E. Pozzetta, ed, *The Immigrant Religious Experience.* New York: Garland Publishing, 1991. Pp. 419–54.

Turner, Victor W. "Religious Specialists." In Arthur C. Lehmann and James E. Myers, eds., *Magic, Witchcraft, and Religion: An Anthropological Study of the Supernatural,* 2nd ed. Mountain View, Calif. Mayfield, 1989. Pp. 85–92.

Wigle, Laurel D. "An Arab Muslim Community in Michigan." In Barbara C. Aswad, ed., *Arabic Speaking Communities in American Cities.* New York: Center for Migration Studies, 1974. Pp. 155–68.

Williams, Judith. *The Youth of Haouch el Harimi: A Lebanese Village.* Cambridge: Harvard University Press, 1968.

Williams, Peter W. *Popular Religion in America.* Urbana: University of Illinois Press, 1989.

Wolf, Eric R. *Peasant Wars of the Twentieth Century.* New York: Harper and Row, 1968.

Wuthnow, Robert. *Producing the Sacred: An Essay on Public Religion.* Urbana: University of Illinois Press, 1994.

Index